Colonial Complexions

EARLY AMERICAN STUDIES

Series Editors
Daniel K. Richter, Kathleen M. Brown,
Max Cavitch, and David Waldstreicher

Exploring neglected aspects of our colonial,
revolutionary, and early national history and culture,
Early American Studies reinterprets familiar themes
and events in fresh ways. Interdisciplinary in character,
and with a special emphasis on the period from about
1600 to 1850, the series is published in partnership with
the McNeil Center for Early American Studies.

A complete list of books in the series
is available from the publisher.

COLONIAL COMPLEXIONS

RACE AND BODIES IN EIGHTEENTH-CENTURY AMERICA

SHARON BLOCK

PENN

UNIVERSITY OF PENNSYLVANIA PRESS

PHILADELPHIA

Published by
University of Pennsylvania Press
Philadelphia, Pennsylvania 19104-4112
www.upenn.edu/pennpress

Printed in the United States of America
on acid-free paper
1 3 5 7 9 10 8 6 4 2

Library of Congress Cataloging-in-Publication Data

Names: Block, Sharon, 1968– author.
Title: Colonial complexions : race and bodies in eighteenth-century America /Sharon Block.
Other titles: Early American studies.
Description: 1st edition. | Philadelphia : University of Pennsylvania Press, [2018] | Series: Early
    American studies | Includes bibliographical references and index.
Identifiers: LCCN 2017046033 | ISBN 9780812250060 (hardcover : alk. paper)
Subjects: LCSH: Race awareness—United States—History—18th century. | Racism—United
    States—History—18th century. | Human skin color—Social aspects—United
    States—History—18th century. | Human body and language—United States—History—18th
    century. | Advertising, Newspaper—United States—History—18th century. | Missing
    persons—United States—History—18th century. | Fugitive slaves—United
    States—History—18th century. | United States—Race relations—History—18th century.
Classification: LCC E184.A1 B559 2018 | DDC 305.800973—dc23
LC record available at https://lccn.loc.gov/2017046033

For Casey

For Ripley

*May you each continue
to embrace the amazing bodies
that house you*

I don't describe [my characters] very much, just broad
strokes. You don't know necessarily how tall they are,
because I don't want to force the reader into seeing what I
see.

—Toni Morrison

Whenever you introduce a character, you don't have to
specify that they are wearing pants. Most readers will
just assume that they are wearing pants unless you say
otherwise.

—Zadie Smith

CONTENTS

INTRODUCTION

Colonial Complexions grew out of two related questions: What were the meanings of black, white, and red in the colonial eighteenth century; and how did Anglo-American colonists describe people's appearance? A desire to explain the intersections of colonial Anglo-American racial ideologies and physical appearance led me to question historians' deployment of skin color categorizations as stable identities. No matter how natural visible racial divisions may seem to modern readers, they have not transcended history.[1] Revisiting these anachronistic applications of modern racial taxonomies led me to colonial interpretations of bodies and persons that have been lost to us through the overriding violence of racism. By treating physical appearance as unremarkable or by employing classifications of white, black, and red as self-evident, scholars risk giving short shrift to the daily creation of constructed corporeality that lay the foundations of racism among early America.

We can see such shifting notions of race, complexion, and identity by comparing two pieces of early modern writing. Shortly after his return to England in 1671, John Josselyn published a travel narrative that described the Massachusetts, Mohegans, Narragansetts, Pequots, Pokanokets, and other Native Americans he had encountered in the lands that would be known as New England. Josselyn paralleled indigenous peoples' appearances to those of Europeans with whom his English readers might be more familiar: "as the *Austreans* are known by their great lips, the *Bavarians* by their pokes under their chins, the *Jews* by their goggle eyes, so the *Indians* by their flat noses, yet are they not so much deprest as they are to the Southward."[2] Pronounced-mouthed Austrians, Bavarians with goiters, goggle-eyed Jews, and flat-but-not-too-flat-nosed Native Americans: these physical stereotypes likely do not resonate with most modern readers, because perceptions of physical appearance are historically and culturally bound.

Almost a century later, Benjamin Franklin again tied identity to appearance. He described Africans as "black or tawny" and Native Americans (and Asians) as "wholly tawny," and he noted that most Europeans (Spaniards, Italians, French, Russians, Swedes, and some Germans) were "of a swarthy Complexion," leaving only the English as "White People."[3] Franklin's commentary suggests both the ways that racial scripts had developed since Josselyn identified people by facial features and how familiar racialized terms held historically specific meanings. Whiteness was not necessarily a synonym for European heritage in the eighteenth century, where humorally influenced interpretations of complexion continued to hold sway. Both men's descriptions point to the power of a writer's frames of reference and the ways that power relationships could be produced through descriptions of bodily features.

By the beginning of the nineteenth century, skin color began to consistently be privileged as *the* sign of racial identity in literary, legal, and public arenas.[4] Race science would be born out of these shifts, as skin color became the primary tool to mark slavery, freedom, and presumed innate racial qualities.[5] But the linkages between bodies, race, and freedom were not inevitable. Historian Barbara Fields's explanation of race is still one of the most eloquent: "Race is not an element of human biology (like breathing oxygen or reproducing sexually); nor is it even an idea (like the speed of light or the value of *pi*) that can be plausibly imagined to live an eternal life of its own. Race is not an idea but an ideology."[6]

To understand the arc of American racial ideologies, *Colonial Complexions* chronicles the quarter century (c. 1750–75) *before* skin color became increasingly equivalent to race. In this time period, missing persons advertisements were an established genre in colonial newspapers, regularly including categorizations of sex, race, and status; aspects of the runaways' appearance and behavior; details about items carried with them; and sometimes a discussion of past relationships that aimed to pinpoint where the person might be headed. The thousands of late colonial print descriptions of missing persons gathered from these advertisements reveal the kinds of daily racial scripts that naturalized writers' beliefs about race and gender, status and hierarchy, health and illness, labor capability and material reality. These newspaper descriptions of physical appearance were widely disseminated throughout colonies where they could both enforce and sustain particular ideologies of everyday racism. This book thus complicates understandings of eighteenth-century racism beyond a catch phrase of red, white, and black.

The title, *Colonial Complexions*, intentionally nods to my interrogation of eighteenth-century meanings of complexion and aims to remind readers that complexion was not the equivalent of skin color. Historians have productively traced the "racially ambiguous men and women [who] *passed as free* in the fluid, bustling, and multiracial world of the eighteenth[-] century mid-Atlantic," but how did colonists determine what "racially ambiguous" looked like?[7] Because complexion could be interpreted as a sign of health, behavior, or emotions, it did not yet hold a predominant racial meaning. I build on literary scholar Roxann Wheeler's conclusion that black and white have become powerful "cover stories for a dense matrix of ideas as closely associated with cultural differences as with the body's surface."[8] Representations of physical appearance gave daily meanings to racial ideologies that reflected historically specific social, economic, and cultural needs.

The chapters of *Colonial Complexions* range from the macro to the micro, from the quotidian to the noteworthy, and from the transatlantic to the local. Sources include scores of colonial and British publications as well as occasional private writings, but this study is based primarily on more than four thousand newspaper advertisements for runaway servants, slaves, and other missing persons issued between 1750 and 1775. Amassing large numbers of these brief advertisements has allowed me to analyze aggregate trends of print descriptions for laborers and other missing persons in early America. Appendix 1 offers an extended discussion of sources and methodology.

At the same time, the subjects who populate this book were far more than the sum of their body parts. I begin here with a story about one runaway's life as seen through print advertisements to offer context for the book's aggregated use of such sources. In the summer of 1769, a Virginia man named Barnaby escaped enslavement. Why he chose that moment to challenge his slavery remains unrecorded. Maybe his family situation had changed. Maybe he decided the unknown dangers of escape outweighed the known horrors of chattel slavery. Or perhaps Barnaby had sought freedom repeatedly, without leaving historical records, and his enslaver chose this occasion to advertise publicly for his return. We know about Barnaby's bid for freedom in 1769 because three weeks after his departure, Augustine Smith paid for an advertisement in the local newspaper to recover his self-liberated property. Augustine described Barnaby to readers as a twenty-year-old "Mulatto boy" who "stutters a good deal when surprised." He ran another advertisement the following week, adding an eye-catching woodcut and modifying Barnaby's description to "a Mulatto fellow," who was "5 feet 5 inches high" (Figure 1A).[9]

It is not known whether the physical descriptions in these advertisements helped anyone capture Barnaby; perhaps Virginians who already knew Barnaby had located him near York, where it was rumored his brother David might be living. However it happened, Barnaby apparently returned to Augustine's Shooter's Hill plantation: two years later, Augustine advertised for the return of his again-fugitive slave. This time, he described Barnaby as "a dark Mulatto Man," who was about five feet two inches tall, "artful in his Answers," and "has an impediment in his Speech." Augustine added a description of Barnaby's clothing, evidently hoping that the man had not had time to replace his inexpensive coarse "suit of dark coloured Russia Drab" (Figure 1B).[10]

Perhaps because Barnaby seemed determined to end his enslavement, Augustine Smith may have deemed his chattel to be more trouble than he was worth. Whereas he'd offered £5 for Barnaby's return in 1769, his 1771 advertisement offered only 20 shillings for anyone who found and jailed his property (Figure 1B).[11] Perhaps the downturn in the Smith family fortunes, and not Barnaby's repeated self-liberations, led to Barnaby's subsequent sale. Barnaby was apparently no more willing to serve his new enslaver. In July 1772, Thomas Crauford placed an advertisement that sought Barnaby's return, describing him as "a Mulatto Fellow" who "stutters a good Deal in his Speech." Thomas modified other aspects of Barnaby's appearance: in three years Barnaby had aged from twenty to twenty-five years old and was now described as being "of a low stature" rather than a specific height. Thomas added a new description of Barnaby's clothing but noted, as did many other advertisements, "as he carried other Clothes with him it is probable he may change them."[12]

Several months later, Thomas had not found Barnaby and offered readers some new details. While Barnaby was still described as twenty-five years old and of a "low" stature, he was now "well made" and his stuttering had been downgraded from "a good Deal" to "a little." Thomas also noted more about the circumstances of his departure: Barnaby had fled with his wife, a "young Mulatto Wench" named Belinda "who is short and very fat," and they were expected to head back to the Smith family's Middlesex plantation (Figure 1C). Barnaby's final appearance in early American print occurred on December 31, 1772, when James Wortham, the Middlesex jailer, confirmed that Barnaby had, as predicted, traveled several days' walk northeast toward the Virginia coast. On that last day of 1772, James advertised that he had "a middle sized Mulatto Fellow" named Barnaby who said he had recently been sold from Augustine Smith to Thomas Crauford (Figure 1D).[13]

These advertisements for Barnaby's capture could be used to craft a variety of rich narratives about his life in early America. Historians have mined such ads to trace the social connections among enslaved people, the geography of slavery, or enslaved people's struggles for freedom.[14] Other scholars have investigated the economic value ascribed to missing slaves or enslavers' public presentation of their mastery.[15]

The variety of details used to describe Barnaby by at least three people over four years also reflects the degree to which appearance was very much in the eye and for the purposes of the beholder. Even when ostensibly written by the same owner, recollections could change and significance could shift. Besides Barnaby's name, only the imposed categorization of "Mulatto," signaling both slave status and adjudged heritage, appeared in every advertisement. Some advertisements focused on Barnaby's clothing, others on his character, some on his age, many on his height, and a few on his body shape. His sex was alternatively signaled by references to him as a man, boy, or fellow. Barnaby was of either low or medium stature, somewhere between five feet two and five feet five inches tall. He may have been dark complexioned and/or mulatto-like in appearance; he may have stuttered a little or a lot, or perhaps only when surprised. Barnaby's most distinguishing feature could have been his artfulness or his physical strength. Through the range of these descriptive choices, advertisers communicated the features that they deemed significant for readers to know and revealed shared assumptions about bodily norms.

Runaway advertisements like those describing Barnaby form the backbone of *Colonial Complexions*. Departing from the kinds of social histories often told from these documents, this book aggregates advertisements to create a cultural history of race in eighteenth-century British North America. Yet I offer Barnaby's story as a reminder: advertisements document the struggles and strategies of untold numbers of people whose place in the historic record has been otherwise erased.[16] My focus on physical appearance as a commonplace tool of race-making means that extended life experiences rarely appear in this book. Instead, we see only glimpses of individuals who make up trends in eye color and hairstyle; in height and age; or in attire and character. Creating a narrative about the cultural

MIDDLESEX, July 17, 1769.

RUN away from the subscriber, about three years a-o, a Mulatto man named DAVID DAY, about 5 feet 8 inches high, has a down look, is very artful, and will attempt to pass for a freeman. He is supposed to have made for the southward. Also a Mulatto fellow named BARNABY, about 20 years old, 5 feet 5 inches high, and stutters a good deal when surprised. He went off about three weeks ago, and was seen at York, from whence I imagine he has attempted to get to the other, who is his brother. Whoever delivers them to me shall have 5 l. reward for each, if taken 50 miles from home; if higher, in proportion. T. AUGUSTINE SMITH.

MIDDLESEX, May 7, 1771.

RUN away, a dark Mulatto Man named BARNABY, about five Feet two Inches high. He is artful in his Answers, and has an Impediment in his Speech. Had on a Suit of dark coloured Russia Drab. Whoever will apprehend him, and have him committed to Jail, shall have TWENTY SHILLINGS Reward.
(Tf.) AUGUSTINE SMITH.

RUN away from the Subscriber, in Brunswick, a likely Mulatto Fellow named BARNABY, who is about twenty five Years of Age, low and well made, and stutters a little. He had on a white Russia Drab Coat and Jacket, black Lasting Breeches, with Shoes and Stockings; he also carried with him a Pair of Leather Boots, and a Velvet Cap. He formerly belonged to Mr. Augustine Smith of Middlesex, and I imagine is gone that Way. A young Mulatto Wench, named BELINDA, went off at the same Time, who is short and very fat. I purchased her of Mr. George Blair of Smithfield, where she possibly may go, but more likely with the Fellow, who is her Husband. I will give FIVE POUNDS to any Person who brings them to me, and Half that Sum for either. THOMAS CRAUFURD.

COMMITTED to the Jail of Middlesex, two Negroes; one of them is a short black Fellow, named WATCH, and formerly belonged to James Mills, Esquire, of Urbanna, who sold him to Edmund Wilcox of Amberst; the other is a middle sized Mulatto Fellow, named BARNABY, who formerly belonged to Mr. Augustine Smith of this County, but now says he belongs to Mr. Thomas Craufurd of Brunswick. The Owners may have them on proving their Properties, and paying Charges to
(2f) JAMES WORTHAM, Jailer.

Figures 1A–1D. Newspaper advertisements describing Barnaby, a Virginia man who repeatedly escaped enslavement. *Virginia Gazette* July 27, 1769, May 16, 1771, October 1, 1772, December 31, 1772. Special Collections, John D. Rockefeller Jr. Library, The Colonial Williamsburg Foundation.

meanings of racism is offered as a supplement to the many vital social histories that document life experiences through advertisements for runaways.

These advertisements for missing persons offer a unique opportunity to analyze the arena in which advertisement writers and newspaper readers communicated shared beliefs. Because the advertisements were not explicitly focused on explaining racial ideologies, they reveal the multiple intersecting constructions of physicality that writers relied on as reality.[17] Aggregation is particularly useful for making visible the patterns that underlie individual stories. That Barnaby was identified as having a speech impediment is just a potentially interesting fact until it is juxtaposed with hundreds of commentaries on runaways' speech patterns. Quantification as a tool for cultural analysis allows me to identify how colonial advertisers created textual bodies out of their beliefs, desires, and worldviews. It allows us to show how advertisers wove their ideal and experiential visions of laborers into every aspect of their descriptive choices. Noting, for instance, details about some bodies and not others marked whose bodies were consistently commodified. Advertisements made individual appearances a matter of public concern, turning even basic identifying characteristics into reflections of unstated beliefs about the people they described.[18]

We can see the ways that colonists implicitly marked intersecting racial and gender differences just through the quantity of words they chose to describe individuals. Advertisements provided information for an average of slightly more than six separate descriptive categories per person. European-descended runaways had about one-third more descriptive categories filled than did African-descended runaways. Most strikingly, advertisements for women identified as European descended contained almost 50 percent more information than those about women identified as African descended. This meant that African-descended women had, on average, the least amount of information provided about them (see Appendix 1 and Figure 6, on p. 148). Such quantitative differences provide a starting point to analyze the constructed nature of descriptions of missing persons.

Bodily descriptions gave meaning to intersecting racial divisions by naturalizing dissimilarities. Advertisements were less a formalized recitation of categorical facts and more a mix of desires, beliefs, and impressions about the amount of information needed to identify individuals. In particular, representations of bodily coloration worked as a tool to homogenize people of African descent while individualizing those of European descent. Categorical terms such as "Negro," "Mulatto," and "Indian" were purposefully applied (or erased) to mark boundaries of slavery and freedom through descriptions of physical bodies. Colonists likely believed that they could identify a woman of European descent, a man of African descent, or any other heritage/gender combination by sight, in part because of the commonly shared language that they reproduced in newspapers across the colonies.

In a book on the development of racial ideologies, even the descriptive terms used to categorize individuals can be fraught. Scholars regularly have to decide how to utilize problematically racialized language when identifying people in colonial America.[19] When possible, I use specific national or cultural terminologies: Algonquian or Angolan; Wampanoag or Welsh; Igbo or Irish. But this level of specificity is often not supported by the extant sources. Historians are left to decide how to best represent, yet not endorse, the colonial gaze. After much consideration, I decided to purposefully use the somewhat awkward phrases of "African descended," "European descended," and "Native American descended." Sometimes I use even more unwieldy phrases, such as: "a man identified as being of African descent" rather than "an African man"; "a woman described as being of multiple heritages" rather than "a mixed-race woman"; "a runaway noted to have been born in England" rather than "an English runaway." On occasion, I use in my own text the now-outdated terms that colonists used to classify individuals, such as "Negro" or "mulatto," because those terms best represent the specific categorization I am discussing. While labeling an individual "Black" or "African American" is less jarring, it also risks ahistoricizing the racist ideologies this book aims to deconstruct.

Given that this book seeks to untangle how racial boundaries are institutionalized and made real through written language, these narrative disruptions mark that many of the terms we often use unquestioningly to categorize people—like "black," "white," and "red"—can inadvertently misrepresent material realities and historical contexts. My inelegant phrasings aim to serve as a gentle reminder that such categorizations were constructions of who someone was, not the reality of their own identity. Descriptions of a person's appearance reflected racial hierarchies that were cultural artifacts, not self-evident facts.

A second decision about terminology relates to the names I use for the thousands of individuals I mention. More than half of the historical actors in this book were enslaved people whose surnames do not exist in the public record. While I discuss the significance of names in Chapter 4, I did not want to reify it in my own discussions of free and enslaved people. Thus, after an initial introduction, I have chosen to use only the given name of runaways. The one-time use of surnames recalls but does not permanently reinforce that racialized naming convention. I have, however, retained the traditional practice of using surnames to refer to published authors and historical figures who were not the subjects of runaway advertisements.

These linguistic choices call attention to the ways that Americans' popular discourse still reflects the heritage of eighteenth-century racial formation. Unwinding the associations between racism and presumed physical reality only occurs when we reckon with the ways that race was made through centuries of daily assumptions and assertions. The expected divisions of black, red, and white—divisions that historians use regularly in our writings on the period—did not yet hold the purchase in eighteenth-century America that they would in later centuries. Long before such racial descriptors became common parlance, colonial Americans translated physical differences into rationales for disciplining and controlling bodies. *Colonial Complexions* traces the power of bodily description in the creation of early American racial ideologies.

CHAPTER 1

Complicating Humors
and Rethinking Complexion

An eighteenth-century writer conjured an image of Christopher Columbus for his readers. Basing the description on Ferdinand Columbus's purported recollection of his father, the author told readers that Columbus was "moderately tall and long visaged, his complexion a good red and white, he had light eyes, and cheeks somewhat full, but neither too fat nor too lean; that in his youth he had fair hair, which turned grey before he was thirty years of age; that he was moderate in eating and drinking . . . that he was naturally grave, but affable to strangers."[1] This re-creation of Columbus's appearance incorporated a seemingly odd mixture of descriptive elements: the dimensions of his body and face, his behavior and character, and his hair, eye, and skin color. These features were not random. In both the details offered and the judgment tendered, they built on centuries of ideas about humoralism that proposed to explain how bodies worked and how bodily workings manifested in one's appearance.

European beliefs in humoral medicine offered a means to interpret individual health, character, and behavior through various aspects of physical appearance, including complexion in particular. The humoral sense of complexion gave significance to external signs of the body's internal workings. In contrast to the racial meanings of skin color that would gain prominence in the nineteenth century, complexion in the eighteenth century revealed an individual's internal health. In both popular and medical usage, a person's outward appearance had literally deeper meaning, reflecting internal constitution and temperament. What one did, thought, and felt became who one was, and all were legible in bodily appearance because emotions and beliefs could transform a person's physiology enough to make a visual impact on the body. Rather than being a shorthand for categorical skin color, complexion signaled individual health, character, and behavior.[2]

Humoral understandings of complexion also functioned beyond individual bodies, as part of a system that purported to explain humanity as a whole. Multiple changes in western European epistemologies gave such wider interpretations of the body particular salience. Colonial expansion, including the institutionalized enslavement of people from Africa, bequeathed descriptive authority to those who had seen new people and new lands, thus incorporating two centuries of global encounters into early modern understandings of humanity. Medicine's increasing emphasis on visual observation and anatomical explanations paralleled natural science's reliance on the power of observation and empiricism.[3] The eighteenth century also saw increasing interest in humanity's ability to categorize the natural world, which was understood to include humanity itself.[4] Together, these shifts set the stage for eighteenth-century uses of external appearance to signify internal truths about the health and functioning of individuals' bodies.

In European thought, humans existed on a hierarchical continuum that was reflected in the variety of humanity's corporeal features. Travelers and naturalists used humoral theory to offer taxonomies that described entire continents of people with whom they (and their readers) were largely unfamiliar. Writers debated the relationship between climate and complexion, between who someone was and where they lived. Whether discussing the color of newborns, the inherent nature of national character, or an assessment of proper temperament, British American writers fell back on humoral understandings of health and complexion to organize their world.

And yet humoral understandings of complexion could not provide definitive answers to Anglo-Americans' growing need to differentiate and rank New World residents: complexion still was embraced more as a sign of health than a means to mark racial hierarchies. Despite the fact that Europeans had spent well over a century attempting to categorize the natural world in light of their new global experiences, even terms such as "race" and "species" did not have settled definitions in this period. The threads of humoralism, inchoate racial divisions, and longtime understandings of ethnic and national divisions remained a site of theoretical inconsistencies in the eighteenth century. Describing corporeal appearance in everyday life was one way to solidify a more coherent worldview about bodies and identities. Understanding the ideologies and histories that European colonists brought to these descriptions of individual appearance begins with humoral medicine.

Constituting: Bodies in Early Modern Medicine

Views of health and disease that had been documented by the ancient Greek physicians Galen and Hippocrates had long permeated European culture under the banner of humoralism or humoral medicine. They promoted a view of the body as a unified, balanced whole where health was affected by physical, emotional, and environmental influences. Colonists were familiar with versions of ancient physicians' theory of the balance of the four internal humors (black bile, yellow bile, blood, and phlegm) and generally believed in the influence of the environmental "non-naturals" (air; sleep/walking; rest/exercise; excretion/retention; passions/emotions) on health and overall well-being.[5] Under this formulation, individuals had unique constitutions based on their ideal balance of humors. Humors were categorized into constitutions or temperaments that reflected an individual's particular humoral balance: choleric, melancholic, phlegmatic, or sanguine. For instance, blood, the sanguine humor, was understood to be associated with a wet and moist constitution, while yellow bile, the choleric humor, led to a hot and dry constitution. An excess of any one humor would shift an individual's bodily constitution toward its corresponding element with negative consequences. Regulating one's constitution meant achieving the most appropriate balance through intake and outflow and was believed to keep an individual in ideal (though perhaps unachievable) health.[6]

While such understandings of the body continued to hold explanatory power, they also adapted to new and scientific developments and global experiences. William Harvey's 1628 treatise, in which he described the circulatory system as distinct from the digestive, was just one of a range of challenges to ancient medical views by the eighteenth century. Alchemy, Arabic medicine, astrology, autopsies, Cartesian thought, folk medicine, midwifery publications, rational physiognomy, and a general rise of materialism and natural science had begun to transform early modern understandings of the body and would undermine traditional medical understandings of temperament. Colonial settler and imperial excursions offered experiences that challenged Europeans' inherited knowledge. Concern over bodily integrity reflected some of the ongoing instability of the relationships between humors, geography, genealogy, and the natural world.[7]

Despite these shifting ideas, eighteenth-century English colonists still largely accepted that humors affected a person's somatic makeup, which meant that medical perspectives on the working of human bodies greatly influenced discussions of individuals' appearance. By the middle of the eighteenth century, a growing belief in physiognomy would reinforce humoral beliefs, allowing physiological and psychological features of one's internal character to be seen through a diagnostic evaluation of angles, facial structures, and other external characteristics.[8] The holistic approach of humoralism made it flexible enough to categorize not only physical bodies but annual seasons, elements, and geographic regions. This flexibility, however, also meant that its terms could be applied with a relative lack of specificity. For instance, writers might interchangeably use "complexion," "constitution," and "temperament" to explain the collection of humors that characterized all living creatures. While modern meanings of these terms might be stable—complexion as skin color, constitution as physiological makeup, and temperament as psychological tendencies—they were far less so for British colonists. For instance, eighteenth-century physician Bernard Lynch wrote of "Temperament, or Nature of our Constitution," using the two terms to explain the same concept.[9]

Because temperament, complexion, and constitution were necessarily interrelated, many eighteenth-century people used complexion as they did other forms of humoral analysis: to convey information about both character and bodily qualities. The term derived from the Latin "complexio" and the Greek "crasis," meaning the temperament made by a balance of bodily elements. The Middle Ages elaborated on these Galenic ideas to affirm that all living things were "complexionate"—each plant or animal had its own individually appropriate complexion or temperamental balance. One late seventeenth-century health manual shows this expansive use of complexion far beyond human skin color: it explained how humoral-based complexions manifested in oxen and sheep.[10] Thus an individual's complexion was a means of identifying their particular bodily workings and form throughout their lives.[11]

At the same time, the porousness of the human body meant that what an individual ingested and experienced could change humoral balances and thus a body's external appearance. Even the clothing one wore could affect the body's ability to keep a proper humoral balance. William Byrd believed that in the Carolinas, colonial settlers ate so much pork "that it fills them full of gross Humours" and causes them to be "markt with a Custard Complexion" that leads to yaws, pox, and collapse of the bridge of the nose.[12] Thus, as Trudy Eden has shown, European colonists might be particularly wary of North American food, lest their constitutional balances be transformed into those more appropriate for indigenous North Americans.[13] A body's exterior offered a window onto its internal secrets, its past actions, and its state of health.[14]

Complexion was particularly useful to determine the state of an individual's internal soundness. According to Swiss physician Samuel Tissot, the "temperament and complexion of the patient" provided a guide to appropriate medical care, because "as it is for the outward complexion, so it is for the inward constitution."[15] One doctor explained the humoral workings that led to such complexion differences: pale-skinned people were those for whom "the Blood is viscid, or circulates with little Force," while "leucophlegmatic" people have skin that reflects "the Colour of the Water or Serum under it."[16] Examples of the health status conveyed by one's complexion abounded: A pale complexion was a symptom of epilepsy, and a florid one could signify rickets or a slow fever. Scurvy would lead to a sallow complexion.[17] Women were vulnerable to sex-specific complexion-affecting maladies: a vaginal discharge condition known as "the whites" would leave women with a "pale complexion," and excessive menstrual discharge would lead to "a sallow complexion."[18] The various kinds of skin discolorations articulated in medical guidebooks were repeated in everyday life as well: A lieutenant in the American Revolution, for example, evaluated the people of Virginia as having "a pale, sickly appearance, inclining to the Yellowish color."[19] The Boston physician and prolific writer William Douglass noted that some Indians are "of a milk-white Complexion, which is not natural and hereditary" but rather the result of a bad constitution.[20] In all of these examples, the coloration and appearance of the skin reflected the body's internal state.

Complexions were tied not only to physical health but also to an individual's emotional well-being. Personalities reflected particular humoral complexions: a red or florid complexion corresponded to a sanguine personality, yellow to a bilious one, black to melancholy, and so forth.[21] (The word "melancholy," still today signifying depression or despondency, derives from the Greek words for black and bile, originally labeling the emotional imbalance believed to be caused by an excess of that humor.) Human emotions and passions were one of the influences that Galen believed could wreak havoc on bodily constitutions and vice versa. So, as one health manual explained, "a Constitution of the *Humours* can affect the *Passions* of the *Mind*," and the "*Passions* of the *Mind* . . . [can] plunge the Constitution into great Disorders."[22]

Because humoral understandings of the body did not differentiate between physical and behavioral features, a person's external markings would reveal "hidden intentions" as well as past practices.[23] As one traveler opined, "Habits and Customs leave deep Traces, and lasting Impressions, upon the more solid Structure of the human Frame."[24] So a Pennsylvania newspaper advertisement touted a wet nurse's "healthy Constitution," alongside her "good Character," because both presumably were desirable qualities for the woman providing sustenance to an infant.[25] A mid-century almanac likewise noted that putting an infant "to the Breast of a Nurse who differs in Constitution from the Child's" is against the child's "Nature" as much as "one Species differs from another."[26] Other commentaries directly offered humoral explanations for behavior: a teacher noted to a student's stepfather that "the chief failings of his character are that He is constitution-ally somewhat too warm."[27] In a world where the interior of the body was largely inaccessible, external physical features and behavior were used to explain one another.

The Africans and Native Americans who populated eighteenth-century North America also held beliefs that emphasized the connections between people's external and internal worlds. For example, people from the west-central coast of Africa, who made up the majority of the colonial British American enslaved population, connected spiritual forces to bodily health under practices known by various names, including Obeah and Vodun.[28] Many West African people did not separate social, spiritual, and physical well-being. European travelers, implicitly paralleling their own beliefs about the influence of "intake" (i.e., food and drink) on humoral health, claimed that various groups in West Africa believed that certain foods would cause illness or death.[29] West African cosmologies connected physical, moral, and supernatural influences on health, often with an emphasis on the role of blood's diagnostic powers.[30]

North American indigenous people emphasized a balance between the spirit and the physical world, within and beyond an individual body. Bodily health could be disrupted by natural causes, witchcraft, or an individual's own thoughts, and even the supernatural could continue to take human form. The Haudenosaunee (Iroquois), for instance, saw the soul existing as a shadow counterpart to the physical body, with its own head, trunk and limbs.[31] Broadly speaking, eastern indigenous Americans shared beliefs in the permeability of bodies to the world around it—be that world corporeal or invisible. Native American beliefs in the permeability of the human body meant that colonial English and Eastern Woodland healing practices had significant overlap.[32]

Like Native American and African peoples, western Europeans recognized the relationship between terrestrial and spiritual worlds in the somatic state of individuals. Religious convictions could be revealed in physical appearance. Even the central idea of an unachievable ideal humoral balance could be understood as the corporeal result of Adam and Eve's fall from grace.[33] Perhaps reflecting the Great Awakening's emphasis on behavioral signs of conversion, one mid-century health writer promised that "just as your Souls thrive under the means of Grace; I'll make the Complexion of your Soul visible in the outward Condition of your Body and Affairs," noting that a "florid Complexion" indicated "a sound and healthful Soul."[34] Christian authors repeatedly discussed "the Complexion of the Soul" or used complexion to signify ingrained religious belief.[35] Complexion was a useful descriptor in these circumstances because its association with a balance of humors marked it as changeable, affected by how one lived.

The influence of behavior on bodies meant that one's affect had a visible impact on corporeal processes. A mid-eighteenth-century health writer explained the physiological workings of high emotion on complexion: when passions "become extreme, they drive about the Blood with such Violence" that the body becomes overwhelmed, which "renders the Complexion pale and ghastly."[36] Or, conversely, "the Vapours, or Hysteric Passion" to which the female sex could be subject was blamed on "an Accumulating of the Blood."[37] In either case, passion "discolours the finest Complexion."[38] Writers expected that heightened emotional states would be externally visible, as in an about-to-be-executed soldier who surprisingly showed no satisfaction at his pardon, "either by his complexion or otherwise."[39] The modern descendant of such beliefs via the language of humoral medicine continues in the phrase that someone's "good humor" signifies their positive emotional state. Indeed, it was not until the nineteenth century that the humoral notion of temperament became widely used to suggest a purely mental disposition.[40]

The expansive uses of complexion also could refer to strong beliefs. Benjamin Franklin, for example, repeatedly referred to a political viewpoint as a complexion. He advised waiting to submit a particular proposal until the "Complexion of Ministers and Measures" had changed, and wrote about "the Complexion of the next Assembly."[41] Revolutionary propaganda condemned the British parliament as having the "blackest complexion," applying a metaphorical understanding of blackness.[42] Complexion linked the internal to the external by tying thought, emotion, and character to corporeal appearance.

Complexion could also reflect the influence of one's social position on appearance. A medical manual noted that "children of the same rank in life and circumstances" will "seem pretty much of the same complexion, and live much in the same manner."[43] An almanac blithely noted that "Company" could "alter complexions."[44] In both medical and common parlance, complexion was a reflection of who one was and how one had lived.

Connecting complexion to internal health and external experiences meant that it was not reducible to observational colors of bodies. So Christopher Columbus's "good red and white" complexion was about far more than the color of his face.[45] "Red and white" was not an uncommon descriptor in the period. A mid-eighteenth-century account of English people living on an island off the coast of West Africa noted that they had "red and white" complexions that reflected an atypical "bloom of health" for people living in "warm climates."[46] Benjamin Franklin hoped for the expansion of "the lovely White and Red" in the Americas.[47] At first glance, it could seem that Franklin was, perhaps in William Penn's tradition, endorsing the notion of the "red" Noble Savage alongside the "white" Anglo-American. But that misinterpretation signals the modern distance from eighteenth-century meanings of complexion. "Red and white" was a humorally based complexion that marked a healthy body. It was not a categorization based on innate skin color. Franklin's "lovely" red and white referred to the perceived clarity of the skin that allowed it to reveal emotions through blushes or exertion through reddening cheeks. As such, it was a reflection of the workings of internal blood and humors.

The positive value imputed to red and white skin has a lengthy history. Ancient Greek masks used red and white to mark physical prowess and athleticism. The Prophet Muhammad apparently described Jesus as having

" 'a moderate complexion inclined to the red and white colours.' "[48] William Shakespeare repeatedly marked women's beauty with reference to their red and white complexions.[49] And in the American context, Thomas Jefferson would famously contrast "the fine mixtures of red and white" in opposition to the presumed dark skin of African-descended people in his *Notes on the State of Virginia*.[50]

By the eighteenth century this complimentary contrast between ecru-colored skin and blushing cheeks not only suggested a particular strain of English identity, it did so by underscoring the internal bodily process that complexion was meant to reflect. Clarity in the skin combined with the perceived health of appropriately flowing blood to create the coveted red and white combination. By juxtaposing the two colors, writers pointed to an ideal humoral balance that created that contrast, rather than an external all-over innate skin color. It was not *a* skin color, it was complexion as a signal of bodily function.

The lengthy European fascination with a red and white complexion is particularly striking because of how those colors would change in the American context. Anglo-Americans' focus on red and white as a sign of health would become less prominent as Native Americans became red, Euro-Americans retained the label of whiteness, and African Americans became increasingly categorized as black. Historians, too, have traced and deployed such color identifications, as an implicit recognition of the growing racialization of complexion as skin color by the end of the eighteenth century.[51] But such usages were neither transhistoric nor consistently applied. As in the use of the "white and red," colonial writers continued to merge humoral discourse to what would only later fully become racist markers of difference.

Thus, medical perspectives on the working of the human body influenced discussions of individuals' appearance. Humoral beliefs offered options beyond a surface reading of innate skin color because individuals' humoral balance could be read in their external complexion. Eighteenth-century transatlantic writers continued to hew to the idea that each individual had a perfect humoral balance that was inseparable from their physical, emotional, and spiritual well-being.

Complexion also reflected external influences. Indeed, the almanac that noted that "company" could alter complexion referenced another influential factor in the same phrase: "Company, *like climates*, alter complexions."[52] The author expressed a widely held belief that people's constitutions, as revealed through their complexions, were tied to their geographic location and communities. It was such beliefs that gave European travelers the ability to use complexion as a means to explain, divide, and rank the people who populated the eighteenth-century Atlantic world.

Dividing: Complexion in the Wider World

In conjunction with the rise of European settler colonialism, humoral ideas profoundly influenced attempts to identify, create, and distinguish among groups of human beings from different geographic regions. Beyond telling the internal truth of an individual, complexion could identify the innate characteristics of a people. As Mary Floyd-Wilson summarizes, "humoralism, for the early modern English, was ethnology."[53] Early modern Europeans were used to reading external bodies for information about both individuals' and an entire people's character, behavior, and constitutions. They brought this knowledge to their descriptions and classifications of people living in Africa and North America.

There is little question that Anglo-Americans saw fundamental distinctions between geographically defined groups. While they used terms that, for modern readers, can appear to reflect a form of nineteenth-century scientific racism, in the early modern period Europeans defined "race" and "species" multivalently. At its most basic, "race" was a marker of shared origins that could be used to signify family heritage or kinship relationships. Thus Thomas Shadwell's 1676 poem: "I am the last of all my Family; my Race will fail, if I should fail."[54] It was not until the nineteenth century that the term would assume the meaning of innate biological difference.[55]

The term "species" was less tied to kinship for early modern Europeans and originated in categorizations of physical substances (e.g., chemical compounds) more than people. It derived from the Latin for appearance or form, as a portrayal of essential qualities. According to the *Oxford English Dictionary*, "species" was first recorded as a synonym for the human race in the early eighteenth century and had been a marker of animal and plant categorization at least a century earlier.[56] One eighteenth-century English dictionary defined "species" as "a common nature [or] idea agreeing to several individual beings."[57] Accordingly, early modern writers might write about species of disease, of livestock, of humanity, or use the term to talk about inanimate categorical divisions.[58]

"Race" seemed to be more widely applied to a variety of human relationships and characteristics in the eighteenth century, underscoring writers' comfort with its lack of specificity. "Race" could be an appropriate
characterization whether referring to humanity, national character, or a
mythical society of female warriors. Tracing how the word was used in the
voluminous family papers of John and Abigail Adams reflects the flexibility
with which it could be applied. Repeatedly, the Adamses used "race" to
mean humanity—whether referring to the "Race of Adam," "the whole
human Race," "the present Race of men," or "all human Race."[59] But on
other occasions, "race" served to mark a group of people united through
what we might call national heritage. John Adams's draft of a letter for
publication in 1765, for example, referred to the inhabitants of America as
being "descended from a Race" that had crossed oceans "for the sake of
their Liberty and Religion."[60] Abigail Adams bemoaned, on the eve of the
Revolution, that Americans came from a "race" of villainous Britons, and
John Adams referred to "the present Race of Brittons." And of course,
Abigail famously noted that if provoked, American women would face their
enemies as "a Race of Amazons."[61]

On other occasions, the Adamses' use of the term implicitly reflected
the humoral links between behavior and bodily temperament. "Race" could
categorize people who acted in concert or who shared ideas. In John's
words, there was the "irritable Race" of men who were determined to
enforce the Stamp Act, as well as the Philadelphia Quakers whom he
dubbed "the Race of the insipids."[62] People could be grouped into a "race"
by how they acted as much as where they came from or to whom they were
related.

The notion of "race" as a flexible label for a group sharing characteristics or beliefs was repeated in various print venues. In one colonial newspaper, "Cato" noted that "hereditary succession does not ensure a race of
good and wise men," while in another, a story about court actions referred
to a leader among "the present Race of pleaders."[63] These uses of "race"
emphasized that in colonial British America, the term was not just, or even
primarily, a physiological construct. It was certainly a means of classification, but paralleling the overlap of temperament and bodily constitution,
"race" was not limited to biological lineage, national heritage, or phenotypical appearance.

Colonial experiences that introduced Europeans to people visibly and
culturally different from themselves helped push race toward physiological

meanings. But there remained inconsistencies. Travelers regularly sought to describe Native American and African exoticism for European audiences, and in an era before evolutionary nomenclature, they employed "race" or "species" interchangeably to mark human differences. Welsh naturalist Griffith Hughes referred to Indians as "a distinct Race," while Scottish historian William Robertson described Native Americans as "men of another species."[64] Dutch naturalist Bernard Romans described people from the African continent alternatively as the "black race" or "Negroe species."[65] In 1750, the *London Magazine* published a reaction to Buffon's natural history that sought to identify different "races of men" from "all the varieties of the human species."[66] It appeared to be an unnecessary—or at least unsettled—distinction if indigenous Americans and Africans were separable human species, distinct races, or each made up of multiple races, as long as the term could serve to mark a significant degree of difference from people familiar to European readers.

Terms such as "race" and "species" could be expansive in part because they conveyed differences of many types. There was no consistent agreement that people from African or American regions were fundamentally separable from European populations. The degree to which phenotypical variation developed out of innate or inherited differences as opposed to external influences would remain a subject of considerable debate through the eighteenth century. At the center of many of these debates were attempts to stretch, modify, or transform humoral understandings of the body in light of Europeans' colonial experiences and interactions.

Humoral explanations of external appearances remained malleable tools for categorizing the world through the eighteenth century. In 1767, *The New Book of Knowledge* used humoral complexions to describe a variety of chronological and geographic divisions: the seasons, the times of day, the stages of life, and the "four Quarters of the World" were all mapped to sanguine, choleric, melancholic, and phlegmatic complexions.[67] Thus it was not a leap to apply the flexible explanatory mechanism of humoral constitutions to a range of gendered, racial, and regional differences in human features.

In its universal applicability, humoral theory united bodies from diverse regions while also providing an explanation for observed differences in individual appearance and among discrete populations. Even before early modern imperial expansion, Europeans were already accustomed to dividing people along humoral lines. Men's humoral balance, for instance, was seen as hotter and drier than women's, which was thought to incline women to being cold and moist. But colonization would challenge these categorizations. The coldness of "women" was not the all-inclusive category of femaleness that its name purported it to be: Europeans believed that African women, for example, had hot constitutions.[68]

Early modern European expansion created a range of challenges and revisions to humoral beliefs. New environments brought added importance to reading bodily health through external appearance. Colonists recognized that seasoning would be necessary for their bodies to adapt to new climates and geographies. The omnipresence of death and disease in early colonial locales offered lessons about the suitability of English physiology and attuned colonists to the influence of environmental circumstances on their permeable bodies.[69] Interactions with people from other regions, climates, and continents would lead to debates about humoral divisions, human origins, and scientific workings of bodies.

Humoralism proved flexible and long-lasting, however. Even though Carl Linnaeus's mid-eighteenth-century cartographic classification of humans would become one of the foundations of scientific racism, his writings were strongly grounded in traditional understandings of bodily constitution. His descriptions of human varieties offer humoral characteristics directly after his complexionate descriptions. Thus Native Americans ("Americanus") were "rufus, cholericus"; Europeans "albus, saugineus"; Asians "luridus, melancholicus"; and Africans "niger, phlegmaticus."[70]

Even with an increasing emphasis on anatomy and the reproducible evidence of experimentation, humoral understandings of the body persisted in Europeans' interpretations of life in lands new to them. Humoralism meant that colonists had good reasons to fear the impact of new environments on Europeans and European bodies. This fear was not simply about external appearance—that English people would come to look like indigenous Americans or Africans. Rather, they feared that they would no longer *be* English: that they would not behave like English people, that they would suffer from decreased rationality and increased passion and cruelty, that they would become more like their imagined versions of savage natives.[71] Eighteenth-century writers strove to identify and account for geographic variations in ways that allowed them to balance humoral views, national needs, and colonial projects.

Just as it had been for individuals, "complexion" could be a useful term to explain an entire people's character. A commentary published around

1700, for example, listed distinctions of "Nations, Complexion, Temper or Genius of Mankind, under several Climates," and a mid-century sermon referred to "Truth and Equity" as the "Character and Complexion of a People."[72] Tying complexion and constitution to nation and region reflected beliefs about heritage, political boundaries, and imagined histories—about where people belonged and, consequently, who they were. Philadelphia physician Benjamin Rush identified "stateliness, proportion, and fine complexions" as the "principal outlines of national characters."[73] For this reason, travel narratives regularly described complexion as a primary means to understand the population of regions largely unfamiliar to Europeans. In his history of North America, William Douglass titled a section on Native Americans "As to their Make and Complexion," emphasizing the centrality of complexion to understanding bodily constitutions.[74] Other writers more specifically emphasized Native Americans' choleric temperament as an explanation for their supposed warlike demeanor.[75]

The ties between climate, region, and bodily constitution meant that complexion was mapped to where one lived as much as to someone's heritage. Naturalist John Mitchell promoted the power of climate on bodies, explaining that "the different Colours of People have been demonstrated to be only the necessary Effects, and natural Consequences, of their respective Climes, and Ways of Life." He offered as proof that "I have been an Eyewitness" to Spaniards living in "the Torrid Zone" becoming "as dark coloured as our native *Indians* of *Virginia*." Mitchell added his assumption that behavior would change constitutions as well as complexions: if the Spanish continued to live "the same rude and barbarous Lives" as Native Americans, "in Succession of many Generations, they would become as dark in Complexion."[76] Experience changed who one was and how one's progeny would look. This was a potentially fearful outcome for nations in the midst of settler colonialism.

British and American writers slotted African complexions into their existing worldviews. Even as English writers focused on the unique-to-them appearance of West Africans, they had a long history of associating Africans' darker skin with that of others around the globe. In 1623, Richard Jobson described both "Tawny Moore" and "Tawny *Fulbie*" people; more than a century later, Anthony Benezet described the West African Fulis as being "generally of a deep tawny complexion," similar to that of Moors.[77] An eighteenth-century writer described enslaved people from Madagascar, off the southeast coast of the African continent, as "somewhat inclined to the

Tawny; yet still a Degree blacker than the Indians."[78] Such descriptions set African complexion alongside that of people of other regions and continents. They described difference not as an exception or opposition but as a comprehensible piece of a geohumoral worldview. These portrayals emphasized the relation of African people to others around the world. A British *Philosophical Transactions* publication made this explicit, noting that the cutis in African people was "somewhat like the Skin of many brown-skinn'd white People" and "somewhat like the Colour of an *Indian or Molatto*."[79] Anglo-American writers made sense of human variation by incorporating distant communities of people into preexisting knowledge and experiences.

Descriptions of indigenous Americans made similar connections to people in other regions. In his mid-seventeenth-century exploration of skin color, Robert Boyle described Native Americans as "Tawny-Mores." An eighteenth-century reprint claimed that "the natives of Canada" have a "colour, which approaches nearer to ours." William Wood ranked Native Americans as "more swarthy than Spaniards."[80] Tying Native American appearance to their place in an imperial world would both make them more legible for Europeans and implicitly engage the issue of the environment's impact on bodily constitution.

Since at least the seventeenth century, a burgeoning field of self-styled European scientists debated the origins of differences in bodily appearance. They proposed theories as diverse as biblical sin, the impact of "seminal imagination" at conception, exposure to sun, a divine plan, and medical arguments related to humoral constitution. They also took note of others' origin stories: an eighteenth-century summary of a travel narrative described West African people's beliefs that "the Whites and Black are two Species, that God created them both in the Beginning."[81]

Competing theories of monogenesis (one common human ancestor) and polygenesis (separate geographically distinct ancestors) abounded in the eighteenth century and were integrally tied to how early modern Europeans understood geohumoralism.[82] Many natural scientists supported single-origin theories. A 1763 supplement to Voltaire's "Essay on Universal History" asserted monogenesis against Voltaire's polygenetic theory, arguing that "we may, indeed, rank all mankind, if we please, under one species. . . . But this species will appear to be really divided into many others, both by physical and moral distinctions."[83]

Explanations for human variation were an ongoing concern among people whose circumnavigation had brought them into contact with communities of people who had markedly different appearances, traditions, and practices. Colonists showed a growing need to define and segregate, not just for the sake of science, but in the service of settler colonialism, a nascent race-based slave system, and hierarchical orderings of national and cultural belonging.[84] Interest in creating cohesive explanations for human variation would eventually lead to the scheme of scientific racism of the nineteenth and much of the twentieth centuries. Yet there was no formal changeover date. Instead, humoral and ethnographic categorizations could be complementary and overlapping in their colonial eighteenth-century applications.

European humoral theory underlay the purported causes of visible differences in skin color around the globe. One natural history writer left it to anatomists to discover "in what part or membrane of the body that humour resides which tinges the complexion of the negroe with a deep black," while Bernard Romans maintained that dark skin color was produced by the "sable race" having additional "vesicles, filled wish [*sic*] a black ink-like humour."[85] Others promoted theories more in line with their belief in monogenesis. Seventeenth-century British philosopher and scientist Robert Boyle concluded that black coloring was only on the "outward skin," based on others' reports of dissection of African bodies.[86] He may have been referring to Voltaire's claim, supposedly based on a dissection in Amsterdam, that a "mucous membrane . . . between the muscles and the skin, is white in us, and black or copper-coloured" in "the Negro race."[87] The claim of skin color being only surface deep was repeated in at least one mid-eighteenth-century natural history of Barbados, suggesting the claim's influence and longevity.[88] However, John Mitchell, a Virginia doctor and naturalist, forwarded a rejection of these explanations that would be repeated and reprinted through the second half of the eighteenth century. Based on anatomical research, Mitchell argued that skin color was related to the thickness of the skin, not due to any "black Humour in the Skins of Negroes." Instead, "those who have such thick and coarse Skins, are never of so perfect and pure a White, as they who have a thin and fine Skin." Thus he concluded, as the heading of one section announced, that *"The Colour of Negroes does not proceed from any black Humour"* and "that there is not so great, unnatural, and unaccountable a Difference between Negroes and white People, on account of their Colours." By arguing that skin thickness related to how much of the body's workings—"the white and red Parts below"—could be seen, Mitchell blended humoral beliefs with anatomical evidence. He continued to assume a relationship between behavior and appearance, arguing that beyond the sun's impact on the skin's thickness, "the nature and Temper of the Country" and "The Ways of Living in it" could thicken and consequently darken the skin.[89]

Such experiments in the name of scientific investigation depended on Europeans' ability to do unrestricted violence to African-descended bodies. John Mitchell's treatise on skin color, published in the Royal Society's *Philosophical Transactions* in 1746, relied on the North American slave system, which gave him the liberty to experiment on African people. Many of Mitchell's conclusions about the structure of Africans' skin came from his analysis of the consequences of "Blistering with *Cantharides*," a beetle secretion that causes severe chemical burns when applied to skin. Mitchell proclaimed that "I have macerated the Skins of Negroes" in his scientific search for a black humor in the skin. Other findings suggest that he tortured African-descended burn victims in his pursuit of science. He "scraped off" layers of skin on a slave's thigh to find a "third membrane" that was only visible after blistering "in a living Subject."[90] Mitchell was not creating these experiments out of whole cloth: as early as 1618, a French anatomist conducted similar blistering and skin dissections on an African person.[91] These experiments and the resulting conclusions were made possible by a transatlantic slave system that deemed African-descended bodies to be a commodity available for mutilation.

Europeans gave less attention to (and perhaps had fewer opportunities for) dissection and anatomy of Native Americans, and instead strove to convey the exact complexion of residents of North America. Native Americans' complexion received extensive attention as European travelers tried to describe the people who filled the American continent. Some referred in basic terms to the "Copper Complexion of the Natives," while others were more expansive: "Their Complexion is of a splendid redish Brown, or metaline Lustre, which is well expressed by a Copper Colour," or "their colour resembles that of cinnamon, with a copperish cast."[92] Referring to Native Americans in terms of exotic spices and the "splendid" coloring of a valued, lustrous metal suggests the influence of the bountiful world in which many British writers believed that Indians lived, and their hope that that bounty would positively affect English colonial bodies as well. Here complexion conveyed not a need for scientific analysis but a seeming desire to emphasize the positive impact of living in North America on physical bodies.

Other colonists seemed to ally Native American complexion to terms familiar to transatlantic readers. A late seventeenth-century travel narrative offered multiple complexion descriptors: Indians were "pale and lean Tartarian visag'd" and had "reasonable good complexions." Early in the eighteenth century, John Norris introduced Native Americans to his European audience by describing them as "a sort of Red Dun, or Tan'd Skin'd People." A mid-century newspaper described Indians as having "reddish brown skin."[93] A 1763 English translation of Voltaire's work asserted that "the Iroquois, the Hurons, and all the people of that tract, as far as Florida, are olive-coloured." William Robertson covered a range of complexionate possibilities by describing indigenous complexions as being "of a reddish brown, nearly resembling the colour of copper," and "of a dusky copper colour." "Tawny" was also repeatedly used: a Revolutionary-era traveler described "their complexion [as] a little tawny, or copper coloured," while Benjamin Franklin simply identified them as "tawny."[94] In Anglo-American eyes, North Americans were copper, reddish brown, red, red dun, cinnamon, olive, tanned, dusky, tawny, or swarthy. This was far from a specific, reliably identifiable categorization based in a single color–marked complexion of Native Americans as a separate race.[95] Instead, they were terms that linked Native Americans to others around the globe.

Paralleling geohumoral debates, some travelers asserted that Native American coloration was more a product of their environment and behavior than a reflection of any innate differences. James Oglethorpe explained that Native Americans in the Carolinas "are somewhat tawny, occasioned chiefly by oyling their Skins, and by exposing themselves naked to the Rays of the Sun."[96] Describing Native Americans' skin color as a result of external modifications gave colonists hope that they could protect themselves from the danger that their new environment could change their essential Englishness.[97]

For European colonists, a changed complexion carried a potentially fearful significance about people becoming someone other than who they were before crossing the Atlantic. In *New-England's Prospect*, republished throughout the eighteenth century, William Wood argued for the supremacy of New England by pointing out that while Virginia's hot summers and diseases changed "lusty" English bodies from swarthy to pale complexioned, in New England, "men and women keep their ordinary complexions . . . fresh and ruddy."[98] William Douglass noted that while Europeans may become more tan in the colonies, "Transplantation or Transportation recovers their native Complexion."[99] Colonial settler expansion meant that Anglo-Americans had a vested interest in minimizing the effect of climate. This could ameliorate concerns over colonists' ability to maintain their own bodily integrity as English people, even in new environments.[100]

Scholars and laypeople repeatedly focused on the degree to which climate determined bodily appearance. In the seventeenth century, Boyle reported on the multiple debates among "Learned Men" and weighed in against a climatological explanation of human difference, noting that African nations' degree of blackness did not directly correspond to distance from the equator and that there appeared to be no black-complexioned natives in the Americas.[101] But concern over the impact of regional climates on people's constitutions continued throughout the eighteenth century. There seemed to be repeated interest in Greenlandic Inuits—their comparatively lighter complexion was used to confirm an association between cool climate and lighter skin color.[102] Such divergent reports highlighted the contested role of geohumoral theories in interpreting appearance and suggest the vested interest of British colonists in debunking climate influence on constitutional temperament.

If humans were scientifically divisible by cartographic regions based at least in part on climatology, then early Americans needed to engage with the possibility that they could, through a changing balance of the humors, become someone new by living somewhere new. In the mid-eighteenth century, writers might uncomplicatedly assert that "climates sometimes change mens [sic] complexions, and have a great influence in altering their constitutions."[103] The author of *Sketches of the History of Man*, originally published in 1774, felt the need to challenge climate's role in determining skin color, offering that "there are many instances of races of people preserving their original color in climates very different from their own; and not a single instance of the contrary, as far as I can learn."[104] Though reports of experiments on Native American people were less common than those on African people, James Adair's history went to great lengths to explain the "anatomical observations" of Indians that identified a "fine cowl" in their skin that contributed to their complexion color. Yet he still hedged his bets, also noting that "their constant anointing themselves with bear's oil" led to the "Indian colour."[105]

Whichever geohumoral argument they supported, writers used these discussions to buttress their political, cultural, or ideological beliefs. For people opposing race-based slavery, environmental influences on complexion showed the fallacy of racial divisions. It was no accident, for example, that an American antislavery publication pointed out the inconsistency in using skin color as a proxy for status. It argued that "there are many honest weather-beaten Englishmen, who have as little reason to boast of their complexion as the Indians," and elaborated that "northern Indians, have no difference from us in complexion, but such as is occasioned by the climate or different way of living."[106] Thus skin color was not a valid rationale for enslavement. Conversely, supporters of American slavery identified fundamental differences in African people's bodies that would not be affected by the workings of the environment. John Mitchell offered an analogy to explain the increasingly obvious: that dark-skinned Africans did not automatically become light skinned in Europe or America. Mitchell analogized that just as it was easier to dye a white cloth black than dye a black cloth white, the thickening of African people's skin that led to their dark coloration was not easily undone.[107] A Revolutionary-era natural historian forwarded an opinion on the (non)effect of climate with a reproductive example. He noted the existence of "four complete generations of negroes in Pennsylvania without any visible change of color: they continue jet-black as originally."[108] This purportedly firsthand evidence against climate theories of complexion implicitly offered a rationale for perpetual enslavement of African-descended people. Complexion could be proof that people of African descent were climatologically unaffected by life on North American soil across generations. It also reassured readers that Anglo-American colonists would remain Anglo-American in any environment.

The invocation of reproduction in debates over human origins and geo-humoralism was not accidental. More than a century of the transatlantic slave trade offered innumerable instances of the potential transformative properties of reproduction. It was unlikely to have escaped notice that the children who were populating the British (and other) colonies had features that suggested an amalgamation of African, English, and Native American heritages. Yet humoral theories offered alternative explanations, most notably, the impact of imagination on a fetus. Jane Sharp, the renowned early modern midwife, noted that by "the strength of imagination . . . sometimes the mother is frighted or conceives wonders . . . and the child is markt accordingly by it."[109] Just as passions could affect an individual's physical appearance, strong emotions could affect the appearance of future offspring.

Reproduction offered a fertile ground for climate and origins theories. Robert Boyle linked a theory of seminal impression to geohumoral explanations, arguing that "Organical parts" like skin color or facial features could have been formed through strong feelings at the time of conception, leading to different-looking groups of humans around the world. Writers focused on human beings' complexion at the start of life to argue for monogenesis. In both the seventeenth and eighteenth centuries, writers concluded that "Negro" babies were not born black. Boyle noted that they were "almost like the Reddish Colour with our European Children" and darkened in a few days.[110] An eighteenth-century writer expressed a similar belief: that the "Negroe species," "like all others of the different species, and varieties of the human genus are born white, which colour soon changes."[111] Such writings supported a belief that all humans originated from a shared ancestry—and specified that that shared ancestry was defined by a European appearance.

Indeed, many eighteenth-century writers insisted that children born of one European-descended and one African-descended parent should be understood as lightened rather than darkened. William Douglass infamously observed that "some dissolute Planters are said to wash the Blackemore white, by generating with the Successive Shades of their own Issue, Children, Grand Children, &c, the Progeny at Length becomes blonde, or of a pale White."[112] A natural history advised that children of mulatto or black and European parents "will gradually lose their Copper-colour Complexion." This author applied "copper coloring," a term regularly used in reference to Native American complexions, as an intermediate complexion of a child descended from African and European parents. In the same passage, he alternatively described the complexion of someone who had an African ancestor six or seven generations back as having "what we call in *England* a Nut-brown Complexion."[113] Writers expressed confidence that English bodies would prevail in determining the appearance of future generations, marking supposed superiority through descriptions of the appearance of multi-heritaged offspring.

William Byrd's multiple comments on reproduction reinforced the idea that the European form would prevail in a somatic parallel to their presumed imperial success. He noted that European- and Native American–descended children would eventually become lighter skinned: "if a Moor may be washt white in 3 Generations, Surely an Indian might have been blancht in two." Byrd reiterated that "their Copper-colour'd Complexion wou'd admit of Blanching, if not in the first, at the farthest in the Second

Generation."[114] In a disturbing bawdy story in his commonplace book, Byrd turned to reproduction between Europeans and Africans. He told the tale of a white man who had a "Mulatto" child with "an Ethiopian Princess." The white man then committed incest with his "Mulatto" daughter, and they produced a "daughter of the Portuguese complection," whom he also impregnated. This final daughter was "perfectly white."[115] Unlike Aesop's fabled impossibility of "Washing the Ethiopian White," Byrd's immorality tale insisted that European constitutions would prove the most powerful in colonial settlements. Determining what the children created by people originating in different parts of the globe would look like mattered to the future of colonial projects. Colonists countered fear of the impact of new environments with insistence that European constitutions would have the most impact on the appearance of colonial Americans—European patriarchal heritage would be visible on children's faces.

These commentaries on the workings of complexion held significant economic and political import. Byrd noted that Indians would have "had less reason to Complain that the English took away their Land" if the English had assumed the property through marriage to "their Daughters." Not only would this have prevented "much Bloodshed," it would leave no question that whitened-complexioned people would be in control of large swaths of the North American continent.[116] British men's sexual relations with Indian women (in Byrd's formulations, only Indian daughters were available for producing soon-to-be-blanched babies) would lead to a more successful settler colonialism. A continuum leading inexorably toward European complexions marked imperial success. And by the eighteenth century, legislating that slavery followed the status of the mother would remove any legal liabilities for centuries of sexual exploitation of enslaved women.

Writers mobilized complexion in transatlantic discussions of political and ideological divisions as well. As noted in the Introduction, Benjamin Franklin notoriously expressed his opinions on complexion and national belonging in his mid-century "Observations concerning the Increase of Mankind and the Peopling of Countries." Franklin complained about German colonists as "Palatine Boors" who threaten to "Germanize us instead of our Anglifying them." He noted that the Germans "will never adopt our Language or Customs, any more than they acquire our Complexion."[117] Franklin conveyed humoral understandings of complexion here, tying behavior to appearance. Complexion differences were not binarily racial.

Complexion performed double service as skin color and temperament. Franklin concluded this essay by noting that "perhaps I am partial to the Complexion of my Country, for such Kind of Partiality is natural to Mankind."[118] Franklin was using complexion as a marker of national heritage: English people had an English complexion that encompassed far more than a spot on a color palette. It signified belonging, outlook, and natural affinity. Similarly, when John Adams claimed that New Englanders were superior because of their "purer English Blood," he saw this as a result of behavior more than any notion of blood quantum. Adams explained that their purity resulted from New Englanders being "descended from Englishmen too who left Europe, in purer Times than the present and less tainted with Corruption."[119] Both men assumed that temperament and appearance were interrelated features of national heritage. Complexion's fluidity, and the conflicting theories of its relation to climate, geography, and bodily stability, meant that writers could apply it instrumentally to support their own political beliefs.

*   *   *

The eighteenth-century description of Christopher Columbus that opened this chapter reflected a humoral understanding of personal description. Columbus's portrayal interspersed descriptors of health (a face "neither too fat nor too lean"), of temperament ("naturally grave"), and of character (ate and drank in moderation) and used complexion as a reflection of internal bodily functions and temperament (good red and white), rather than a categorization of specific racial heritage.

Such humoral interpretations were not transhistoric. Toward the end of the eighteenth century, Presbyterian minister Samuel Stanhope Smith published a lengthy essay in opposition to racial classifications. Titling his essay "Variety of Complexion and Figure in the Human Species," Smith sought to identify the "diversity of mankind." The word "humors" did not appear even once.[120] Likewise, an early nineteenth-century reading and spelling book defined "complexion" unequivocally as "color of the skin," without any indication of its broader humoral and constitutional meanings.[121] Complexion as an indication of one's personal health had transformed into a marker of cultural, national, or racial divisions. By the start of the nineteenth century, complexion had been largely replaced by skin color in American discourse.

An emphasis on skin color transformed complexion from a reflection of internal bodily workings into an immutable racialized identity. Color became a labeling mechanism rather than a tool of revelation. Instead of reading a continuum of humoral balances, external appearances were understood as determinative, reflecting from the outside in, not the inside out. Skin color determined the inner truth of groups of individuals, rather than one's exterior complexion reflecting that individual's changeable inner balance.

Yet these nineteenth-century versions of complexion that were increasingly divorced from the word's humoral roots did not yet dominate the world of eighteenth-century British colonial thought. That earlier time intermittently mixed national, regional, individual, and humoral meanings of complexion. Centuries of European beliefs in the skin as a reflection of physical, moral, and environmental experiences made complexion a particularly useful explanation in an expanding imperial world. Complexion displayed a being's temperament, its inner nature, and was malleable enough to allow eighteenth-century Americans to manipulate, modify, endorse, or reconfigure systems of belonging and difference within its framework.

We make a mistake if we equate complexion to skin color to race in the transatlantic world of the pre-Revolutionary British colonies. Complexion was neither reducible to nor separable from skin color. Instead, complexion allowed viewers to tie bodies to geographic regions, to experiences, and to ideological and economic purposes. A series of unsettled questions about the relationship between constitutions and environment, between lived experiences and temperament, and between bodies and behaviors undermined any easily marked divisions among humanity. The ability to marshal complexion for political and colonial aims was a direct result of the flexibility of the term.

These circulations of conflicting, overlapping, and transmuting ideas in the eighteenth century provide a necessary base for understanding descriptions of appearance. Common people rarely explicitly debated—at least in the historical record—their thoughts on complexion or humoral expression. They did not overtly state what black or white or red meant to them in a given context. But they did selectively employ a range of beliefs about constitutions and complexions, colors and climates, regions and populations.

When British colonists offered descriptions of individual people, they drew on the place of bodies in centuries of medical, scientific, and popular thought. In keeping with the humoral emphasis on reflections of bodily health, colonists commented on the shape, size, health, strength, and weaknesses of bodies, as well as on behavioral and character features. Complexion, signifying far more than skin color, was just one of the qualities that could be used to distinguish individuals from one another. The published descriptions of missing persons in eighteenth-century North America are most legible when read in the context of European humoral understandings of constitutions, temperament, and bodily workings.

CHAPTER 2

Shaping Bodies in Print

Labor and Health

In any given year, hundreds of colonial Americans escaped their homes in a bid for freedom. Newspaper advertisements narrated many of these self-liberations. With just a few lines of text, an advertiser attempted to describe a runaway servant's or slave's appearance so that readers could envision a three-dimensional person. A runaway laborer's size and shape, age and health, general looks, and specific idiosyncrasies might all be potential identifying factors. Advertisements were filled with lusty and likely bodies; down looks and surly affects; well-set and straight-limbed frames; long visages and full faces.

Descriptions of missing persons turned observation, belief, and imagination into corporeal characteristics. The many features noted in advertisements reveal as much about the appearance of runaways as about colonial understandings of bodies. Never islands unto themselves, bodies were always in relation: in relation to perceptions of an individual's laboring abilities; in relation to beliefs about sex and race; and in relation to how external appearance reflected internal health and character.[1] While Chapter 1 focused on broad understandings of bodies within early modern European expansion, this chapter moves squarely across the Atlantic to explore how colonists connected humoral beliefs to appearance and labor capabilities. The range of descriptive choices in advertisements—whether to list a given characteristic, whether to describe measurable features quantitatively or qualitatively, or how many details to include—all contributed to colonial understandings of how particular kinds of laboring bodies were expected to look and behave.

Determining the relationship between visible variations and the influence of racial ideologies is no simple task. Even though advertisements reflected the describer's worldview, some descriptions related to material variations in bodies. Yet advertisements were not textual replicas of bodies: they were cultural transformations of individual lives into print. Masters may have lived and looked more closely at people of European descent. Gender and sartorial practices left some bodies more visually accessible than others. To analyze the culturally specific ways that different groups of laborers were described does not deny the physicalities undergirding descriptions. Rather, it notes which features, out of the hundreds that could be usefully described, were naturalized as innate features on which bodies in this specific historic context.

In lieu of observable, measurable details, African-descended bodies were transformed into chattel through their owners' evaluative descriptions. This served both to commodify enslaved human beings and create racial difference with criteria beyond ethnicity, nationality, and skin color. Labeling of Negro or European heritage may have been a prerequisite for identification, but its assertion was accompanied by a wide array of features that reified categorization into physical reality. For instance, health, illness, well-being, disability, and ability served as markers to define race in the colonial eighteenth century even without explicit recourse to ideas of racial difference. By more often specifying the age and height of European-descended runaways, advertisers focused on self-represented details for these free laborers, while regularly classifying enslaved laborers with evaluations made by the people who owned them. Likewise, advertisers emphasized free laborers' specific ailments but more generically described enslaved people's ill health.

By making such subjective distinctions, colonial advertisers reified racial ideologies. When they relied on humorally based interpretations more for European-descended than for African-descended laborers, they were transforming opinions into physiological realities and cementing race as a category of difference. A wide expanse of laborers' physiological and psychological features were transformed into material capital by constituting what it meant to be identified as a person of European or African or (less frequently) Native American heritage. This process, labeled "racecraft" by historian Barbara Fields and sociologist Karen Fields, did not require that European and African bodies be set in opposition to one another.[2] Instead, incompatible standards for evaluation of appearance reaffirmed colonists' social, economic, and ideological divisions on a daily basis.

A Frame for Laboring: Age and Height

Colonial advertisers emphasized age and height in their searches for runaways. In my topic modeling study of the eighteenth-century *Pennsylvania Gazette*, for instance, some of the most likely descriptive words to appear in reference to runaways were "years old," "feet," and "inches."[3] Whether the person was old or young, tall or short: these were presumably visible features that provided a literal framework for identification. Age and height simultaneously conveyed information about health. When colonists chose to describe someone by a qualitative term such as "young," "middle aged," or "elderly," they were conveying an evaluation of appearance in lieu of a specific age with the expectation that readers would share their perspective on what an "old" or "young" person would look like. Likewise, descriptions of "short," "tall," or "middling" spoke to an implicit set of shared beliefs. Even numerical representations of height conveyed more than numbers on a measuring stick. Height could serve as a proxy for strength, health, and the effect of life history on bodies. In the contexts of servitude and enslavement, age and size provided a way to mark differentiated life experiences and reinforce racialized expectations of laboring bodies.

Even though runaways largely clustered into a youthful subset of colonists' life span, age was a common descriptive criterion. One historical study of an early American newspaper found that two-thirds of advertisements listed the runaway's age.[4] In the thousands of advertisements analyzed here, slightly less than two-thirds of runaways had their numerical age listed in advertisements. Unsurprisingly, runaways were usually on the young side of the adult population, with half of all missing persons identified as being between twenty and thirty years old. New England runaways with specific ages listed in advertisements were slightly younger: the age of the middle 50 percent fell between eighteen and twenty-eight years old, likely reflecting the traditional New England system of apprenticing out teenaged children. Conversely, criminals who had escaped from jail were older than other runaways, averaging thirty years old. Beyond these variations, there was little deviation among the average numerical ages for runaways, with most subgroups averaging twenty-four or twenty-five years of age.[5]

Age might seem like one of the most objective features in bodily descriptions, but it was not necessarily an exact count of the person's years on earth.[6] In a phenomenon known as age heaping, runaways were much more likely to be listed at an age that was a multiple of five: for example, twice as many runaways were identified as being twenty-five years old as twenty-four or twenty-six years old.[7] This may be partly why Barnaby, the recidivist runaway discussed in the Introduction, aged from twenty to twenty-five years old in only three years.

Whether owners knew their laborers' exact ages was less important than their ability to decide the public age of missing persons in their absence. In many cases, owners and masters knew the specific age of their laborers. Indentured servants and apprentices often had ages entered into legal documents that their masters could have consulted. Many slave owners recorded their property's age at times of sale or as regular bookkeeping practices. But the nearest half decade often seemed accurate enough for identification purposes. An exact numerical age was probably an unnecessarily specific descriptor for a visual identification—someone being twenty-two rather than twenty-six years old, for example, would not make a consistent difference in their appearance. In 1758, one owner said that missing slave Hercules was "about 27 years of Age." When Hercules ran away again two years later, his new owner referenced that advertisement but estimated that Hercules was now "about 26 years of age."[8] Even a factual characteristic like numerical age reflected advertisers' views of how old their property seemed to be.

Colonists emphasized the numeric age of some runaways but the qualitative age range of others. Advertisers' age categorizations of African-descended people used old and young as labor divisions under slavery, while European-descended servants were most likely to have specific, enumerable details of their age noted in advertisements. Almost seven in ten European-descended runaways were described by a numerical age, as compared to only about one in two African-descended runaways.[9] Some scholars theorize that the absence of a known numerical age could reflect an individual's lack of quantitative literacy. Economists suggest that recording numerical age can reflect levels of societal numeracy, and they use that numeracy to trace the rise of "human capital."[10] But the term has an entirely different meaning when applied to enslaved people, who were, literally, capital themselves.[11] Recordings of age in runaway advertisements were not self-presentations by those who had become missing persons. Rather than a lack of self-knowledge, age categories more likely reflected a slave owner's comparatively lower interest in the precise age of his chattel.

African-descended people were far more likely to have their age described with a qualitative judgment—about five times as often as people of European descent. There were undoubtedly more "elderly" enslaved people than servants in colonial America because enslavement was in perpetuity. And indeed, almost every runaway identified as elderly was of African descent. A man identified only as an Angola slave was described as elderly and Fortune was called "an elder fellow" when they were each imprisoned in a South Carolina workhouse.[12] Youthful status—referring to someone as a young adult—was also far more employed as a descriptor for African-descended people. Sam, Sue, Sylvia, Starry, Sill, Syphax, and Simon were all described as young in advertisements for their capture.[13] New England, with its preponderance of Anglo-American servants, offers a reminder that colonists were choosing whether to use categorical or numerical terms: New England advertisements averaged the numerically youngest population of runaways but did not qualitatively emphasize their runaways as "young."

Again, *quantitative* ages listed for runaways were largely similar, with less than a year separating the average African-descended and European-descended runaways' ages. And given the harsh treatment of individuals who were slaves, African-descended people may have looked older than how European-descended colonists expected a particular age to appear. Medical anthropologists have described the "structural violence" of poverty, oppression, and violence that leads to physical decline and illness.[14] The qualitative evaluation of age thus served as a marker of a body's life experiences as much as any number of years and days lived.

Advertisers disproportionately chose to describe the age of their African-descended runaways in general categories rather than as reflections of specific, individual lives lived. Disproportionately focusing on the qualitative age status of enslaved people emphasized external evaluations of African-descended bodies. An exact age reproduced a person's features as a form of identity: it allowed individuals to track their own life history. Choosing categorizations over exact ages effectively linked a non-racialized feature of physical appearance to a racial categorization.[15]

The exclusion of exact ages from advertisements was a decision by the slave owners and copywriters, not an indication of a lack of numerical self-knowledge by people of African descent. Enslaved people knew their own numerical ages and those of their family and their community members. Olaudah Equiano recalled that he had "turned the age of eleven" when he was first captured into slavery and "was near twelve years of age" when he arrived in England.[16] Harriet Jacobs noted when she was "fifteen years old"; wrote that an "old black man" who joined a Baptist church was "fifty-three years old"; and commented on the ages of numerous children.[17] Another ex-slave narrative noted that a man named Ebenezer Hills had become "free when twenty-eight years of age" and died in 1849 at 110 years old.[18] These former enslaved people recalled specific ages as a significant marker of their personal life experiences.

Owner-determined age categorization emphasized an externally commodified value for enslaved people. As chattel, enslaved people's ages were tied to their long-term labor capability rather than short-term expectations of changes in servitude or service. Owners who identified their missing property as "young" were implicitly noting the lengthy timeline for which they might be deprived of their enslaved runaways' labor. Age specificity mattered far less in reference to a lifetime laborer than to a servant with limited years of obligation. Rather than just being an approximated descriptor of appearance, enslaved people's age conveyed their bodies' economic value through their description.

From the day of their first capture and sale, enslaved people were commodified into productivity and reproductivity groupings that were heavily reliant on their apparent age. This lack of a self-produced numerical age meant that the judgment of the enslaved person's owner—was their slave young, old, or somewhere in between—substituted for what could have been a concrete descriptive marker. Thus Virginian John Thornton wrote unhappily about the human cargo of the ship *Othello* in 1773: "those left on hand you may believe must be of less value than the others, being 9 old women 4 Men, 3 of them old, 4 small girls & 4 very small boys which are very unsaleable."[19] Combined with sex divisions, too old or too young conveyed a reduced economic value. Slave merchant Henry Laurens was more specific about the age range of the "young People" he thought would sell best: "males from 14 to 20 or 25 years of age, & the females from 14 to 20."[20] A South Carolina advertisement more generally described the "choice Cargo of young healthy Negroes" that had just been imported from Angola.[21] The age-range designation of youth—which, as Laurens's request shows, was quantitatively younger for enslaved women than men—may suggest why more African-descended women were marked with a status of agedness: enslaved women were seen to reach old age half a decade before enslaved men. Oldness was a relative judgment: more women have been prematurely perceived as elderly because women's value was more directly tied to the ability to reproduce.[22]

This emphasis on age as a proxy for labor capabilities continued past the slave market and into daily life under enslavement. Documentation from George Washington's plantation offers some useful examples. A 1762 list of enslaved people included the ages of only the children: Belinda was recorded as five years old, Milly as four, and Boson as just a year old.[23] Adult laborers' ages went unmentioned; instead a monetary value substituted for mention of their ages. A 1780s list of Mount Vernon slaves again noted the ages of children, while implying the advanced age of others in direct relation to their labor capabilities: Doll was "almost past service," "Alce [sic]" was "old and almost blind," and Schomberg was "past labour." The list also included a notation of "Women old[:] 10."[24] Age categorizations were a determinant of enslaved people's labor value. As John Adams noted of debates over the counting of enslaved people for tax and representation purposes in the Articles of Confederation, "the young and old Negroes are a Burthen to their owners."[25] Substituting owners' judgments for African-descended people's self-identified markers of their own life spans reproduced the values of a race-based slave system onto physical bodies.

Height was the other common quantifiable description of runaways. Overall, about three-quarters of advertisements for men and close to half for women mentioned the height of the runaway. Much like age, stature was described in both quantitative and qualitative terms.[26] Using economic, demographic, and archaeological data, anthropometric historians have tried to reconstruct the heights of people who lived before the modern era. One study of skeletal remains puts the average height for eighteenth-century colonists at five feet seven and a half inches tall for men and five feet two and one-quarter for women. A study of the stature of men (race unspecified) in the United States in the first decades of the nineteenth century found their average height to be about five feet eight inches. An evaluation of slave ship manifests found that African adult men averaged about five feet seven inches and African adult women almost five feet three inches. Native American historic heights have been less systematically analyzed; one of the few studies, of late nineteenth-century Plains Indians, found their average height to be just shy of five feet eight inches.[27]

The heights of people described in my own collection of advertisements for missing persons are in line with these anthropometric findings: heights of European-descended men averaged five feet seven inches tall and women five feet two inches tall. The middle 50 percent of European-descended men ranged from five feet five to five feet nine inches, and for European-descended women, these two middle quarters ranged from five feet to five

feet four. Men identified as African descended averaged five feet seven as
well, while men identified as having Native American heritage, though relatively few in number, averaged about an inch taller. African-descended
women were reported as averaging two inches taller than European-
descended women (five feet four versus five feet two inches).

In many descriptions, however, evaluative judgments of height substituted for a specific number of feet and inches. An enslaved woman was
"above the middle stature," a Dutch woman was "middling tall," and an
Irish runaway was a "short Woman."[28] A numerical height was an absolute
descriptor: two people who were five feet five inches tall would be the same
height in any circumstance. But descriptors like short, tall, and middling
size were relative criteria that only made sense in comparison to a shared
norm and, as such, particularly reflect the writer's viewpoint.

As with age, precise physical stature was used most frequently for
European runaways. More than half of European-descended people had
their height described numerically, compared to only about four in ten
African-descended runaways, and, although the numbers are too small
for definitive conclusions, less than two-fifths of runaways who were
identified as being of Native American descent. In an era of growing
emphasis on rationality and empirical observation, advertisers paid more
attention to the physical details of European-descended runaways' bodies.
The decreased attention to the exact size of African-descended bodies
would be repeated in numerous areas of physical description, where
advertisers replaced specific details with evaluation.

The perception of tallness added value to human chattel. South Carolina planter and merchant Henry Laurens claimed that the "finest slaves"
were "tall able young People." He further noted that "People like tall Slaves
best . . . & strong withall" because "such as are small, meagre, or other ways
ordinary" would not sell well.[29] In an era where adequate nutrition was not
a given, especially for enslaved people who did not have the liberty to pro-
cure their own food, height could be a proxy for health.[30] As such, it substituted an owner's assessment of his property for factual details of height.

A list created upon Lawrence Washington's death in 1754 shows the
commodified meanings of age and height together. In a "Division of the
Negros," adults were listed by their sale value, children were identified by
height, and only infants, whose height could presumably not be reliably
measured, had their ages listed. Adults named Abram, Barbara, and Tom-
boy were listed as worth £40 each, and Bell, Will, and Anteno were worth

£10 each. Sue was two feet eleven and one-half inches, and both George and Prince were recorded as three feet seven and a half inches tall, while Farrow and Tobey were listed as one month old; no infants and children had an explicit valuation assigned.[31] On this list, height and size substituted for a child's age in terms of labor value. Moreover, the detailed half-inch heights suggest that owners did carefully track the size of at least some of their human chattel, even if they did not necessarily include that information in advertisements.

The height of Native Americans also captured colonists' attention. While relatively few Native American–identified runaways appeared in advertisements, travel narratives and diarists repeatedly commented that Indians were, on average, a tall people. William Byrd asserted that "Indians are generally tall," as did William Smith and John Lawson.[32] Other travel writers described Native Americans as "of a good stature" or claimed that "many of tham [sic] [are] about six feet high."[33] Although Native American–descended runaway men's average numerical height was no more than one inch greater than that of other runaways, writers embraced an image of Indians as generally tall. This likely reflected views of Native Americans as unencumbered by the diseases that visibly affected European bodies and served to mark the overall healthy environment of North America.

The ways that advertisers chose to describe the age and stature of their runaways reinscribed both cultural beliefs and economic practices. European-descended people were most represented as individuals with specific and absolute features. African-descended people, on the other hand, were more likely to be described through terms adjudged by their owners. The measurable facts of their bodies and persons were subsumed under owners' reformulations of the importance of those characteristics to their performance of the labor of enslavement. Relationships of enslavement were textually re-created in descriptions of physical appearance. This would become even more marked in the many descriptions of bodily shape that emphasized strength and fitness.

Shaping Labor and Health

How well a body functioned was an essential characteristic in British colonies where labor was in particularly high demand. Advertisers regularly conveyed their sense of a runaway's strength and health through descriptions of their general appearance. Many runaway advertisements implicitly referenced an individual's health without pointing specifically to an illness, disease, or bodily failing. Overall body shape, individual body parts, and even behaviors were notable signs of an individual's well-being. Advertisers were more likely to label people of African descent by their perceived labor capabilities. Just as Henry Laurens's request for "able" and "strong" young slaves reflected an imaginary ideal for his toiling property, so too did owners of enslaved runaways seek to emphasize the labor value of their missing chattel through the shape of bodies. In contrast, descriptions of European-descended laborers were more likely to acknowledge the impact of disease on their bodies. These descriptions reified racial and gender divisions, naturalizing evaluations of strength and health.

Descriptors of bodily shape were fairly common, appearing in more than 40 percent of missing persons advertisements. These included phrases such as "well made" and "well limbed" or less physiologically specific terms, such as "likely" and "lusty," that suggested a constitutional robustness rather than a particular shape, size, or form. "Well made" was a common descriptor, signifying a strong or admirable physique. Like many terms used to describe the shape of bodies, it was disproportionately applied to particular groups. Overall, men were more than twice as likely to be identified as "well made" as were women. John Skelton, from Scarborough, England, was said to be "strong and well made," and Benjamin Parrot from Buckinghamshire was described as "pretty well made."[34] Dick, Boston, and Peter were all described as "strong, well made," and Ned was "remarkably well made for strength."[35] Yet this was not a simple gender distinction that incorporated the assumption that men's bodies were generally stronger than women's: it was a reflection of the raced labor expectations of particular bodies. European-descended women were almost never referred to as "well made," but African-descended women regularly were. In fact, both African-descended men and women were more often described as "well made" than were their European-descended counterparts. Two South Carolina enslaved women were labeled "Well made," as was a woman named Tabb. "Well made" was not linked to a specific body size: Hannah was five feet five and Doll was described as short, and both were said to be "well made," suggesting that the term was a judgment of a person's capabilities, as much as a description of specific bodily features.[36]

By making "well made" an evaluation disproportionately applied to enslaved people of African descent, colonists wrote the realities of race-based slavery onto appearance. One enslaved woman's description explicitly emphasized the labor implications of being well made: Venus was "well made for labour."[37] Mapping aptitude for physical work onto a description of appearance emphasized the purpose that African-descended bodies—both male and female—were meant to fulfill in settler colonialism. "Well made" was a description of potential physical labor capabilities.

It could be that enslaved people, forced to undertake more physically challenging labor, had more developed musculature than servants and that this might contribute to the disproportionate use of "well made" in reference to African-descended bodies. It may have been that fewer layers of clothing left enslaved people's musculature more visible to owners or that slave owners enriched their own self-image by emphasizing the strength of the people under their power. But advertisers had many descriptive options to note physical prowess: they could have talked about people being strong or about bodies being fit or muscular. Even if enslaved and indentured laborers' work led to average differences in strength and robustness, advertisers chose to capture such differences with the disproportionate application of "well made" to African-descended bodies, verbally turning the results of labor and circumstance into innate bodily differences. This translated enslaved people's lived experiences into how their bodies were said to appear.

An emphasis on men's strength and labor capabilities, in particular, would be emphasized in other bodily descriptors: almost every person described as "straight bodied" or "straight limbed" in advertisements was male. Both African- and European-descended men were classified with such terms. Jonathan, a runaway slave, was described as "straight made," and a German man was described simply as "strait." Daniel and Portsmouth were described as straight limbed.[38] Having a straight body or limbs suggested a lifetime without major structural illness or deformity. A morality tale aimed at children told of the unpleasant child who insulted the looks of "people that happen'd not to be so strait and well shap'd."[39] Straightness was a desirable attribute for both labor and admiration, and as such, it could offer masters a language with which to discuss the desirable appearance of their economic subservients.

Although Native American–descended people appear only in small numbers in advertisements, many travel narratives commented on the straight-bodied appearance of New World residents. Europeans described Native Americans as straight, well made, or well-set as a way to complimentarily indicate healthy lives of vigor and abundance. William Byrd noted of the Cheroenhaka that their "Shapes are very Strait and well porportion'd [*sic*]." Other travelers described Indians as "well limbed," a "well-made people," "well shaped," "generally streight-body'd," and "generally speaking, well made, of a good stature, and neatly limbed." William Wood complimented the "strait bodies" of the "Aberginians," calling them "healthful and lusty," without deformities or birth defects.[40] Indeed, settler colonial projects around the world had a long history of describing indigenous people as strong and healthy. One of the first descriptions of Native Americans, published in English in 1511, had called the indigenous people of America "well shaped in body." An eighteenth-century travel narrative referred to the indigenous people of Guam as a "well-limbed people." A scientific writer on Captain Cook's second voyage complimented people of the South Seas for being "well limbed, athletic."[41] With these kinds of commentaries, European-descended writers used indigenous bodies to signal the bounty and health of worlds new to them.

Native Americans were not the only people who were described with such terms. Men identified as being of African descent were almost twice as likely as European-descended men to be described by the strength and form of their limbs in runaway advertisements. African-descended men were described as "strong limbed," "well limbed," "clean limbed," and "stout limbed."[42] This embodied language of strength and labor potential was not just for human chattel; it was also terminology applied to workhorses. A 1771 husbandry manual recommended draft horses for farmers because they are "strong, well limbed." John Jay complimented the "very active and well limbed" mules who pulled carts in Madrid, having had "no Idea of there being animals of this Kind in the World so fine."[43] "Well limbed" was a marker of strength, of suitability for strenuous labor. Hence it seemed an appropriate term for European-descended owners to apply to their enslaved, largely African-descended laborers.

European-descended women's fitness for strenuous labor may have escaped regular commentary, but their body shape did not go unnoticed: they were the runaways most likely to be described as "fat." While African-descended women might occasionally be described as "fat" (such as Ibbe, who was "very fat and clumsy"), the term was used about five times as often in reference to European-descended women. Eleanor Kinney, an Irish runaway, was "a very fat thick Woman," and Jane Jackson was "a stout fat woman."[44] We might assume this was a reflection of European-descended people having opportunity to eat enough to gain weight, but adult men were rarely described as fat. Male fatness was instead limited to European-descended boys. John Wyer was thirteen years old when he was described as "fat," and a nine-year-old German runaway was described as "a fat boy."[45] Colonists' designation of fatness suggested its association with softness and a lack of masculine strength that was not as easily applied to adult men or laboring chattel.

Fatness was used to imply health and a non-muscularized robustness beyond runaway advertisements as well. Elizabeth Drinker wrote in astonishment that her two-year-old son had been "fat, fresh and hearty" just a week before his death. In a 1778 letter, Deborah Norris noted that she had been "in the best height of my plumpness." Philip Vickers Fithian complimented a Miss Corbin as looking "*fresh* & plump as ever."[46] Women of European descent and children were described as desirably "fat" or "plump" because they were not expected to show muscular strength. Such evaluations relied on raced and gendered assumptions about whose bodies would show the effects of physical labor.

There were other terms that could refer to the healthiness of adequate weight. "Stoutness"—referring to a powerful, strong, healthy build, not to corpulence—was disproportionately applied to African-descended men's bodies. They were described as "stout" more than twice as often as were African-descended women or European-descended runaways. London was a "pretty stout fellow" and Cesar was "uncommonly stout," while James, Jemmy, Jupiter, and two men named Jack were each described just as "stout."[47] Stoutness was often paired with a commentary on well-made bodies, suggesting a reference to a solid muscularity rather than excess fleshiness.[48] It was a sign of strength and labor capability—which was why it also repeatedly appeared in sale advertisements for male slaves.[49]

Other terms used to describe health and labor potential were more divorced from specific bodily shape. "Lusty" was one of the terms frequently used to describe the state of runaways' bodies. Through the early 1600s, "lusty" connoted a pleasing appearance. This meaning appeared to have faded by the eighteenth century, when the word was employed to more explicitly convey health, strength, and vigor for both people and animals.[50] In advertisements, "lusty" referred to the constitution of bodies. Beck, a runaway slave, was described as "thin in her person when she went off, but naturally lusty," implying that lustiness signaled an innate health. Harry Cooke was "lusty and very well made," as was a "Negroe Man, named Sam." Hannah Galley was described as "strong, lusty." Lustiness was not necessarily tied to a particular body shape: a pregnant runaway was described as "a lusty hearty woman." Other runaways were "lusty and fat," "lusty big boned," or, more commonly, "lusty and well made" or "lusty well set."[51]

Other writings confirm the eighteenth-century use of "lusty" in reference to health: when William Wood referred to "lusty" Englishmen, he was commenting on their naturally healthy and hearty disposition. William Fleming recalled his Native American captors saying "as I looked young and lusty they would not hurt me," because his youthful wellbeing could be put to better uses. An eighteenth-century account of a slave uprising referred to a "lusty slave" who struck his captor hard enough to break bones.[52] In these contexts, lustiness conveyed an image of a healthy and hearty physique.

European-descended women were labeled "lusty" about twice as often as any other group. Mary David Philips, Rebecca Wooley, and Magdalen Hakaliver were all said to be "lusty."[53] Numerous women of European descent were described as "lusty" alongside a body-size or strength reference, suggesting it served akin to the male-focused appellation of being "well made." Mary Lee was "lusty and strong," Mary Dugan was "a tall lusty woman," and Frances Yetts was "of a lusty size." Some female runaways of European descent were described specifically as lusty and of a larger than average size. Rose Flanagin was "stout and lusty" and Catherine Smith was "thick and lusty." Mary Parker, Nelly English, and Alice McCarty were all described as both "fat" and "lusty."[54] Such descriptors offered a way to convey a healthy build without recourse to the implication of a specific muscularity inherent to other laborers' bodily classifications.

Lusty seemed to have different meanings when used in reference to women of African descent, when it was repeatedly accompanied by an additional focus on sexuality, breeding, and reproduction. "Lusty" was a common descriptor in advertisements for the sale of slaves, usually conveying generic positive value. But when runaway advertisements applied the term to women of African descent, they were also remarking on women's reproductive value. A "lusty black wench" ran away with her "child of a brick colour," raising the specter of her having engaged in sexual relations with someone of non-African descent. A Virginia enslaved woman was "very lusty" and "supposed to be pretty far gone with Child." And in the most overt advertisement, a "Mulattoe" woman was described as a "very lusty Indian looking hussy."[55] For women of non-European descent, lustiness seemed to have a closer relation to its more modern sexual connotations. This tied African-descended women's value to their reproductive capacity, labeling the appearance of their body through their owners' implicit judgment of their laborers' generative potential.

The association of lustiness with sexual availability and procreative possibilities was even more explicit in advertisements for the sale of enslaved women. One woman offered for purchase was a "lusty Negro Wench, without a Character." Another advertisement offered a "lusty able breeding Wench" for sale. Notably, that advertisement offered her husband for sale as well and mentioned her (presumably their?) child, but did not call the "able Negro man" lusty.[56] That designation was reserved for women who could be imagined as using their healthy, sturdy bodies to breed more laborers for those who owned them. In the context of enslaved women's bodies, lustiness signaled a capacity to breed. Unlike indentured servants, enslaved women's reproductive, not just productive, capacity was a noteworthy sign of their value.

A second common descriptor of overall appearance was "likely." Likeliness appeared in about 6 percent of all advertisements. James Hammond, a runaway "mulatto man servant," was described as "likely" and "well built," while James Hamilton, a deserter, was described simply as "likely." Jane Pain, an English runaway servant, was described as "pretty likely," and Kate, a runaway slave, was described as "very likely."[57] The *Oxford English Dictionary* defines early modern European uses of "likely" as being of a "seemly or comely appearance."[58] Occasionally runaways were described as having a "likely face," suggesting this meaning of attractiveness.[59] "Likely" could also convey a person's suitability or promising nature for a given purpose—and in advertisements that purpose seemed to generally be laboring capacity.

The likelihood of likeliness as a descriptor for runaways varied markedly: almost one in eleven African-descended runaways was labeled "likely," as compared to about one in fifty European-descended runaways. The word had a long history in the European trade in African bodies. It was one of the terms regularly appearing in slave sale advertisements—someone offering a "likely Negro wench" for sale was common. One slave merchant specifically requested "very likely healthy People" for sale, tying likeliness to the labor value of his future property. A broadside boasted "A CARGO Of 170 prime young likely" slaves for sale.[60] In the context of African-descended bodies, likeliness was meant to convey a fitness for enslaved productivity. The frequency of the use of the term in advertisements for the sale of enslaved people suggests its widely understood economic value. As Stephanie Small-wood summarizes, terms such as "likely" offered "a special lexicon" for merchants "to cast their human wares in the mold of the qualities buyers desired in the people they purchased . . . the image of the ideal slave."[61] Smallwood rightly identifies the imposition of commodified terms as a means to transform African people into enslaved bodies. Likeliness was a measurement of labor potential wrapped in economic value for enslaved people.

Associating enslaved runaways' likeliness with their youth further signaled the term's relation to labor potential. Multiple advertisements substituted a descriptor of "likely young" status for specific ages of slaves. Cuffee was described as a "likely young Eboe" man. Scotland was described as "a likely young Negro Fellow."[62] The phrase was not simply a replacement for an unknown age: other advertisements supplemented a specific age with the phrase "likely young." Daniel was "a likely young negro fellow . . . about 18 Years of Age." Lot was "a likely young Negroe fellow . . . about 24 years of age." An unnamed "likely young mulattoe woman" was "about 22 years of age." The sheriff of Augusta, Georgia, described Poll and George as "likely young slaves" who "seem to be about 20 years of age."[63] In all of these cases, the combination of youthfulness and likeliness offered an evaluation of productive (and for women, also reproductive) capabilities.

"Likely" was not just used to describe human chattel: as they did with "lusty," colonists used the word to describe draft animals. Advertisements repeatedly mentioned a "likely horse" for sale.[64] Horses that were described as "likely" even appeared alongside descriptions of runaways. A tradesman took with him a "well-set, likely" horse, and a twenty-three-year-old servant took a "likely Bay Horse" when he ran (or more accurately, rode) from his Virginia home. In a 1764 advertisement, William Ball first described his missing servant, William McCreary, then noted his sale of "two likely young Negroes," as well as "a likely young Saddle Horse."[65] Even in the same advertisements, colonists might overlap the language of domestic husbandry with that used for enslaved human beings, describing both through their relative productive value.

"Likely" was not only more frequently used to describe African-descended runaways; it was more often used as a totalizing term. Mentions of African-descended likeliness repeatedly occurred without other bodily descriptors. Of eighty-six individuals whose body was described by the word "likely" with no other detail, only six were of European descent. The rest of the "likely" runaways were identified as mulatto or Negro. Milly, Robin, Sue, Tarresman, Sarah, Rank, and many more people who had escaped slavery had their bodily appearance described only as "likely."[66] In contrast, for European-descended runaways, likeliness infrequently appeared alone without other specific descriptors of body shape. John Hutchinson, an English servant, was described as both "likely" and "stout"; deserter John Greenwood was "likely well built"; and Daniel Hooseman was "well set, appears a likely fellow." Other European-descended runaways were "likely well made," "likely well set," "likely built," "likely slim clean limb'd," or "likely" and "thick set."[67] "Likely" was a totalizing description predominantly for African-descended people.

Thus descriptors of bodily shape, health, and strength marked the social and economic status of bodies, coding the work that people were expected to do into textual portrayals of their appearance. Descriptions marked the slave status of African-descended people by turning physical appearance into a commodified value through a disproportionate emphasis on corporeal strength. By applying terms that codified physical features into a master's evaluation of his human property's relationship to enslavement, African-descended bodies became reflections of their slave status. In contrast, European-descended runaways often had more multifaceted descriptions that represented their appearance beyond the singular axis of strength and labor capability.

Signs of Sickness

While many runaways were noted for their well-made, likely, or lusty bodies, others appeared to suffer from an array of observable health problems, long-term injuries, or chronic conditions. Because ill health was believed to be readable on the body, it could be worth mentioning as an identifying feature.[68] Advertisements commented both on the overall ill health of individuals and on specific features that they believed signaled a medical problem. European-descended runaways were more likely to be described by specific ailments, while African-descended runaways were described more directly by physical signs of illness. The ideas of humoralism that connected interior bodily processes to external features was more often applied to European-descended runaways' descriptions. There seemed to be little effort to explicitly relate health implications to the bodily features of slaves of African descent: the appearance of their bodies took precedence over the internal workings that appearance might humorally represent. Thus African-descended runaways were marked by the external state of their bodies more than the internal processes that led to changeable appearances.

Thinness was often a generic sign of unwellness. Mary Conolly was "very slim, and looks sickly." Jessath Rainbord "looks thin, having been lately sick with Fevers," while a runaway convict servant "looks thin at this Time, occasioned by a venereal Disorder."[69] In all of these cases, being underweight was associated with ill health. An advertisement for a family missing from a German ship explicitly opposed sickness to fatness. The mother was "a sickly woman with a sore leg, age about 45 years," her son was "a fat boy about 9 years old," and her infant was "a sickly child aged about 5 months."[70] These descriptions contained parallel information on age and health, and contrasted fatness to sickness when conveying the run-aways' overall well-being. In a society where an array of illnesses affected appetite and digestion, extra weight could be a sign that people were healthy.

The shape of someone's face was mentioned in close to 10 percent of descriptions, and here, too, thinness could be a sign of internal sickness. An eighteenth-century British serial contained a description of an ill man that noted his "thin, pale, sickly Visage."[71] Runaways were described as having a "thin visage" or a "long visage" as opposed to being "round faced" or "full faced."[72] A thin face could be read as a sign of a body operating at less than peak efficiency. Chelter was said to be "rather thin visaged for so sturdy a young fellow," conveying the expectation that a full face was a sign of strength and well-being. William was so "ill looking" that his "cheek bones [were] sticking out." Other advertisements noted the thinness or roundness of a runaway's face without explicit recourse to the health sig-nificance. Deserter Joseph Blinn was "thin visag'd" while his fellow runaway Edward Price was "full fac'd." An escaped servant named Mary Halls was described as having a "round Vissage, and fresh Complexion," while James Gordon had a "thin visage" and was "pale faced."[73]

Overall, only a handful of advertisements noted a runaway's specific illness in lieu of the features that signified a disease, and usually these were catastrophic ailments. Runaways who were liable to suffer from seizures might have their being "subject to convulsion Fits" noted.[74] In one of the most detailed descriptions, James Lee, a runaway British convict servant, was described as "until reduced by sickness, remarkably strong and braw-ney; but having been long afflicted with a cachexical complaint, he still has a dropsical appearance, his belly and legs being swollen, and his face sallow and bloated." Clearly James had been chronically ill over an extended period, and his master combined a listing of his body's physical changes along with interpretations of their medical causes. Likewise, John Stanton was usually a "likely well looking lad when well, but has now the ague every third day." [75] When advertisers described African-descended appearances, however, they were less likely to emphasize a specific illness as a cause of their bodily abnormalities. For instance, a slave named Ned was described in a Virginia advertisement in 1775 as being five feet tall and having a "flat face and long head, which is remarkably sharp on the top"; in addition, "some of his fingers grow together." [76] The advertiser claimed that Ned's syndactyl fingers were caused by a childhood injury. Modern medicine might suggest that Ned suffered from Saethre-Chotzen syndrome, a chro-mosomal defect that causes short stature, a flat face with a cone-shaped head, and webbed fingers. [77] While we would not expect eighteenth-century colonists to make that diagnosis, the advertisement offered no medical or humoral explanation for Ned's obviously atypical appearance; it referred only to an acquired injury.

Ned's description underlies that advertisers decided which health or medical issues were relevant to a public description of their laborers' bod-ies. For instance, bloodshot eyes were an easily identifiable feature and had long had a humoral association to choleric excess as well as multiple health problems. [78] Thomas Peters, a self-described London botanist, advertised in a Pennsylvania paper that he could cure "sore eyes" with plants and herbs "according to the constitution" of his patients. A turn-of-the-century news-paper listed "turgid red eyes" as a symptom of smallpox. Proverbs 23:29, on the other hand, linked bloodshot eyes to drinking alcohol. Some historians of medicine have suggested that red eyes may have been a result of vitamin deficiency—lack of Vitamin A and riboflavin could lead to dry eyes that might appear red. Red eyes could also be perceived as a reflection of strong emotions, tying physical symptoms to emotional affect: Thomas Shepard ascribed Native Americans' red eyes during conversion to "the mighty power of the Lord." [79]

Most of the commentaries on European-descended servants' eye red-ness focused on a specific cause, an additional explanation, or its unusual nature. The red eyes of John Stuart, Dennis Daley, and Joseph Byard were all described as "remarkable."[80] Other European-descended servants' red eyes were more explicitly connected to particular medical issues. Joseph Wright "has a blemish in one of his eyes, which looks very red." James Harn was "fond of spirituous liquors, by which means his eyes are generally very red." Lawrence Reddy had "very weak eyes, looks red."[81] Connecting red eyes to a humoral effect, Elizabeth Prugelin was characterized by her "melancholy temper, red eyes."[82] Some servants' eyes were described just in terms of the appearance of soreness, presumably relying on readers to understand that sore eyes would look red or inflamed. Mary Chambers "looks as if she had sore eyes." George Sharswood, David Fitzgerald, John Hughes, and Thomas Jones each had "sore eyes." Jane Shepherd had "one of her eyes always watering."[83] Such descriptions emphasized the relationship between a medical problem and appearance and suggested an individualized interpretation of the causes and meanings of reddened eyes.

In contrast, more people of African descent were described simply as having red eyes, without additional qualifications or specifications. In over one hundred mentions of runaways with "red eyes" in the *Pennsylvania Gazette*, *Virginia Gazette*, and *South-Carolina Gazette* from 1750 to 1775, only a handful of people of European descent were described just as having "red eyes," without the kind of additional details mentioned above. In contrast, Coco, Decipher, Dick, Jack, Lucy, Moses, Ritty, Scipie, and at least two men named Tom, for instance, all were described as having red eyes without additional explanation.[84] Hannah's owner went to the trouble to spell out that "the Whites of her Eyes [are] remarkably red" but did not provide any further information about the cause.[85]

The standardization of commentary on African-descended red eyes contrasted to the specificity of causes of red eyes for runaways of European descent. Enslaved people of African descent were categorized as red-eyed, as opposed to the myriad contributory explanations offered for runaways of European descent. Perhaps this was a cultural carryover of medieval beliefs that the curse of Ham or association with the Devil resulted in Africans having red or inflamed eyes.[86] Regardless of its origins, advertisers chose to offer details about specific effects on European-descended runaways (soreness, watering eyes, remarkableness) but summarized their conclusions about African-descended runaways (red eyes).

Slave owners were accepted as the public experts on determining, rather than explaining, other unusual features of African-descended bodies as well.

Advertisements repeatedly mentioned the unusual size or shape of African-descended runaways' legs. African-descended people were more likely than European-descended people to be described with less than desirable limb form.[87] Cook was "a little bow-legged," an unnamed enslaved boy was "knock kneed," and Caesar was described as "bandy legged."[88] In contrast, descriptions of European-descended runaways were more likely to offer an explanation, such as that James Penticost had "remarkable bandy shins, occasioned by having both legs broke."[89] Enslaved people may have suffered higher rates of rickets and childhood malnutrition that could lead to bow-shaped legs. But as discussed earlier, African-descended people were also more likely to be described as "straight limbed." Rather than a direct representation of the level of malformation, the state of African-descended slaves' limbs seemed to reflect particular concerns of owners who expected people of African descent to conduct decades of back-breaking labor. Commentaries on the shape of limbs reflected an ability to work, not inner workings, making this a term more commonly applied to people of African descent.

Similarly, the many references to the large legs of people of African descent seem to have been a commentary on their health as reflected through the shape of their body. Cyrus, a "Negro Man Servant," was "well built" with "Legs and Feet somewhat large." Frederick had remarkably large feet, and Ned had "large limbs."[90] Many of these oversized legs and feet can likely be traced to edema, described by one contemporary medical manual as "a puffy swelling of the feet, legs, and thighs."[91] Swollen limbs could result from medical conditions as diverse as congestive heart failure, kidney disease, lymphatic system damage, thiamine deficiency, and liver dysfunction. They could also result from the leg irons placed around enslaved people's ankles to prevent escape or as a punishment.[92] Sickle-cell anemia could also cause a swelling of hands and feet, due to sickle-shaped blood cells blocking the blood vessels that supplied them.

European-descended people were not immune from health problems that caused edema. But when European-descended runaways' leg size was mentioned, advertisers more often included additional information explaining the illness behind the runaway's swollen limbs. Thomas Painter's legs were "a good deal swelled, owing (he says) to his being confined on shipboard." John Farrell was "a sickly looking Man . . . his Legs seem to be swelled." Thomas Agnew "has exceeding bad sore legs, ulcerated and swelled."[93] Confinement, sickness, soreness—these were representations of an individual's experiences, not just observations of the appearance of a body part.

It is worth noting that regardless of the disability, runaways still used those infirm legs to leave their masters. There is a certain irony in the repeated notations of runaways' damaged legs and consequential irregular gaits: slaves and servants made bids for freedom even if they had to hobble away to do so. An enslaved man named Peter was crippled yet escaped from his Virginia home in 1771, and the elderly Jemmy's "clumsy Legs" (likely nerve damage) did not deter his escape in 1770.[94] Many runaways were missing toes, and several had lost a leg, emphasizing the toll that colonial life took on bodies.[95] A venereal disease apparently caused one convict servant's limp, and a boyhood knee injury caused another to drag his leg. Hugh McCarnon "has had his Right Leg broke, which is crooked, and bends inward from his Ancle to his Knee."[96] An unusual walking gait not only offered a means to identify individuals, it reflected some of the ways that advertisers interpreted how ill health and permanent injury manifested in appearance.

Despite undoubtedly harsher living conditions under slavery, we should not assume that African-descended runaways were necessarily described as being more infirm than were European-descended runaways. Within my collection of almost 4,000 advertisements for runaways, almost three times as many runaways of European descent were described as stooping as were people of African descent. For instance, Maria Kummersfield "has a hobling walk, and stoops pretty much." James Clark "stoops in his Shoulders, and walks with his Knees close."[97] A search in multiple online collections of newspapers confirms this. *Accessible Archives* contains upwards of 4,500 advertisements for runaway servants and a roughly equal number for runaways identified as "Negro" or "Mulatto" from 1750 to 1775. Yet only 1 percent of those identified as being of African descent by those terms were said to stoop. In contrast, 4 percent of runaways identified as non-African descended servants were described as stooping.[98] Through aggregated differences like these, people of European descent were portrayed in terms of what they did, while people of African descent were described by their bodily appearance. These were daily enactments of racial divisions: people of African descent were presented through others' evaluation of their external features, not by detailing the individual underlying causes or experiences.[99] For people of African descent, physical appearance was the end point in and of itself, rather than a means to understand an individual's internal character and constitution.

One final set of illness-related commentaries again shows the emphasis on the inner workings of European-descended bodies. The notation of smallpox scars—"much marked with the Small-Pox," "pock fretten," "pitted with the Small-Pox"—appeared in about one in ten advertisements.[100] Smallpox did not yet seem to be associated with lower-class and non-white communities as it would be in the late eighteenth and nineteenth centuries, when the wealthy could take advantage of inoculations: in the colonial period, smallpox could and did strike anyone.[101] Commentary on smallpox was common in slave sale ads. Slave merchants regularly noted whether the offered chattel had already survived the deadly disease as a way to assure potential buyers that they would not be bringing an infectious or potentially short-lived laborer to their home. When describing runaways of African descent, however, colonists did not generally reference that history of illness.

In fact, mentions of smallpox scars were far more common for runaways of European descent, accounting for about three-quarters of its appearance in advertisements. This was consistent whether individuals were described as very pockmarked, only slightly pockmarked, or just pockmarked with no degree of scarring mentioned. One twentieth-century study found that upwards of 80 percent of unvaccinated adults under forty years old displayed at least five visible facial pockmarks.[102] Given the endemic nature of smallpox in the eighteenth century, it seems that colonists were choosing to notice and comment on smallpox scars primarily on European-descended laborers. It might have been that colonists paid more attention to European-descended faces generally. But even if that were the case, it reflected the notion that it was important to mention the effects of illness on European-descended laborers in a way that it was not for African-descended laborers. Smallpox scars were not relevant to advertisers' description of enslaved people's work capabilities. Individual physical markings seemed less relevant to African-descended bodies unless they could be made into a sign of their labor value.

In commentary on an array of seemingly observable health concerns, advertisers formulated descriptions out of their expectations for particular groups of laboring bodies. We might imagine it unlikely that runaway slaves, who were subject to literally backbreaking labor, would stoop less than European servants, who often labored for others for a limited number

of years in markedly better living conditions. Likewise, it may be that stooping was less worth noting about African-descended people because it was a
default result of slavery. Every descriptive choice reflected a belief in the
relevance of that feature to that body. Regardless of individual advertisers'
rationales, the aggregation of such details served to construct a naturalized
version of race through accounts of individual bodies' shape, size, and
functions.

* * *

During the American Revolution, George Washington instructed his plantation manager to make sure his latest purchases for Mount Vernon would
be "tall and strait bodied."[103] Washington's instruction used common
descriptors of the ideal body shape of valuable slaves. But in this case, he
was actually describing the locust trees he wanted his manager to acquire.
Both trees and enslaved humans would be more valuable for their straight
and tall status. The overlap of terms for inanimate and human property
reiterates how descriptive language created a textual picture out of expectations and assumptions. More than offering a replica of objectively observed
physical features, textual constructions of physical bodies were powerful
because they appeared to be reasonable reflections of sight and observation.
In reality, however, descriptions of missing persons naturalized race, status,
and gender divisions by differentially emphasizing specific aspects of physical form. Missing laborers were described with terms that prioritized their
strength, health, and potential value, signaling their value as laborers.

Most striking are the ways that the demands of enslavement were physically written onto African-descended bodies, turning supposedly objective
descriptions into commodified evaluations. Slaveowners reformulated self-
reported life history or self-determined age into an evaluation of work capability and economic worth. Whether a decision about describing a missing
person's age with quantitative or qualitative terms, determining whether
someone counted as old or young, or whether age even mattered: these
were not just decisions to convey information about a person's appearance.
Whether a focus on leg formation versus gait or notation of a symptom
versus a cause of a disease: advertisers created, enforced, and reified cultural
beliefs into materiality through bodily portrayals. Advertisement writers
reiterated race ideologies in every runaway's description. Enslaved people

were marked as chattel by transforming owners' evaluations into seemingly objective corporeal features. Racial differentiation could be accomplished by making bodies seem naturally different in their purpose, form and function, even without recourse to complexion, color, or black and white binaries.

CHAPTER 3

Coloring Bodies

Naturalized Incompatibilities

A runaway servant named Ishmael Mux was about twenty-eight years old when he left New London, Connecticut. He was headed, his master thought, either eight hours north to Lebanon or five hours east along the coast to Stonington. Likely hoping someone might notice him on one of these routes, he further described Ishmael as "having a white Complexion . . . wears his own hair."[1] A few years later in Lancaster, Pennsylvania, a man known as John Daily ran from his home with apparent hopes to gain freedom by passing himself off as a soldier. His master noted that John was about nineteen years old and had a "black Complexion, bushy Hair."[2] Another runaway, Andrew Vaughan, was believed to have headed south to North Carolina when he disappeared. His master told newspaper readers that Andrew stood five feet ten inches tall, with a red complexion, and had an unusual hairstyle that involved shaving the front of his head.[3]

Without supplemental information, it might seem reasonable to assume that the white-complexioned servant named Ishmael was of European descent, the black-complexioned John who hoped to pass as a free soldier was of African descent, and the red-complexioned Andrew with the partially shaved head was of Native American descent. But complexion and hair color descriptions were not so neatly divisible in the colonial eighteenth century. White, black, and red complexion did not automatically parallel European, African, and Native American heritages, respectively. In fact, Ishmael was described as mulatto; John as Irish; and Andrew was listed as an infantryman in the British 40th regiment, as born in Philadelphia, with no nationality or ethnicity specified. Skin and hair appearance were features related to, but not constitutive of, ethnic or national background.

African- and European-descended people were not described through oppositions of black and white skin color in the colonial eighteenth century. African-descended complexion was generally read along an imagined monochromatic scale of dark to light that was a tool to categorize rather than personalize. In contrast, advertisers regularly noted tonal and textural variations in the complexions of people of European descent, identifying their appearance across numerous axes. For people of European descent, descriptions could convey health and reflect gendered expectations of bodily appearance rather than any single innate European-ness. For African-descended runaways, however, complexion offered a means to categorize from the outside in, rather than explain from the inside out. Complexion was primarily used to mark African-descended people's relationship to an imagined norm of Negroness. Rather than complexion serving to mark variation for people identified as mulatto or mustee, their complexions classified their place in a system of racial categorizations that their existence otherwise challenged.

Descriptions of hair and eye color followed similar patterns, classifying people of African descent in terms of their perceived Africanness while differentiating among people of European descent. In contrast to the multiplicity of details offered about European-descended hair texture and color, hair descriptions of non-European-descended people were primarily used to parse out African and Indian heritage. Though advertisements less frequently offered descriptions of eye color, these too transformed the privileges of European heritage into salient bodily descriptions.

Assuming that black, red, and white corresponded to complexion categories wrongly naturalizes skin color descriptors as a phenotypical reality. Bodily complexion was not equivalent to race in the mid-eighteenth century. Categorizations of Negro were not equivalent to blackness, categorizations of whiteness were not a reflection of explicit skin color, and categories of redness had little to do with Native American runaways. Despite advertisers' presumable interest in describing their missing bondpeople with as much detail as possible, they could not describe what they did not recognize, did not take note of, or did not believe was relevant to the laboring bodies they owned.

Colors of Complexion: Categorization and Division

Despite the existence of racially oppositional categories of black and white, individual runaways were not described as black (African) or white (European) complexioned. We could imagine colonists creating a complexion system primarily around a range of browns (brown-tan-beige-ecru) that might seem to better match human flesh tones. It might be even less of a leap to assume an early America with red Native Americans, yellow/brown Africans, and white Europeans. Yellow could have made sense from a humoral perspective, with its connection to people from warm climates and the preexisting association of yellow complexion with some African groups. However, these were not the primary color ranges offered by colonial American advertisers. Instead, they employed less regularized skin colors, mobilizing complexion in more subtle ways than simple color opposition or unbroken linear ranges from dark to light.

Advertisers gave meaning to the significance of complexion in when, how, and for whom skin color mattered. The lack of detail about African-descended runaways' complexions seemed particularly marked. African-descended people's complexions were described in just over one-quarter of the advertisements, while European-descended complexions were described more than half of the time. European-descended runaways came in a veritable rainbow of complexion colors, including black, brown, dark, fair, freckled, fresh, light, pale, red, ruddy, sandy, swarthy, tawny, and yellow.[4] These numerous options did not correspond to any specific European ethnicity. People described as "pale" heralded from England, France, Germany, Ireland, Scotland, and the American colonies, as well as from unspecified national backgrounds.[5] Dark-complexioned people of European descent covered a similarly wide range of nationalities.[6]

In contrast, African-descended complexions generally required little description once the term "Negro" was applied. The most frequent complexion color used to describe African-descended people was black, but it still appeared in only about one in ten advertisements. Rather than a statement of color, black complexion was primarily a notation of exceptionalism. Runaway slave Jenny was "remarkably black," Tom was "of the blackest sort," Will was described as "middling black," and Prince was "not very black." An unnamed "Bamba born" man was "very black," while Sterling, also born in Africa, was "not of a very black."[7] All of these comments remarked on the color of African-descended runaways' skin in terms of its deviation from advertisers' (unstated) standard of what a Negro person should look like.

Blackness was not limited to people of African descent: there were dozens of European-descended people also described as having a black complexion. Black-complexioned Europeans were a relatively small percentage of the diverse complexion options (about 4 percent), but they still included Irish, Dutch, English, German, Scottish, and Welsh people, as well as people with no national identity noted.[8] For example, aside from numerous men named John (Croane, Peritt, Quin, and Shirley), there were Richard Poole and Richard Pritchard, Thomas Duel and Thomas Davis.[9] Such European-descended runaways were described as just black complexioned, not by their degree of blackness; they were not remarkably or middling or not very black.

People of European descent who were described as having a black complexion undoubtedly did not have ebony-colored skin. By the end of the nineteenth century, the often derogatory term "Black Irish" would be used to identify an Irish person with dark hair and a dark complexion or eyes. But this was not used in colonial British America. The only mentions of "black Irish" in colonial print were in reference to black Irish linen, not people.[10] In the eighteenth century, Europeans' "black" complexion may have suggested a sense of relatively dark coloration rather than just a specific focus on skin. When noted, the hair color of these servants was generally also described as black. Blackness could also be a reference to a humoral notion of complexion, where a swarthy appearance resulted from an excess of black bile.

Because "Negro" already carried physical meanings that did not need to be explained to readers, complexion could focus on the degree to which African-descended runaways fit advertisers' imaginings. The word "Negro" was certainly associated with the color black. Its etymological roots in Spanish or Portuguese derived from the Latin *niger*, meaning black or dark, and appeared in reference to people from Africa as early as the sixteenth century. By the colonial eighteenth century, "Negro" was replacing the use of "Ethiop" or "Ethiopian" in Anglo-American texts, and had expanded beyond a reference to presumed African descent to signal a person's status as a slave.

"Negro" coloration, however, was still not a common explicit descriptor. The *Oxford English Dictionary*, although not always ideal for demarcating shifting North Americans' conceptions of race, notes that the use of

"Negro" as a term meaning color did not appear until the nineteenth century. A comparable evaluation can be gleaned from Google Ngram, which
confirms that the phrase "negro complexion" was virtually nonexistent
until the end of the eighteenth century.[11] On rare occasions Negro status
would be invoked in a complexion description as part of a comparison, not
as a substitute for color. For instance, Peter had "a very light Complection
for a Negro."[12] Such usages left "Negro" as a category tied primarily to
slave-labor status rather than an explicit skin color description.

Neither were the terms "white" and "black" regularly used to categorize
an individual by their appearance. In 1760, a British dictionary offered a
humoral definition of "black," as "a cloudy countenance; sullen." That dictionary's only association of whiteness to complexion or a nationally based
categorization was a reference to Spanish White, a treatment "used by ladies
to heighten the complexion."[13] As long as complexion continued to signal
internal workings of some bodies, it was less useful as a marker of
unchangeable external appearance. Explicit association of color to racial
categories was not a necessary precursor to racist ideologies that viewed
people of African descent as a lower form of humans. For instance, the
same dictionary reflected the early modern belief that male apes and African women would have sexual relations; under the definition of "chimpan-
zee" it noted that "it's said, [they] will set upon and ravish the negro
women, when they meet them in the woods."[14] The categorization of
"Negro" and the development of race-based slavery left no question that
Europeans viewed people of African descent as subservient and animalistic.
But they did not yet set that inferiority expressly and primarily upon skin
color.

It may seem counterintuitive for advertisers to have limited the details
about any of their missing runaways. If they were trying to recapture their
missing property, why would advertisers leave out gradations of skin color
that might distinguish one individual from another? Perhaps owners
expected that slaves walking freely through communities would automatically be suspect, so placing an advertisement served more to trace a found
individual than to identify a missing one. As with other bodily details, it
was also likely that advertisers genuinely did not notice the precise complexion of their property. There has been extensive modern research on
cross-race identification bias that suggests that people are more competent
at recognizing and identifying individuals from their own racial group.[15]
Colonial advertisers may not have expected their presumed newspaper

readers to note nuances among people of African descent. Instead, the category of "Negro," with its frequent use as a synonym for "slave," replaced a recitation of individual details.

This lack of attention to complexion may explain why very few African-descended people were described as any shade of brown. Despite brownness being an utterly appropriate descriptor for the skin color of people of African descent, a brown complexion was more than ten times as likely to refer to a person of European descent as to one of non-European descent. For example, Dutch servants Michael Holingshow and Christiana Fothergale each had "a brown complexion," as did Irish servants Catherine Smith, Richard Bryant, and Robert Marchel.[16] Numerous English and American servants as well as those with no specific national heritage listed were described as having brown complexions.[17] Some advertisements even added specifications to brownness, as in Robert Gower's "dark brown Complection" and Joseph Ellvie's "brownish Complexion."[18] The few African-descended people labeled with a brown complexion were disproportionately those with multiple heritages. One advertisement noted a "very brown" mulatto man, and another a woman with "Mustee Hair" and a "brown Complexion."[19] As with degrees of blackness, advertisers noted an African-descended person's brown complexion to mark deviation from a norm through physical appearance.

Unlike black and brown, white was one of the most infrequent complexion descriptions, accounting for less than 1 percent of all complexions. A few European-descended runaways were described as "whitish," and a Virginia newspaper described a servant boy as having a "whitely complexion."[20] These advertisements added a derivational suffix to use the less definitive "whitish" or "whitely" (a term that referred to the appearance of whiteness). They did not categorize European-descended individuals as white people or white complexioned.

In fact, runaways identified as African descended were about four times more likely to have their complexion described as exhibiting some degree of whiteness as were European-descended runaways. Almost all of the white-complexioned people of African descent were described as being of mixed heritage. A mulatto runaway was "of a whitich [sic] cast, very much freckled in the face." Otho was described as a mulatto runaway with "very white" skin, Jerry, a runaway South Carolina slave, was described as a "remarkably white" mulatto man, and Annas, a Virginia woman, was identified as a "very white Mulatto wench."[21] Rather than describing an absolute color of whiteness, advertisers made these commentaries about degrees of whiteness to mark the unexpected lightness of some African-descended people's complexions. Such skin color concoctions served to mark racial status, tethering the appearance of physical bodies in perpetual reference to a normative racial constitution for people with any African heritage.

Using a white complexion primarily in the context of mulatto status created a category that European-descended people did not themselves inhabit: mulatto-identified people could be described as white complexioned in consequence of their partial European heritage. A white complexion only gained color-related meaning for people who straddled preexisting categorizations and who needed to be described in terms of their atypical coloration. Labeling a mulatto person white complexioned was not viewing them with criteria used for people of European descent; it was creating new descriptors that signified their exceptional status.

On the infrequent occasions when colonists did categorize European-descended people simply as "white," it was not a specific commentary on an individual's complexion; it was a comparison to someone described as "Negro" or "Indian." When an English runaway "took with him a Negro Lad," their master offered "*Five Pounds* for the white Man, and *Five Pounds* for the Negro." Hugh Sutherland was labeled "white" when he broke out of jail with an African-descended slave; John Brookes was described as a "white indented servant" when he went away with a mulatto slave; and Ann Gootey was labeled a white girl in comparison to a Negro man named Plymouth.[22] A designation of whiteness appeared when the European-descended person was contrasted with people of Native American heritage as well: "There is not one Indian or white Man," noted one newspaper story. Another described "an Indian, who has a white woman to his wife."[23]

These European-descended people were identified as white to distinguish them from their association with non-European-descended people, not as a reflection of their individual appearance. To wit: one of the few designations of a white European-descended runaway not accompanied by a person of African descent was a "WHITE man" named John Stanforth. In this case, John was also described as having "an Iron Collar, with two Prongs to it, about his neck."[24] Wearing an iron collar often used to punish slaves likely made the designation of whiteness seem necessary. In all of these cases, whiteness was used as a categorical comparison more than to explain the specific coloration of a European-descended individual.

That the category of whiteness was a different descriptor from complexion is made clear in newspapers that occasionally identified European-descended people as white and then described their non-white complexions: James Henson was described as having a "dark-complexion" and was identified as one of "two white men," accused of theft. Sarah Benfield was identified as a "white Servant Woman" with a "dark Complexion." Similarly, when an owner noted that a runaway mulatto man named Jack "may pass for a white man," this was not just a description of his complexion but rather an interpretation of how Jack could use his body to deceive viewers about his status as a slave.[25] Whiteness in this instance represented a category of freedom more than a specific skin color.

The ongoing instability of racial categories is evident in the application of "yellow" complexion in runaway descriptions. By the nineteenth century, yellow would largely become associated with the appearance of people of a mixed African-European heritage.[26] In the colonial period, advertisers noted a yellow complexion about a range of individuals. In one major digitized colonial newspaper collection, twenty-nine people who were called "Negro" and about twenty-two people identifiable as of European descent were described as yellow complexioned.[27] English servant John Nicholas and "Irish Servant Man" Edward Godfrey both were so described, and a sailor named Cuddie Cockren was said to have a "yellow complexion" when he ran away from his master in 1751.[28] Yellow did not yet have sole use as a racial marker of mixed-race heritage.

There was a group of eighteenth-century European-descended runaways who were particularly likely to be described as yellow complexioned: Mediterranean or Spanish-descended individuals. Francis Pidginett was labeled a Portuguese man with a yellow complexion, and Francis Rodrigo was identified as a Spanish servant with a yellow complexion.[29] Using yellow as a marker of Spanish heritage likely reflected British attempts to differentiate themselves from Spanish imperial challengers. The association of Spanish people with a particular complexion reflected a world where geo-humoral notions had long marked specific national heritages. One Anglo-American writer described a recent arrival to Fort Pitt in a 1763 letter, noting that the man "seems to have got almost the Colour of a Spaniard."[30] Yellow suggested a natural link between complexion and nationality that had long been a hallmark of humoral understandings of the body.

Advertisers did not regularly use "yellow" to mark nationally specific humoral features or independent coloration for runaways of African descent. Yellow complexion descriptions of African-descended bodies marked variation from a standard, not a standard variation. About 10 percent of people of African descent were described as having a yellow-related complexion, making it the second most common color applied to them. Runaway slave Harry Bedlo was "yellow faced," and others were "yellow-looking" or "yellowish."[31] "Yellow" was also used in reference to an assumed blackness of complexion. The description of Josee, a runaway Virginia slave, explicitly contrasted the two colors, stating that she was "rather inclined to a yellow than black complexion," while Caesar was described as "not a right black, but a little on the yellowish cast," and Betty was described as having "a yellowish or dingy black Complexion."[32] Yellow-complexioned Spanish people, however, were not more yellow than swarthy or less yellow than brown. In fact, European-descended complexions had no parallel set of descriptions for these yellow/black oppositions: they were not a little dark, or brownish white, or inclined toward sandy.

Some of these yellow-complexioned individuals were simultaneously identified as having a multiple-heritage background. Jerry Clark, a "lusty yellow" slave, was described as "Part Indian and part Negroe," and the "yellowish" Tabb was identified as a mulatto woman. Peter was one of two "dark mulatto slaves" who ran away, and he was said to have "a yellow complexion." Another man was "of a yellow Complexion being a mixed Breed." Yellow's imagined association with multiple heritages was made clear in the description of Guy. He was a "Negroe" slave who had "a Yellow Complexion, much like a Mulatto."[33] Yellow could be used as a marker of in-between status, a signal to readers that the missing person might not look like the imagined archetype of a Negro runaway.

But the wide use of yellowness did not require a mixed heritage; instead, it reflects the unstable nature of racial categories throughout the colonial eighteenth century. Accordingly, some African-descended people described as yellow were categorized as "Negro," not "mulatto," which destabilizes notions of a necessarily parallel relationship between skin color and mixed-race heritage. Multiple advertisements for slaves with yellow complexions noted a specific African heritage: people were "of the Eboe Country," "Guiney," "Angola," "Malimbo," or "Kinshey."[34] Plenty of American-born Africans were described as having a yellow complexion as well, including Milly, London, and Zeb.[35] In fact, yellow complexions appeared about half as often in reference to mulatto-or mustee-identified runaways as they did to Negro-identified runaways.

This is not to say that the complexion of people of multiple descent went by unremarked: runaways identified as mulatto or mustee were almost 40 percent more likely to have a complexion described than were those identified just as Negro. Fully half of these complexion commentaries referenced whether these people of multiple heritages appeared dark or light.[36] People who were of solely African heritage were not monolithically skin toned. But advertisers were largely uninterested in imagining the range of brownness (buff, ebony, hazel, hickory, mahogany, sepia, tan, umber, etc.) or identifying the specific tone that could have been used to describe individual African-descended runaways' complexions. Instead, advertisers sought to mark variations from a perceived norm, to label people lighter or darker than they believed they should be.

The complexions of Native American–descended runaways were described in ways similar to those of African-descended runaways. As discussed in Chapter 1, Indians' complexions were regularly featured in travel narratives and natural histories. But runaways identified as having Native American heritage had complexion descriptions in only about 20 percent of their advertisements, a frequency slightly lower than that of people of African descent. There was no single particular color used to describe Native American complexions; rather, descriptions often focused on how light or dark the person appeared: Charles was an Indian man with a "light Complexion," a "white *Indian* Woman" was reported missing, and an "Indian Fellow" was described as dark.[37]

Despite the red, tawny, and copper complexion descriptions in travel narratives and natural histories, advertisements for runaways of Native American descent almost never referred to complexion in those terms. By the middle of the eighteenth century, advertisers certainly associated Indians with the classification of "red."[38] But this was not necessarily because they considered an individual Indian's complexion red colored. There seem to be few print associations of individual people of Native American descent with red complexion before the Revolutionary era.[39] Instead, a "red" or "copper" Indian complexion was a description of bodily decoration, not a permanent feature. For instance, Thomas Hutchinson's history of Massachusetts described a Canewaga man who visited "in his Indian dress and with Indian complexion (for by means of grease and paints but little difference could be discerned)."[40] "Indian complexion" was not a common phrase—this appears to be the only publication in either *Early American Imprints, Series I: Evans* or *Accessible Archives'* newspapers with this phrase before the 1790s.

Neither were "tawny" and "copper" regular descriptors of Native American–identified individuals' complexions; they were more used to describe people of African and European descent. This included numerous people labeled as "Negro": Solomon was described as "tawny black"; Jack was of a "yellowish, tawny colour"; and Dick was "dark tawny." A runaway apprentice called T—— H—— had a tawny complexion, as did Elizabeth Johnston, an Irish woman, and Joseph M'Nabb, an English man. Toney was described as a mulatto "of a light copper Complexion," and Sam was a "Negro" of a "dark Copper Complexion."[41] A Virginia boy, taken captive by the Shawnee in the 1760s, was described as having "a tawny Complexion" when he was returned to Pennsylvania soldiers. Perhaps the food the boy ate, the dress he wore, or even his "Indian name," Wannimen, led to his complexion being described with the imagined color of an Indian native.[42]

Native Americans may have been described as red, copper, or tawny when in their "native" habitat, but when they were escaped laborers, colonists seemed to scrupulously avoid these color descriptions. Rather, in keeping with race-based slavery, escaped people of Native American descent were described in terms connected to supposed "Negro" appearance. Indeed, copper- or tawny-complexioned people who were identified as being of African descent may have simultaneously been of Native American heritage. Colonists would not question that people of African descent were enslavable, but Native American heritage ran the risk of signaling wrongful enslavement, giving advertisers an economic interest in negating any descriptors pointing to that possibility.[43]

The use of complexion in individual descriptions was far more complex than a binary categorical division. The same colors—like black or brown or white or yellow—were used to convey fundamentally different meanings on differently categorized bodies. For European-descended bodies, complexion was a means to identify an individual among a wide range of pigmentation variance. For enslaved bodies, complexion primarily compared an individual to the monolithically imagined categories of enslavable "Negroes."

Complexion Beyond Skin Color: Humoral Evaluation and Racial Exclusion

Because African-descended complexion descriptions focused largely on dark-to-light linear variation, humorally influenced understandings of complexion were less often seen as applicable to African-descended runaways. In contrast, advertisers used European-descended complexion features to convey bodily specifics beyond a color palette, including gendered expectations of bodily appearance. European-descended women's complexions, in particular, were noteworthy beyond a color commentary through terms that prioritized evaluation over observation.

Some observations of European-descended complexions clearly reflected humoral understandings of bodies. Peter Hakens was "of a sanguine complexion," as were George Lambeth and David Ludwick Thomas. Other advertisements referred more generally to health status via complexions: one runaway servant had a blooming countenance, Francis Correy was "of a healthy complexion," and John Sprague had a "pretty good complexion."[44] Some descriptors were less obvious commentaries on health or constitutions but still showed the impact of humoral understandings of the skin as a reflection of other bodily processes. These kinds of humoral and health descriptors focused overwhelmingly on people of European descent.

"Freshness" was a repeated complexion descriptor that did not constitute a specific skin color so much as the skin's ability to reflect other qualities. About one in ten advertisements for European-descended runaways referred to their "fresh" complexion. Freshness did not correspond to any overall coloring, skin quality, or national heritage among European-descended runaways. Fresh-complexioned people heralded from all over Western Europe, including England, Germany, Ireland, Scotland, Wales, and Norway.[45] Hannah Galley, an Irish servant, was "fresh coloured," and Elizabeth Petters, a Dutch runaway, was "of a fresh complexion." Neither was freshness limited to a particular complexion color on European bodies. Margaret Hurly had a "fresh coloured, dark Complexion," while Sarah Robbins had "a fair complexion, fresh coloured." Thomas Erwin was of a "fresh colour, of a sandy complexion," and Elizabeth Boyd had a "fresh Colour, but swarthy Complexion."[46]

In the eighteenth century, the adjective "fresh" meant blooming, healthy, or youthful; fresh was more a judgment of a state of being than a proximal replication of a hue. One diarist in the period overtly set fresh in opposition to death: Isabella Graham insisted that a doctor confirm that her husband was indeed deceased, because "how fresh the colour; how every way like life" his corpse seemed. Advertisements promised products that would deliver "a fresh and healthy Complexion." One almanac offered recipes to create "clear and fair" and "fresh coloured" complexions.[47] Freshness could convey health, vitality, youth, and a pleasing appearance.

Despite the varied applications of "freshness," the term was not univer-
sally utilized: I have yet to find a reference to a Negro or mulatto-identified
runaway having a fresh complexion. Plenty of dark-complexioned Europeans were described as "fresh," suggesting it was not a synonym for fair skin.
But early Americans did not map freshness onto African-descended bodies.
This was at least partly related to eighteenth-century understandings of
anatomical differences between European and African bodies. Virginia doctor and naturalist John Mitchell maintained that Negroes "never look[ed]
red in Blushing," and their veins "do not appear blue, till the Skin is cut."
Thus, Mitchell concluded, "the Skins of Negroes transmit no Colour thro'
them."[48] By understanding paler skin as transparent and darker skin as
having a fundamentally different opacity, a central aspect of humoral
understanding—reading the truth about bodies that could be seen through
the skin—was deemed largely inapplicable to African-descended bodies.

That social meanings could be inscribed in complexion is evident in the
fact that European-descended women were more than twice as likely to be
described as having a "fresh" complexion as were European-descended
men. This was, by far, the most gendered of complexion descriptions. Runaways named Ann Smith and Ann Jones; Elizabeth Beaver and Elizabeth
Burnet; Margaret Sliter and Margaret Welsh: all were described as fresh
complexioned.[49] Other print genres also used freshness as an attribute of
feminine appearance. A girl in a children's book had "pretty plump cheeks
[that] had a freshness that made them often kiss'd and admir'd." When
arguing that women benefited from fresh air and exercise, Scottish physician William Buchan contrasted the "fresh and ruddy looks of a milk-maid
with the pale complexion of those females whose whole business lies within
doors." Some used freshness as a sign of an appealing appearance: William
Byrd noted his friends' pursuit of "2 fresh colour'd Wenches," in contrast
to the sallow and scabby complexions of other North Carolinians Byrd had
encountered.[50] Fresh was not only a judgment of a state of health and
appeal, it was an evaluation that male colonists applied primarily to European-descended women.

"Fresh" coloring's disproportionate association with European-
descended women reminds us of the mutability of complexion. All laborers
were judged by their health and labor capability, but advertisers thought it
most important to mention freshness when envisaging missing European-
descended women. This was part of a pattern that relied on evaluative terms
to describe women's appearances. Advertisers emphasized the youthfulness

and health of African-descended women but did not mention freshness in runaway descriptions or slave sale ads because they did not see African-descended people's complexions as potentially revealing. Accordingly, African-descended women's complexions were far less often an eighteenth-century focus of European admiration, whereas European women's complexions had a long history of admiring evaluation. Lady Mary Wortley Montagu, an elite English travel writer, repeatedly remarked on women's complexions: there was Lady R——'s "unsullied complexion," a woman's lovely complexion "unsullied by art," and another woman with "the most beautiful complexion." Pennsylvania leader and eventual founding father Benjamin Rush specified "how great a proportion of beauty a fine complexion forms in a female face." Almanacs might tell of women's cheeks that repeatedly "glow'd with blushes," making them appear "in full bloom and beauty."[51] In all these examples, women's complexion signaled both their internal state (healthy, youthful) and the writers' evaluation of those internal features (beautiful, desirable). The pairing of such terms suggests the evaluative power of a public gaze on women's bodies and offered a potential means to read youthful fertility. Women's youth and health were critical to the success of the colonial enterprise, but how those characteristics were described varied according to the identified race of the individual. Only some women's internal wellness was rendered a visible aspect of complexion.

Like "fresh," "pale" was a term applied almost exclusively to European-descended bodies. Unlike freshness, it often conveyed a lack of health. Timothy Tyrrel, Thomas Taylor, and Robert Rouse were all described as both pale and ill looking. John Southerlan was described as pale and sallow due to a sickness he had in the West Indies, John Mure was "pale faced, just out of a fit of sickness," and John Normani was described as pale and recently sick.[52] Some advertisements made explicit that paleness was separate from a person's innate coloring: Mary Kirby was "of a dark Complexion, pale Face," while an unnamed runaway servant was described as pale and swarthy, and Daniel Wheaton had a "pale sandy complexion."[53] Paleness was a judgment that an individual looked more sallow or fatigued than was normal for their complexion.

Paleness was widely understood as a sign of bodily experiences, such as illness or external influences. An eighteenth-century British serial described an ill man by his "thin, pale, sickly Visage." Numerous publications invoked paleness as a sign of near-death: a young woman deemed incurable from a "putrefaction of the lymph" showed a "countenance [that] was pale and sallow." Revolutionary diarist Sally Wister noted that when Major Stodard had a fever, "instead of the lively, alert, blooming Stodard . . . he look'd pale, thin, and dejected."[54] On other occasions, paleness could be ascribed to time spent indoors or without physical activity: when John Adams described a Dr. Perkins as "a dark Complexioned, [*illegible*] Yet pale Faced, Man," he explained that the paleness was a result of profession, not natural inclination: "I have a great Regard for a Pale Face, in any Gentleman of Physick, [*illegible*] Divinity or Law. It indicates search and study."[55] Less admiringly, the sheriff of Baltimore County noted of the men who broke out of the Baltimore jail that "as many of them have been long confined, they appear pale."[56]

As a reflection of bodily health, paleness could have been used to describe African-descended people's complexions. The conditions of colonial enslavement undoubtedly led to chronically ill bodies, and brown-complexioned people could certainly appear unhealthily pale for their coloration. Recall Mary Kirby, the runaway servant who was described, for instance, as "of a dark Complexion, pale Face." Or instead of paleness, African-descended runaways might have been described, like William Denny, as "ill coloured."[57] But the visible effects of illness on complexion were not as readily applied to African-descended bodies.

Commonly held humoral beliefs should have meant that advertisers would see paleness as a potential sign of ill health for all runaways. But public humoral readings of African-descended bodies were uncommon; advertisers evaluated external, not internal, workings of African-descended bodies. Instead, on the rare occasions that paleness was associated with African-descended bodies, it was used to mark someone's atypical heritage, not their health. Titus, who was labeled a mulatto man, and Toney, who was described as "Mustee," were two of the small handful of runaways not solely of European descent who were labeled pale complexioned.[58] Paleness in these exceptional instances renamed a marker of internal health or life experience into a hierarchical ranking of skin color for people of multiple heritages.

In fact, many health-related complexion notations were consistently limited to descriptions of people of European descent. For instance, European-descended runaways' illnesses might be described in humoral terms, such as Charles White, who had "a sallow countenance, having had the flux lately."[59] The absence of African-descended bodies from these kinds of humoral descriptions did not mean that people of African descent were particularly healthy.[60] But advertisers did not choose to describe illness via the appearance of African-descended people's complexions. An African-descended man named William was described as sick looking and with his "cheek bones sticking out," yet any effect on his skin color went unmentioned. Mary was described as "thin" and "very sickly," and Hallowell was described as "an ill-looking fellow" with no mention of complexion for either slave.[61] Complexion was evaluated along a singular scale for people of African descent: color served to mark deviation from an assumed norm, not the multiplicities of meanings utilized for people of European descent.

Another health-related complexion description that was used for people of European descent was "red" or "ruddy." An unnamed two-year-old had a "red round face," and Richard Smeddle was "red faced." Many runaways were described as having a "reddish" complexion or being "red faced," referring to features or conditions beyond a specific complexion color.[62] Eleanor Kinney had a "sandy complexion" and was "red faced" while John Booker had a "fair complexion ruddy countenance." A warrant described a man as "red faced" and "dark complectioned," and Charles Hunt had a "brown ruddy complexion."[63]

On European-descended bodies, facial coloration caused by visible blood circulation was worth noting because it offered a means to read an individual's physiological processes. The relation of ruddiness and redness to health and blood circulation was made explicit in a mid-century treatise on vampires that explained that their "fresh, ruddy colour" was a result of having "veins ready to burst with blood."[64] A ruddy complexion was caused by an excess of circulating blood, as distinct from redness caused by sun exposure. One advertiser explicitly noted the distinction when he described James Foster as "ruddy, but a good deal sun-burnt."[65] Redness or ruddiness was indicative of internal bodily processes. In fact, a 1772 British dictionary offered "ruddy of countenance" as one of the definitions for "fresh."[66] Thus "ruddiness" was a term akin to "freshness," both reflecting internal health and well-being. A mid-century natural history directly associated both terms with national boundaries, claiming that there is almost "no Place out of *England*, where the Natives have such fresh, ruddy Complexions."[67]

Advertisers would broadly apply "ruddiness" to servants claiming an array of European nationalities, but such humoral features of complexion would not be stretched to individual African-descended bodies: of seventy runaways whose countenance or complexion was described as "red" or "ruddy," only one was not identified as solely European descended.[68] One of the closest descriptors to being "red faced" was that of a runaway slave named Sam, who was said to have "some Colour in his Cheeks when warm."[69] This advertiser did not discuss Sam's cheeks in terms of a specific color, and spelled out the circumstances rather than offering a specific complexion color. People of African descent could certainly show facial coloration changes due to blushing or exertion. But advertisers did not use complexion to note the internal health and workings of African-descended bodies.

For people of European descent, complexion encompassed not just pigmentation but health and life experiences. European-descended women might be particularly prominent in advertisers' assessments beyond coloration in ways that emphasized health, youth, and desirability. For people of African descent, however, complexion was an external identifier perpetually linked to their status as "Negroes" more than a mutable reflection of lived experiences.

Hair: Dividing and Determining

As with complexion, hair was far more frequently mentioned for European-descended runaways, providing yet another opportunity to add descriptive details. In contrast, the hair of non-European-descended runaways was largely described in terms of its relation to their non-European status. Commentary on hair type and color of people of Native American descent, in particular, worked to fit them into a colonial hierarchy outside of their own cultural norms.

Hair color was almost exclusively reserved for descriptions of European-descended runaways, accounting for more than 90 percent of hair color mentions. Black was the most commonly mentioned single hair color. William Ashton, William Day, William Hide, William Nives, and William Thompson were all described as black haired. So were Mary Ann Reyt, Mary Davis, Mary Sournas, and Mary Kirby.[70] Put together, various shades of brown hair appeared most frequently in advertisements—dark brown, light brown, brown, or brownish were all common.[71] European runaways were also described with an array of less common hair colors. Arthur Katin had "yellowish hair," Mary Marshall had "light-colour'd" hair, Henry Berragar had "sandy colour" hair, and John Seymour had red hair.[72] Hair color had little obvious pattern or significance within descriptions of European-descended runaways, where it did not seem to correspond to gender, nationalities, or other identifiable divisions.

Still, hair color could certainly be used as a means to divide and categorize. A Florida captivity narrative republished throughout the eighteenth century recounted how hair color was used to distinguish between Europeans' nationalities. The narrative repeatedly described how Jaega captors tried to determine if shipwrecked Europeans were English or Spanish. Beyond interrogation and linguistic tests, "some of the *Indians* would point to those whose Hair was Black, or of a deep Brown, and say such a one was a *Spaniard* of the *Havana*, and such of *Augusteen*; but those whose Hair was of a light Colour, they were doubtful of; some would say they were no *Spaniards*."[73] If we take this writer's words as a somewhat reasonable parsing of indigenous statements, the Jaega were relying on hair, rather than other bodily features, to distinguish among European nationalities. These indigenous people saw a distinction among Europeans' hair that they tied to national heritage.

Advertisers also might rely on details of hair texture to identify and delineate among European-descended runaways. Welshman David Evans had "short curly" hair, and John Hark's hair was "inclined to curl." Solomon Kissinger had straight hair, and Daniel Viscuop's hair was said to be two inches long and "strait."[74] Advertisers even commented on European-descended runaways' hair beyond particular stylings, color, or texture: Matthew Thorp's hair was "much neglected," and Nelly Jones had "a great deal of hair."[75] In contrast, African-descended runaways' hair texture was rarely commented on. Less than 2 percent of runaways whose hair was described as straight or curly or by any color were identified as Negro, for example.[76]

For advertisement writers, African descent included imagined wool for hair as a descriptive conclusion: details of hair color or texture mattered little once the categorization of Negro was applied. Since the beginnings of European enslavement of Africans, European writers had commented on African people's hair texture. In a passage that defined "the Negro race" as a fundamentally different species "from ours," French Enlightenment writer Voltaire claimed that "the black wool on their heads and other parts, has no resemblance to our hair."[77] Such statements not only segregated humanity, they underscored the association of Africans with wool-covered domestic animals.

A European-descended runaway might have hair that "curls very much" or a "Bushey Head of Hair."[78] But "wool" was a term used exclusively for people of African descent. As one eighteenth-century chronicler wrote, people from western Africa "have wool instead of hair."[79] A description of a "Negro boy" that contrasted him to his white-appearing sibling specified his "woolly hair." In advertisements, "wool" was occasionally used as a synonym for "hair." Boston had "wool" that grew "low on his Forehead," and Sam had a "long Shock of Wool on his Head."[80] These mentions of "wool" did not invoke the word as a description in and of itself: rather, it was a term that instead affirmed assumptions about the nature of Negro bodies.

When hair color and texture was described for people of African descent, it served to racially tie people of multiple heritages to their African parentage. People of African descent who were said to have a yellow complexion were about three times as likely to have their hair described. Lizzy and Hannah were both described as having yellow complexions and long woolly hair.[81] On these occasions hair could serve as a marker for people who might not otherwise be seen by colonial readers to fit the category of Negro. Advertisers might occasionally use African heritage itself as a descriptor: Toney, who was described as light complexioned, had "Negro hair." David, who was "yellowish," had hair "of the Negro Kind."[82] Such descriptions explicitly marked African heritage with the assumption that people originally from Africa had a monolithic hair type, notable for its difference from European hair.

In contrast, a description of bushy hair could be applied to both people of African descent and European-descended people of all nationalities (English, Dutch, French, German, Irish, Scottish). Here, too, the majority of African-descended people described with bushy hair were of mixed heritage.[83] A man identified as "Half Negro and half Indian," as well as numerous people just described as "mulatto," were said to have bushy hair.[84] Advertisers sometimes labeled hair according to the mixed heritage of bodies that they thought it belonged on. An unnamed man who was born in Havana had hair "like that of a Mustee." Sampson had "a curled, Mulatto Head of Hair."[85] Ethnic identifiers transformed into hair descriptions only for people of non-European descent. Hair appearance was used to mark individuals' place on an imagined spectrum of Africanness. Hair gained meaning not just for how it grew out of someone's head but through the perceived ethnicity of the body on which it grew.

Although relatively small in numbers, Native American–related runaways were some of the most likely people to have their hair described:

almost half of their descriptions included a commentary on hair. Most of these advertisements noted their black hair color, length, or straightness. Mary, a native from Canadian territories, had long black hair. An "indian Man Servant John Wamcom" had "short black hair." Charles, "of the Indian Breed," had straight black hair, as did John Peritt, a Nansemond man.[86] The association between straight black hair and Native American heritage was explicit in an advertisement for a runaway mulatto man who "has been seen with his Hair combed out straight" in order to "pass for an Indian."[87] Straight black hair marked Native American status.

Descriptions of Native Americans' hair in advertisements paralleled the attention given to it by travel writers. One writer described Native Americans as having hair that is "lank, strong, black, and long." Another explicitly noted that "their hair is lank, coarse, and darkish. I never saw any with curled hair."[88] Beyond black color and lank (straight, flat) texture, Native American hairstyles had long been used as a sign of their exotic differentiation from European standards of civilized presentation. William Wood cataloged multiple indigenous hairstyles: "sometimes they wear it very long, hanging down," and at other times it was worn short and bound. Some wear it "cut with a long foretop," soldiers and young men "wear their hair long on the one side, the other side being cut short," and "other cuts they have as their fancy befools them, which would torture the wits of a curious barber to imitate."[89] Writers described elaborate Native American hairstyles alongside descriptions of clothing and jewelry as a way of conveying exoticized indigenous customs.[90]

For Native American–descended people, hair, more than skin color, was repeatedly cited as a defining characteristic. Advertisers used the type of hair on the heads of people with Native American heritage as an explicit marker of that background: a mulatto-identified woman known only as B had "short *Indian* hair"; and James Cheshire, a mulatto slave, had hair "resembling an Indian's." One advertiser made sure that readers knew that his missing "indented Indian servant" had "black Indian hair." A Revolutionary-era advertisement described a runaway who had hair "of a different kind from that of a Negro's, rather more of the Indian's, but partaking to both."[91] Readers were expected to understand what Negro and Indian hair looked like and to be able to imagine how their combined characteristics would appear.

Moreover, while advertisers chose to transform straight black hair into Indian hair, they did so only on some bodies. Numerous American,

English, French, German, Irish, Scottish, and Welsh people had "strait black" or even "lank black" hair, but it was not referred to as Indian hair—nor was it attributed to any other nationality.[92] Advertisers did not use hair as an explicit marker of heritage for people identified as being of European descent. There was no Irish hair or German hair. Unlike the increased attention to hair for someone of a purported yellow complexion or mulatto or Indian status, hair descriptions did not serve to link European Americans to a particular heritage or category.[93] But for non-European-descended runaways, descriptions of hair overtly marked racial categorizations rather than adding to individualized descriptions.

Body hair offered another opportunity to make cultural categorizations from descriptions of physical features. Imperial writers had long commented on Native Americans' lack of body hair. Indians were "without the least appearance of hair on any part of the body, except their heads."[94] In the seventeenth century, Europeans took this as one more sign of Native Americans' lack of appropriate masculinity, given that European cultural practices regarded a beard as a sign of male maturity.[95] Eighteenth-century colonists consistently concluded that Native Americans' missing body hair resulted from nurture rather than nature. Bernard Romans claimed that "they prevent the growth of what little beard nature has given them, by plucking it out by the roots; they never suffer any hair to grow on any part of the body except the head." A description of Delaware Indians noted that " 'Tis said that they suffer no hair to grow on their body, only on their head. Some pull out their eyebrows." One writer explicitly noted that "both sexes pluck all the hair off their bodies, with a kind of tweezers" that he labeled an "Indian razor."[96]

For Native Americans, on the other hand, Europeans' beards were filthy, debris-filled signs of their failure to follow appropriate masculine grooming customs.[97] Robert Eastburn noted that his captors shaved him because he had "a long *Beard* which the *Indians* hate." William Wood commented that New England natives would call anyone with a beard "an Englishman's bastard." Henri Membertou was a Micmac leader who was recorded as the first Native American baptized in New France. He had a beard, which led to speculation that his father may have been French: Jesuit missionary Pierre Biard wrote that Membertou was "bearded like a Frenchman."[98] Both Europeans and Native Americans saw facial hair as a symbol of European heritage and culture.

Yet advertisers' commentaries on body hair did not emphasize either of these particular cultural practices; notation of men's facial hair was neither consistent nor common. Almost 5 percent of male runaways had their beards—or lack thereof—mentioned. Many European-descended people were described as having beards of various sizes and colors. John Nickles and Thomas Long had sandy beards; George Newton and Thomas Bolton had red beards; and John Blackburn and John White had black beards.[99] The beards of African-descended men were more often described by their length or absence, not color. London had a full beard, Tom had a small beard, and Quamaner was "thin bearded, but commonly wore it very long."[100] Other men were described for their absence of a beard. Mingo, Ralph, and Jacob were smooth-faced. So was Englishman Edward Rider.[101] Yet no one who was said to be of possible Native American heritage had a beard or lack of beard described. A beard on a Native American–looking mulatto man might have been a distinguishing feature or a signal of Native American heritage. Bodily practices associated with traditional indigenous community practices were not part of the lexicon for runaway laborers.

Perhaps surprisingly, eye color was one of the least frequent descriptors of missing servants and slaves: only a few percent of any runaways had an eye color listed. Indeed, the phrase "eye colour" came into use only at the end of the eighteenth century, suggesting that the color of irises may have been a relatively unimportant identifying feature for colonists.[102] This may be because advertisers described eye color on a different color spectrum from the one used in modern identification schema.[103] Eye color seemed to be constructed on a continuum of light and dark, not a polychromatic range of blue-green-brown. Gray eye color was most common, accounting for more than one-third of all eye colors mentioned. For instance, the eyes of John Chambers, John Grant, John Lawson, John Hunter, John Hoodloss, John McGonnegall, and John Nicolls were all described as gray. Black eyes accounted for another quarter of eye color descriptions. Only a handful of eyes were described as brown or blue, and not a single one as green.[104]

National heritage did not seem to be tied to a specific eye color for European-descended people. People of all nationalities might have eyes described as black, blue, brown, dark, gray, or light.[105] In contrast to this panoply of individual colors, however, people of African descent almost never had their eye color described—eye color appeared in less than one-half of a percent of their advertisements. And of these rare iris color commentaries, almost all appeared in reference to runaways identified as mulatto. Moll was described as a mulatto woman with gray eyes, while Dick, another mulatto-identified runaway, had dark eyes. The eyes of

Watley, a "Gambia negro fellow" who was "of a yellowish complexion," were described with an explicit notation of their uniqueness: they were "remarkable grey eyes, or rather of a yellowish white."[106] For people of African descent, eye color was only worth mentioning for its exceptionality.

This lack of overall attention to the color of eyes suggests that it did not hold the explanatory or classificatory power that other physical features might. Unlike a reddening of the whites of the eyes, the color of the iris was not seen to reflect the health or emotions of European-descended individuals. In this time period, many mentions of eye color referred more to metaphoric meanings: green eyes were known primarily as a sign of jealousy (à la *Othello's* "green-eyed monster which doth mock / The meat it feeds on").[107] Accordingly, some advertisers would describe eyes not by color but by the emotions they saw in them—eyes could be tender, look "something wild," or just have "an uncommon Look out of them." Even general evaluations of character could be seen in the eyes—the occasional runaway was described as having "a sly Look with his Eyes," and many advertisements listed eye descriptions directly after commentary on a runaway's "look."[108]

In fact, the overwhelming majority of comments on the eyes of people of African descent related not to their color but to their shape or setting in the face. People identified as Negro were full eyed, sunken eyed, small eyed, or hollow eyed, for example.[109] And as discussed earlier, many runaways of African descent were far more likely to have the redness of their eyes noted than to have the color of their irises described. Some Europeans had pointed to eyes as a marker of racial difference. Voltaire claimed Africans' "eyes are not formed like ours."[110] Perhaps he was referring to the dark irises of many African people's eyes, or perhaps to his understanding of their shape and function. Either way, Voltaire presented eyes as a way to note a fundamental difference between African and European people. A belief in such innate differences meant that a Negro classification could again replace an array of features on individual bodies—even in advertisements that ostensibly existed specifically to distinguish among similar individuals. Hair and eye color descriptions of African-descended people were primarily used to compare individuals to advertisers' monolithic construction of a Negro person.

*   *   *

In his *Notes on the State of Virginia*, first published in 1785, Thomas Jefferson rejected the idea that emancipated enslaved people could be productively integrated into American society. Jefferson noted African-descended people's complexion, pointing to "the immovable veil of black which covers all the emotions," alongside an array of readily observable innate physical, character, and behavioral differences—"the real distinctions which nature has made"—between people of African and European descent. Jefferson's linkage of skin color to essential differences among people of European and African origins was suggested by almost exclusively referring to these groups as "white" and "black."[111]

We could easily see Jefferson's language as a consequence of the ways that individual bodies had been described in the colonial eighteenth century. Decades of culturally constructed characteristics more than any physiological pigmentation underlay a shift to oppositional identities of black and white. Jefferson's black veil of African skin overtly minimized the relevance of humoral notions of complexion: a covering veil literally prevented reading the mutability of African-descended bodies. Without regularized humoral evaluations of the appearance of individuals of African descent, their complexions became increasingly divorced from an ability to reflect health, passions, and other inner workings. Instead, skin color itself would become a defining feature of nineteenth-century bodies.

Through the colonial eighteenth century, however, descriptions of the surface features of individual runaways were far more complex than either a color palette or racial categorizations might suggest. Colonial descriptions of missing individuals did not use the language of "black" and "white" and did not tie mutually exclusive complexions to racial identities. In colonial advertisements, descriptions emphasized European-descended people's many forms of visual variety while primarily commenting on African-descended people's appearance in terms of its degree of variation from an imagined racial standard.

Thus, historians tread shaky ground when assuming transhistoric relationships between various bodily descriptions, ethnicities, and racial meaning. Colonists made meaningful divisions among bodies through quotidian descriptions of missing persons. Bodily descriptions categorized runaways neither by oppositional descriptions nor by enforcement of black and white. Instead, descriptions of hair, eyes, and complexions marked variation from a norm on some bodies and variation as the norm on others. Humorally influenced interpretations of complexion were applied to people of European descent, while African-descended people were far more likely to be described by the fresh whip marks on their bodies than by their fresh complexions.

CHAPTER 4

Categorizing Bodies

Race, Place, and the Pursuit of Freedom

London was mentioned dozens of times in colonial advertisements for runaways. Thomas Osborne was "born near London." James Alexander was "born in the parish of St. George in the East, London." Thomas Warton was born at Hackney near London.[1] In advertisements for people of African descent, however, London was not a birthplace: it was their name. Twenty-year-old London ran away in Rhode Island. A "sensible negro boy named LONDON" ran away in South Carolina. Another man named London escaped slavery in Georgia. Still more Londons ran away in Virginia and Massachusetts.[2]

These uses of London encapsulate how nationality and heritage were differently applied to runaways of European and non-European descent. In print advertisements, geographically specific narratives embraced European-descended individuals' retellings of their own heritage as markers of their identity. Meanwhile people of African descent saw centuries of cultural, familial, and individual life histories papered over with names, terms, and geographies imposed by those who bought and sold them. This was accomplished not only through individual names like London, which retitled enslaved people with the cities of their enslavers, but also via the European-created categorizations of "Negro" or "mulatto," which labeled certain bodies in racial terms that denoted slave status rather than geographic origin, national affiliation, or other community ties.

The geographic identities that did appear in runaway advertisements embraced European-descended individuals' versions of their life histories. Colonists included this information because they believed that people's origins influenced how they appeared to others, making specific European heritage a necessary identifier. In contrast, people of African descent were overwhelmingly described in terms of their relationship to enslavement, encoding temporal categories of the North American slave system into bodily descriptions. We may take for granted that Europeans monolithically represented African-descended people from diverse cultural and geographic heritages with the label of "Negro." But this common sleight of hand erased entire life histories and replaced people's pasts with European-imposed identities that were based around the temporality of the transatlantic race-based slave system.[3]

The individual names of runaways used in newspaper advertisements likewise marked racial divisions. First names and surnames reflected imposed heritages as well as slave versus free status. Like with the many men of African descent called "London," naming practices were a prime example of the ways that racial differences were inscribed beyond complexion or other racialized physical features. Names reflected assumptions about sex, race, and nationality and highlighted contestations of freedom.

Through various categorization practices, runaway advertisements also sought to minimize the liminal status of people identified as being of multiple heritages (mulatto and mustee). Because Native American and European heritages could lead to a repudiation of slave status, advertisers repeatedly minimized any in-between-ness in descriptions of enslaved runaways, often substituting a description of an individual's appearance for a heritage marker or casting doubt on a runaway's self-stated identity. These contestations simultaneously reveal the many ways enslaved people attempted to use their appearance to pursue freedom.

Marking Heritage

What we might call national or ethnic or racial identifiers—in other words, a nod to place of origin and heritage—were the most common descriptors mentioned for runaways. African-descended people were described as "Negro" or "Mulatto" in almost every single runaway advertisement (over 99 percent of the time), while European-descended runaways' national heritages were mentioned just under two-thirds of the time. Thus Maria Charlotta Hamanin was described as Dutch, Catherine Diel as Irish, and Sally as Negro.[4] The frequencies of these labels were similar for men and for women, reiterating that colonists saw such terms as basic identity markers.

The imposed status of "Negro" overshadowed any specificity of belonging or identifying details of place or nation. A single sentence in a 1760 captivity narrative exemplifies the incongruent application of heritage classifications: Briton Hammon listed people who had been killed: "*John Nowland*, and *Nathaniel Rich*, both belonging to *Plymouth*, and *Elkanah Collymore*, and *James Webb*, Strangers, and *Moses Newmock*, Molatto."[5] Hammon offered three kinds of descriptions of the named individuals: the first two were identified by where they were from ("belonging to *Plymouth*"). Two more were described as "Strangers"—clearly they were not complete strangers, since Hammon knew their full names, but he did not know where they had lived, and given their deaths, could not ask them. But the final deceased person, Moses Newmock, was identified neither by his hometown nor by the lack of information in reference to where he was from: instead, a judgment of his racial status ("Molatto") was used in place of the specific geographic information offered for the other, presumably European-descended, men. It did not matter if Moses were from Plymouth or from an unknown residence. Even in death, his imposed mulatto status overrode the importance of his life history.

Such divergent identification schemes for European- and African-descended people were standard. A writer in the Seven Years' War identified two people who froze to death in the winter cold: "a man of the Royal [infantry unit] of Late Prideaux's and a negro."[6] Even though neither man was named, the first was tied to his British heritage by his membership in Colonel John Prideaux's 55th Regiment of Foot. Yet the "negro's" relation to the military, to Britain, or to any other identifiers (even his male gender has to be assumed) were nonexistent.

Undoubtedly, these labeling practices did not explicitly occur to advertisers when they put pen to paper. But their assumptions turned racialized status into a replacement for other forms of lived identity. For European-descended runaways, heritage markers provided details about the life histories that they, themselves, had likely conveyed to their masters. These histories often cited a specific national geographic place of origin. For African-descended runaways, heritage markers were more likely to be related to the chronology of race-based slavery, minimizing individual differences, marginalizing self-constructed identities, and underscoring supposedly biological aspects of "heritage."

No runaways were generalized as European—what mattered was the national or geographically specific polity to which they belonged (Figures 2

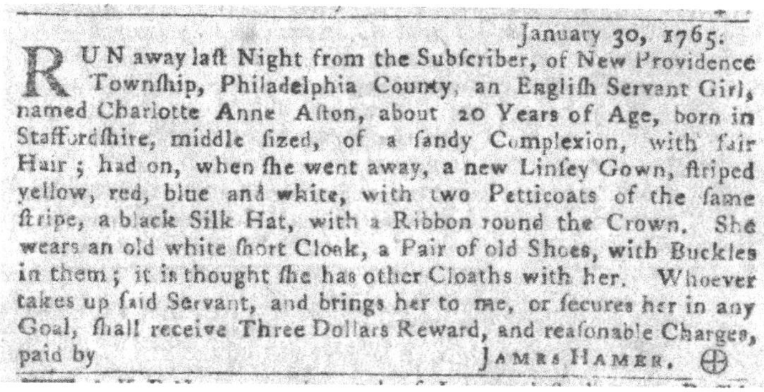

January 30, 1765.

R U N away laſt Night from the Subſcriber, of New Providence Townſhip, Philadelphia County, an Engliſh Servant Girl, named Charlotte Anne Alton, about 20 Years of Age, born in Staffordſhire, middle ſized, of a ſandy Complexion, with fair Hair; had on, when ſhe went away, a new Linſey Gown, ſtriped yellow, red, blue and white, with two Petticoats of the ſame ſtripe, a black Silk Hat, with a Ribbon round the Crown. She wears an old white ſhort Cloak, a Pair of old Shoes, with Buckles in them; it is thought ſhe has other Cloaths with her. Whoever takes up ſaid Servant, and brings her to me, or ſecures her in any Goal, ſhall receive Three Dollars Reward, and reaſonable Charges, paid by JAMES HAMER. ⊕

Figure 2. An advertisement for a missing "English Servant Girl" named Charlotte Anne Aston further specified that she was "born in Staffordshire." *Pennsylvania Gazette* February 14, 1765, p. 3. Library Company of Philadelphia.

and 12, on p. 153). European-descended national identifiers appeared in several forms. Advertisers might assert national heritage (English or Englishman) or a notation of birthplace or origin (born in London, from England). American military deserters were particularly likely to have their residential heritage recorded, probably because it was part of their military records.[7] Advertisements noted that runaway servants hailed originally from all over Europe (Denmark, Holland, Italy, France, Germany, Ireland, Norway, Poland, Sweden, Switzerland). Within the British Empire, advertisements noted runaways' origins in various regions of England, Ireland, Wales, and Scotland, as well as in most of the British colonies. Rose Flanagin had been born near Newry in Ireland; an unnamed Boston runaway was said to be "from Newcastle"; and Ann Jones was "born in Dublin."[8] Even for colonists who had never traveled to Europe, these place-names were likely far more meaningful to them than any African cities might have been.

Belonging to a British colony was sometimes not even a specific enough birthplace, and European-descended runaways might have their exact colonial hometown noted in advertisements as well: there were European-descended runaways from New London, Connecticut; Elizabethtown, New Jersey; Lebanon, Pennsylvania; and Nansemond, Virginia, for example. In a particularly detailed advertisement, William Springate was described as being born in Wales and raised in Bristol, specifically marking his life travels within Great Britain.[9] These kinds of specific geographic narratives reflected the individuals' retelling of their own life histories. Even though most masters could not know, firsthand, where their servants had been born, they generally seemed to accept their laborers' telling of their familial origins.

In contrast, most people of African descent were largely categorized by the imposed taxonomy of "Negro" that corresponded neither to a political state nor to a particular part of the invented region of Africa (Figure 13, on p. 153). Since at least the seventeenth century, Europeans had used "Negroland" to refer to parts of the African continent. London cartographer Herman Moll labeled an inland area of West Africa "Negroland," in contrast to the coastal areas he labeled with terms imposed by European colonizers, like "Grain Coast," "Gold Coast," and "Slave Coast."[10] There was little life story in such imposed extra-national segregating labels. While colonists would not generalize that runaways were European or even British, they would use "Negro" to group an array of people presumed to have an African heritage. This effectively ignored self-described life histories in favor of evaluations of how an individual matched an overarching racial categorization. Colonizers certainly had the knowledge to tie individual people of African descent more directly to their heritages. Eighteenth-century publications noted that "Africa" contained numerous empires. As early as 1704, a commentary explicitly noted that "the Name of Guinea" is "a gross Error. That name is not known to the Inhabitants of the Country, and the kingdom of *Guinea* is an imaginary Kingdom."[11] But knowledge had to be relevant to colonial goals, and disaggregating the kingdoms and cultures of West Africa was not pertinent to a colonial system of race-based enslavement.

When noted at all, the geographic origins of a person of African descent was not usually mention of a specific place. It was a commentary on the person's temporal relationship to enslavement: most commonly "this country born" versus a "new Negro."[12] The common phrase "country-born" categorized a person as a second-plus generation of enslaved Africans; in other words, someone who had been born in the American colonies. "New Negro" status reflected a temporal relationship to slavery by marking the person's relatively recent entrance into the American slave-labor system. Both terms orbited around the single sun of racialized enslavement.

These representations of African-descended birthplace thus marked individuals' relationship to slavery and ownership, not to a national or specific cultural heritage. Newspapers usually specified that a runaway slave was "country-born" without more geographic specification—marking primarily if African-descended people were foreign or domestically birthed.

Colonists may have (and certainly could have) known the birthplace of their enslaved runaways yet they did not view it as an integral part of their description. A birthplace appeared in advertisements when it provided a future possibility, not a past life detail: one advertisement noted that "the said Negroe was born in Maryland . . . [so] it is supposed he is on his way to his old master, to see his father and mother."[13] Parentage and family ties might matter in advertisements for African-descended runaways as a prediction of future behavior and as a means to track missing persons. The expected details of birth did not matter in terms of the ability to identify that missing person by appearance or behavior. Advertisers did not describe the birthplaces of people of European descent because they thought that they were heading back to them. John McGee was not going to be found in "Clownish, county of Monaghan, North of Ireland," Lawrence Flinn was not apt to make his way to Kingsgate, Ireland, and James Lee was unlikely to be headed to Manchester in Lancashire.[14] Advertisers cited European birthplaces as a way to convey what they considered salient details that might help identify how someone appeared.

Gender differences in the notation of birthplaces for people of African descent offer another reminder that advertisers chose when to include a point of origin for runaways. African-descended women were much less likely than men to have their racial status supplemented with mention of a particular place of origin. Almost twice as many African-descended men were tied to an African polity than were African-descended women: Jemmy was an "Eboe Negroe," Jack was "Coromante" born, and Homady was an "Angola fellow." In contrast, Bet and Bess were both described just as "new Negroes," which referenced an entrance into slavery rather than a national heritage.[15] This did not mean that more enslaved male runaways may have been born in African regions: more enslaved men were described as being from a specific location in the colonies than were enslaved women. For example, even though her owner knew Nann well enough to mention childhood injuries, he only described her as "Country born."[16] Overall, about one-quarter of African-descended men had a place of origin specified, as compared to only 16 percent of African-descended women. Because enslaved men could not realistically be more likely than enslaved women to be of African *and* American origins, advertisers were choosing to emphasize men's origins more than women's labor value. Once heritage was divorced from self-identity and life history, it could be considered optional information, to be included only when it was the chosen means for advertisers to categorize their property. Fewer African-descended women may have had a place of origin specified because women's heritage may have mattered less to their owners: African-descended women were generally seen to have fewer notable features overall (Figure 6, on p. 148), and those bodily features that were described tended to be evaluative more than factual descriptors.

A qualitative comparison of male and female runaways from Georgia confirms this gendered difference in amount of information offered. Venus, a runaway slave, was identified only as "Negro," even though the fact that she had her "fore teeth filed" suggests that she may have originally come from one of the West African cultures where that was a common practice. Likewise, Darchus, a runaway enslaved woman, had no place of origin specified but was "much marked in her face with her country marks," suggesting that she had a familial history from somewhere other than the colony of Georgia. Phebe's "three or four large Negroe Scars" might have been a signal that she was not originally from the British colonies, but she, too, was only described as "Negroe." In contrast, Bob was identified as a Negro who had been "born in Virginia" when he ran away, and Caesar was described as a Negro "of the Angola country" when he escaped from his Georgia home.[17]

Notation of specific African places of origin could be a way to commodify national heritages, turning personal history into perceived value under enslavement. Anglo-American sellers of enslaved people held a variety of beliefs about the labor quality of people they purchased from different African dominions. Henry Laurens believed that Gambians were more likely to be "tall robust people" and instructed his purchasers that while that Gambia and Gold Coast slaves were most preferred, "any Country will do, except Callabars." In an oft-quoted passage, Laurens described the hundred slaves he imagined purchasing: "there must not be a Callabar amongst them. Gold Coast or Gambia's are best, next to them the Windward Coast are prefer'd to Angola's."[18] Laurens clearly saw a difference—at least in economic worth—among Africans. Similarly, elite Virginia slave owner John Carter expressed unhappiness with previous shipments of African people for sale and told a colleague, "If you or your friends think fit to send Gambia, or Gold Coast Negroes, I will endeavour to serve you, but will not accept of a Consignment from any other part."[19] A history of Barbados proclaimed that slaves from the "Kingdoms of *Coramantee, Angola, Whiddaw, Ebo,* and *Anamabw*" were most common, but Coramantees (Akhan ethnic groups) were considered the best laborers.[20] These writers shared a belief that African ethnic heritages held distinctive economic value, even if they did not agree on the exact ranking of those values. But once African-descended individuals were enmeshed in colonial slave systems, there was far less attention to the physical and cultural differences ascribed to these heritages.

Comparatively few advertisements identified a specific African birthplace or ethnic heritage for runaways. If we do not include references to the generic "Guinea," the European name for a swath of West Africa, only one in twenty advertisements for people of African descent mentioned a specific African heritage. In fact, most of the advertisements that mention ethnically or linguistically specific African heritages were for enslaved people who self-identified their background, not for missing runaways being described by their owners. Suspected runaway slaves who had been caught and sent to workhouses or jails until masters could claim them were most likely to specify their place of origin. South Carolinians were most likely to advertise slaves who had been found and taken to workhouses and were thus particularly likely to publish details of a specific African heritage.

Even though workhouse advertisements were less than one-fifth of those for African-descended people in my data, they account for about half of the notations of specific African cultural groupings. One runaway who, according to the formulaic language of the *South-Carolina Gazette*, "cannot tell his own or his masters name," was identified as a Negro newly imported from the Angola country, and another, identified only as "D," reportedly came from the "Yallunka" country. Jailers noted that Binab was of the "Fuller" country, Bruse was Calabar, and Diama was Angolan.[21] An African cultural identification in these cases could be important, not necessarily to imply a physical description but rather to alert an owner who would presumably know from where their property had originated (or at least from where the slave trader claimed their salable bodies had originated). That was likely why an unnamed man who had been committed to jail in Virginia was described as an Igbo man, brought to Virginia six years earlier.[22]

Instead of owners deciding what information they remembered about their chattel, jailers could—and did—ask runaways about themselves. While the information they translated into advertisements was still mediated, it did appear to rely on African-descended people's claims to their countries or cultures. It also may have offered an opportunity for captured people to offer misdirection about their personal histories. The fact that jailers noted the heritages of presumed slaves suggests that this information was expected to be known by owners, and thus could have been regularly used as a means to identify enslaved people. In theory, advertisements for missing slaves could have offered this information so that anyone who found a runaway could ask them identifying details. But specific heritage was not a common theme in advertisements for missing slaves. Enslaved people knew these details of their lives, and undoubtedly so did the people on whose farms, homes, and plantations they lived. But their African-based heritages were primarily relevant when advertisers depended on African-descended people to describe themselves.

Recognition of birthplace mattered because assertions of freedom were tied to the ability to self-generate a life history. The incompatibility of a publicly noted life history and enslavement is clear in advertisements that atypically noted birthplaces of people of African descent. Many mentions of a specific birthplace involved people who made claims of freedom. A man named London was "born in the Isle of May" and "is supposed will pass for a free man." "Negro man" John Wellman "says he was born in France and is a Freeman." Jack, a "Molattoe slave," uncharacteristically described as being born in "Allentown, Monmouth county," was said to "intend to pass for a free Negro."[23] The ability to have one's geographic origins recognized supported claims of freedom, which meant that advertisers could be particularly hesitant to publicly apply them to enslaved people.

Sometimes the birthplaces of people of African descent were marked as claims rather than facts to minimize their self-identified life history in comparison to an owner's claim of enslavement. As with London and John Wellman mentioned just above, advertisements frequently noted that enslaved people "said" they were born in a particular location in Europe. "Negro" John Emmanuel "says he was born in Spain." John M'Kae, described as a mulatto man, "says that he was born in Yorkshire, Old England." And Josee "says he is a Spaniard, by his account born at Comana."[24] Advertisers likely used the phrasing of imputed claim because they saw the men trying to cement their free status through a European birthplace. Conversely, advertisers cast aspersions on European-descended runaway servants' life stories only when there were specific reasons for doubt: William Blake had no national heritage listed, likely because he "tells various stories concerning the place of his birth." William Davis was thought to pretend to be an Englishman, and Hugh Dean apparently pretended to be German.[25] But these were rare exceptions and overtly described as suspicious claims. In the overwhelming majority of cases, national heritage of

European-descended runaways in advertisements more likely matched how they described themselves.

As a contrasting example, advertisers showed little suspicion of the numerous European-descended people who were identified as being of French descent. John Fougasse was described as "a Frenchman (born in *Beaurdeaux*)," John Barsterie was a Frenchman "born in Rochfort," while Francis Bertrand was described simply as French, with no birthplace mentioned.[26] Undoubtedly the masters of these runaways did not have firsthand knowledge of their servants' French birthplaces. But advertisers did not question their nationality. These servants' self-presentation, including language skills and their given names, likely matched masters' image of how a French person should look, sound, and behave. Advertisers were willing to accept the life histories of people who claimed to be of solely European-descended heritage. But people who were also of African descent could not as uncomplicatedly assert their self-identity in publicly recognized ways.

This contrast between imposed and claimed self-identities is clear in a Maryland advertisement for the return of two enslaved "Negro" men. One, named John, "says he was born in France," while the other was described as "Jamie, an Eboe Negro."[27] Jamie's Eboe status was taken as fact, while John's French heritage was marked as a less-than-factual claim. This reflected a mainstay of settler colonialism and a labor system where self-identity was not particularly relevant to people of African descent: what mattered was their history as enslaved people. An Eboe Negro was still a Negro slave, but a Frenchman might not be a slave, so John could not uncontestedly claim his French birthright.

Runaway advertisements conveyed a central feature of colonial slavery: people of African descent's relationship to their own heritage was replaced with a temporally focused identification constructed by their owners. The incompatibility of enslavement with a regularized notation of birthplace is explicit in multiple advertisements. When two men ran away together, John Child was described as "born in England," while Ben was called "a Country born Mulattoe Slave."[28] John's self-determined birthplace contrasted with Ben's racialized description of his relation to the slave trade. Another advertisement likewise emphasized how inheritable enslavement changed the significance of personal life history: Colin Campbell described a runaway slave named Solomon as "born in my family."[29] Campbell's lifetime ownership of Solomon would not have an ostensible value to readers of the advertisement; it would not convey much of what Solomon looked or sounded like that could not be conveyed by a "country-born" reference. But it did transform birthplace from a personal heritage into an unequivocal sign of ownership where "family" confirmed slave status.

Control of one's birthplace mattered because it could be used to determine free or slave status. When Thomas Parke leveled charges against Robert Caten, it was for selling "a free born Negroe Woman" as a slave.[30] Negating the specifics of one's heritage allowed a narrative of enslavement to subsume personal identifying features in public descriptions of enslaved people. Those who had birth claims outside of their slave status were a potential danger to the very institution of race-based slavery. Perhaps this is why slavery plots might note, as did the story of one Antigua uprising, that some of "the most active Incendiaries" were "*Creoles* of *French* Parentage."[31] The dangers of enslaved people claiming European-descended privileges of self-identity went to the very heart of slavery.

For European-descended people, place of origin was a means of understanding someone's public presentation of self in an imperial world. For enslaved people, ethnicity served as a more totalizing imposition that marked their exclusion from full membership in that world. In a system where slave status followed the mother, the formal stripping of paternal relations also negated national ties.[32] "Negro" or "Mulatto" was a manufactured invention of who people of African descent were, developed out of the violence of European-sponsored intercontinental trade and colonialism. The terms did not indicate the specific political collection of individuals to whom they might relate, and thus were far less stable for African-descended people than were nation-based markers like "Irish" or "German." Thus a slave named Daniel could be initially described as a "Negro" runaway and a few sentences later be called "a mulatto fellow" in a way that a European-descended runaway would not be alternatively described as, say, English and Irish in the same advertisement, let alone as "European" to begin with. Indeed, it was much more likely to see a comment that an Irish servant was pretending to be English or that a deserter was trying to pass as Welsh.[33] Such advertisements signaled that heritage boundaries, even within the British Empire, were significant and real. Divorced from a specific locale, African-descended bodies could be represented as existing outside of a notion of geographically specific histories. Advertisers instead constructed African-descended runaways' identities around whether people were made slaves or born slaves. Either way, their identity circulated around the chronology of the slave trade and settler colonialism.

Naming Freedom

A runaway's name was usually one of the first details mentioned in an advertisement for their return. Names signaled heritages and labor status and could be points of contention over an individual's identity. Numerous historians have undertaken analyses of African-descended naming patterns as a study of creolization, assimilation, cultural persistence, or other social practices.[34] Advertisements for runaways make clear how names could be used to classify and categorize. Personal names marked gender and racial boundaries both through cultural expectations about the kinds of names people were expected to have and as exercises of power through the naming process. In particular, naming patterns reveal enslavers' efforts to erase signs of freedom for people of multiple heritages.

The names recorded for runaways were an implicit label of sex identification. Most obviously, men and women were expected to have mutually exclusive first names, making a name into a gender marker. Readers could tell, without any other information, that Alice, Bess, and Chloe were female runaways and David, Elijah, and Frank were male runaways.[35] Advertisements showed gendered patterns beyond individual name choices. Female runaways were almost twice as likely to not have their name listed as were male runaways. Occasionally it seemed as if advertisers may have just left off a woman's name—like the unnamed enslaved woman who was middle sized, thirty-five years old, and "impertinent" or the runaway servant originally from Newcastle who was "round-faced and freckled." In other cases, unnamed missing women were described as accompanying named runaways. Polly Murphy and her unnamed mother ran away, and John Zenger's unnamed black-eyed wife escaped with him. Even though enslaved women could not legally marry, they might be described as a wife in lieu of a name in an advertisement. Cornelius's unnamed "mulatto" wife attempted to escape slavery and pass as free with him. An unnamed "mulatto wench" was believed to have run away with Mark Wiley; while she went unnamed, the advertiser noted an additional set of names for Mark, who also apparently went by John May.[36] Women's relationships could turn their given names into superfluous details.

Similarly, people of African descent were far more likely than people of European descent to go unnamed in advertisements. Roughly 10 percent of missing people of African descent had no names listed, as compared to only 2 percent of European-descended people. A fair number of these were recently enslaved people who likely did not speak English. An "Angola fellow" five feet two inches tall with a scar on his left knee, an "Ebo" woman, and a "Negro man, lately imported from Africa," all were described as runaways with no names mentioned.[37] It may be tempting to see this pattern as a necessary result of a slave-labor system that brought together people with little shared cultural or linguistic reference points. But the dehumanization of kidnapped African people was a central feature of race-based slavery that was reinforced with every advertisement for an unnamed person and with every refusal to recognize an African slave's birth name.

As other scholars have noted, we should not assume that names recorded in primary sources "were the only names that slaves possessed."[38] Former slave Venture Smith recalled that his father gave him the name Broteer, but when he was bought by Robertson Mumford for "four gallons of rum, and a piece of calico," he was "called VENTURE, on account of his having purchased me with his own private venture."[39] Olaudah Equiano recalled that every sale of his body led to a new name. Onboard the slave ship, he was "called Michael." The man who bought him in Virginia called him Jacob. When Equiano was sold again and bound for England, his master named him "Gustavus Vasa," after the king of Sweden, but Equiano insisted that he "would be called Jacob."[40]

Advertisements hint at similar conflicts over names imposed by masters versus the names claimed by people of African and Native American descent for themselves. In some cases, it is obvious why enslaved people contested their names. The enslaved man "formerly known by the name of Lowie's Cate" went by just "Cate" when he ran away, rejecting the name that made literal his status as another man's property.[41] In other cases, we can see the conflicts, if not the rationale, behind name choices. Did Achilles prefer to be known as Hercules as a way to embrace a more powerful persona? Did the man in a South Carolina workhouse who would not tell his owner's name choose the name "SMART" as a proclamation? What did the man who was alternatively known as Charles or "Trash" think of his names? His owner claimed that "he will answer to either," but that may have been wishful thinking about the power of his mastery.[42] For people who were born into perpetual slavery, their names could reflect their parents' dreams or fears, their owner's claiming, or some combination of the tangled identities created out of enslavement and all too often wielded by enslavers.

A South Carolina advertisement points to the imposition of names as part of the process of enslavement. "Four new Negroes who can speak no

English," wrote one advertiser, were at the workhouse. He went on to note that "from my fellow who understands their country language," he learned that "their names are Ned, Tom, Dick and Harry." The selection of names is a curious one given that the phrase "every Tom, Dick and Harry" was used in the eighteenth century.[43] Was the writer's "fellow" interpreter providing a list of generic Anglicized names to help the runaway enslaved people with whom he shared a common language avoid a return to their owner(s)? Did the slaves have a single owner who thought this would emphasize the lack of individuality of his chattel? Ads such as this make clear the multiple potential arenas for contestations over the reformulation of identity through names.

Unlike Tom, Dick, and Harry, there were entire categories of names primarily applied only to African-descended people. Names of African-descended runaways included well-known biblical characters, place-names, classical names, and West African names. Many African-descended men had recorded names that seemed to mockingly reference historical leaders: Prince, Pompey, Caesar, and Primus appeared repeatedly in advertisements.[44] While slave owners chose many of these names, it was also possible that enslaved people, powerless in so many aspects of their lives, embraced historically powerful names themselves. Did the enslaved man named Caesar Rich choose his name as an aspirational goal, or was it an irony forced on him by the man who owned him?[45] Rather than place-names or names related to historic greatness, women seemed more likely to have names like "Doll" or "Kitty" that associated these women with the status of an inanimate toy or domesticated animal.[46] Names that might have been chosen by parents or might have carried on family traditions were replaced with Anglicized creations that marked slave owners' fantasies for their property. Name assignments made slave owners into literal kingmakers, with great male leaders under their dominion and docile women just waiting to be petted and played with. One of the powers of slave ownership was the ability to name their property in accordance with their own wishes and desires, claiming the right to create enslaved people's public identities.

A substantial portion of runaways of African descent had West African names. There were numerous people named Cudjoe or Cuffey, Quaco or Quamine, Sambo or Mingo.[47] West African names may have been kept at an owner's discretion, or some owners of enslaved people could have preferred their property to have African-sounding names. One newspaper advertised for Jack, aka July, pointing to a conflict between imposed American and West African naming practices. Perhaps the man named Quaco decided that his West African day name would be too conspicuous in his bid for freedom; he may have believed that going by the name of William Murray would help him blend into colonial settler society as a free person.[48]

Diminutive names were frequently given to people of African descent. Advertisements indicate more than a dozen African-descended people named Robin but not one Robert, the original from which Robin was derived. Conversely, more than three dozen European-descended runaways were named Robert, and not one European-descended runaway was named Robin. Almost every man named Joe was of African descent—perhaps as a shortening of an Ashanti day name, Cudjoe. One Irish man was named Paddy Joe, his heritage perhaps meant as a qualifier to the atypical name usage. Every runaway named Jack, the diminutive of John, was of African descent, while less than one in ten runaways named John were of African descent. While there were dozens of African-descended men named Will, there was only one man of European descent listed with that name.[49] Yet William was one of the most common men's names for people of European descent: there were almost twenty times as many European-descended as African-descended Williams. Likewise, there were scores of European-descended runaway women named Mary, but less than half a dozen African-descended women so named. European-descended women were Charlotte, and African-descended were Chloe. There were European-descended Eleanors and Elizabeths and African-descended Fannys and Floras; European-descended Anns versus African-descended Amys. Individually, names such as Amy and Ann do not seem to be markers of slave or free status. But aggregated comparison of their usage suggests that colonists would have likely recognized the racial applications of such nomenclature.

People of African descent also were generally the only runaways to have geographic locations as personal names, such as the "Londons" mentioned in the chapter opening. City or regional names appeared repeatedly for people who were newly enslaved: Boston was from Angola, Bristol was born in an unspecified African location, Carolina was "of the Guiney country," and both Dublin and Plymouth were "of the Ebbo country."[50] Perhaps named after where the ships that propelled them from freedom to slavery had alighted or where slave traders resided, or just after locales that tickled the owners' fancy, slaves had their actual names replaced with place-names that held meaning to the people who owned them. Occasionally, the rationale was explicit—as in the case of Newport, a runaway who was "born in Newport, Rhode Island."[51]

Surnames offered another means to divide European- from African- and Native American–descended people. For people of European descent, surnames could convey both a family lineage and national heritage. Runaways with a last name beginning with "Mc" or "Mac" were overwhelmingly Irish or Scottish, including Robert M'Cormick, Thomas M'Guier, Jane Mackenzie, Anne McDonnell, and Alexander McCormack. From their experiences living in multicultural British colonies, readers may have recognized surnames like Huffman, Kloss, and Luntz as belonging to people of German heritage. Likewise, the surnames Fougasse, Vilaneuse, Barsterie, and De Boutemant undoubtedly sounded French to many colonial readers.[52]

Those few people of African descent with publicly recognized surnames were likely to be of multiple heritages. Sarah Hammet was a runaway described as mulatto, as were Hankey Sexton and Sally Grey.[53] Overall, about one in five enslaved people who were identified as being of multiple heritages had a surname mentioned in advertisements, compared to about one in thirty runaway slaves who were just identified as "Negro." On top of that, almost one-third of runaway "Negro" slaves with a surname mentioned had it described as an alternative or contested name. Bob was also known as Edward or Edmund Tamar, Tom used the surname Salter, Isham went by the surname of either Randolph or Allen, John went by the name Manly Rattan, another Tom went by the name Thomas Morris, and Dick used the name John Lynch.[54] Surnames could help runaways blend into communities as free persons. This was exceptionally clear in the case of Jemmy, who was also known as James Freeman.[55] His first name rejected a diminutive, and his surname clearly expressed his claim of freedom.

When Mary, described as an "old negro wench," ran away from her South Carolina home in 1770, the advertisement offering a reward for her return noted that she might have headed to a plantation where her "three sons, London, Bob, and Bristol," lived.[56] We can only imagine how two of Mary's children came to be named after cities in England, a country that she was unlikely to have ever visited. Did the person who owned her and her progeny choose those names? Did Mary hope that names taken from imperial metropoles would offer the strength of leadership and freedom to her children? It was not just a lack of surnames that divided African-descended from European-descended runaways. The imposition of first names and the resulting contestation over how people were identified were inextricably tied to enslavement. Names further marked slavery onto the bodies of people of African descent and frequently replaced their public identities with those created by the people who owned them.

Categorizations of Sex and Race

Runaways who were not identified with a specific national heritage were instead generally labeled with categorizations created out of colonial settler ideologies. Historians may have become inured to seeing ethnic and racial qualifiers such as Negro, mulatto, Indian, and so forth in sources. But in taking them as unremarked realities, we risk leaving colonial formulations of racial difference naturalized. Colonists integrated sex and race divisions in advertisements, making gender inseparable from descriptions of ethnic and national heritage. Women of African and Native American descent were subsumed under names like "wench" and "squaw" that reframed their gender into a silent component of their racial designation. European-descended men were linked to their nationality, while European women were described in ways that reflected their exclusion from the national polity. Finally, categorizations such as mulatto and mustee worked to fit the complex reality of multiple heritages into a form that would bolster the colonial race-based slave system.

"Wench" technically referred to women generally. Historically, it was used to refer to a low-status woman. But by the second half of the eighteenth century (at the latest), colonists had reserved its use primarily for missing African-descended women. So Sarah, Nell, Bellow, and Sary were all described as Negro wenches when they escaped from enslavement, as were the majority of African-descended women.[57] In fact, the only runaway of European descent identified as a "wench" was described with the phrase "white Servant Wench," applying the unusual descriptor of "white" to counteract the assumed association of "wench" with African heritage.[58] The degree to which "wench" had become a gendered substitute for a Negro woman is clear in a comment made by John Adams in 1777. He complained to his wife about an unfit employee, describing the man as "A low lived Fellow, playing Cards with Negroes, and behaving like a Rival with them for Wenches."[59] John Adams set African-descended men whose sex was assumed under a Negro identification in direct opposition to African-descended "wenches," whose racial categorization was included in their gendered identification.

Like "wench," "squaw" was an Americanized term that segregated women of non-European descent from the supposedly generic designation of women. The report of the murder of Native Americans in New York described some of the victims as "three Indian Men, two Squaws, and two Indian Children." Letters written from the city of London noted that a British navy captain brought "two Indian Chiefs, and their squaws" with him from Labrador.[60] In contrast to "wench," however, "squaw" marked a female racialized space that was never applied to runaways. "Squaw" was a European nomenclature that signaled indigenous women's social roles in their society: therefore, it was not appropriate for a dependent laborer's description. Squaws were mentioned in advertisements only in reference to a Native American woman who accompanied a missing servant or slave. A slave named Tory escaped from Connecticut with "a Squaw named Lydia," and a "Mulatto Fellow named *Squire*" ran away with "a Squaw named *Charity*."[61] Despite their Anglicized names, these women were not identified as servants or slaves, and no reward was offered for their return. A Native American woman accompanying a runaway could be labeled a "squaw" because she was not in the role of dependent laborer or chattel. The title of "squaw" marked possible participation in Native American communities and life and consequently was not regularly applied to descriptions of runaways who were expected to be members of European American–controlled households.[62] In contrast, a "wench's" direct ties to race-based enslavement, not to any African cultural practices, could be consistently invoked in descriptions of individual female runaways.

A connection between heritage and sex was implicit in descriptions of European national heritage as well. European-descended women were regularly referred to with terminology related to their national heritage: there was no commonly used title to mark national belonging for women. In contrast, colonists frequently referred to men as Xcountry-man, which had no parallel for women—Xcountry-woman was only very rarely used in advertisements.[63] George Pearce was described as an "Englishman" and John Jones as "an Irishman," but their companion was just described as a "woman . . . born in Dublin." In another advertisement, Richard Purcell and Arthur Kelley were each described as "an Irishman," while Margaret

Smith "came from Belfast last summer."[64] These examples are typical: a
search for "Englishwoman" or "Irishwoman" in the *Virginia Gazette* and
Pennsylvania Gazette between 1750 and 1775 yielded fewer than a dozen
missing persons advertisements, compared to well over a thousand examples of "Englishman" or "Irishman." European-descended men's identity
was created through their national belonging, while European-descended
women's heritage was more often mentioned as a moment in their life
histories. This mimicked legal and cultural attitudes toward women's life
trajectories: in western European patriarchies, women were less definitely
bound to their geographic locales and would be expected to join their husband's lineage upon marriage.

Not all runaways of presumable European descent had their heritage
explicitly marked. Almost 20 percent of runaways had no heritage noted.
James Adams and James Ashworth; Henry Sharff and Henry Snissen; Alice
Walker and Alice Biscons—all were runaways without a specific nationality
or ethnicity noted.[65] Various factors suggest that all of these runaways were
people of indeterminate European descent. Some were military deserters,
others were escaped convict servants or apprentices—all positions most
often, but not exclusively, held by people of recognized European descent.
None was noted as enslaved, all had surnames listed, and their given names
were not those common to people of African descent. There were no Joes,
but many Josephs; no Robins, but many Roberts; no Wills, but scores of
Williams. Given racialized naming patterns, it seems reasonable to surmise
that people with unmarked heritage were overwhelmingly of European
descent. It may be likely many were English or American, making their
heritage an unstated default.

Indeed, when people of African descent were employed rather than
enslaved, it appears that their racial status was purposefully mentioned. Sias
was a runaway servant; Kitty was a servant who had previously served the
Virginia governor; Constant was apparently not that constant when she ran
away from her servitude—and all were described as "Negro." Syphax was a
servant described as mulatto, as were Tully, John Dancer, and Cornelius
Gallaghan.[66] Servants of African descent with surnames not only had their
African status noted, but sometimes their exceptional status as freemen
versus bondmen was specified. Peter Holmes, an indentured servant, was a
"free negro." Ben Suson was described as a Negro runaway servant who
"calls himself a free man."[67] While we risk employing a circular logic in
identifying people without a national or racial marker as being of solely

European descent, the exhaustive and seemingly consistent notation of African heritage in advertisements suggests that unmentioned ethnicity was what we might anachronistically label the invisibility of whiteness.[68] Advertisers expected readers to assume a European-descended heritage as an unstated norm.

Mulatto was another created category. It theoretically marked a combination of heritages that included African descent. The word "mulatto" derived from the Spanish and Portuguese term for a mule (the offspring of a donkey and horse), signifying hybridity. The suffix of "-ato" was likely a relation of the Latin "-attus" to denote the young of animals, again connecting people with African heritage to husbandry rather than humanity.[69] As a legally employed category, "mulatto" acknowledged the specter of reproductive sexual relations among people from geographically disparate continents.[70] In an era before formal registration of parenthood or DNA tests, the term was far from a biological fact. "Mulatto" was instead often a situational judgment of appearance. Daniel was described as a Negro who was born of a "dark Mulatto."[71] Daniel's mulatto parent did not override his "Negro" status, despite "mulatto" being the label for someone of multiracial status. "Mulatto" allowed writers to mark bodies while avoiding specific national backgrounds; the word highlighted the appearance of mixture, not specific cultural heritages.

Divorcing "mulatto" from the specifics of parental heritage was a purposeful tactic to racialize divisions. Advertisers sometimes used "mulatto" as a visible skin color. A 1766 advertisement for a missing slave in Prince George County described George as "between a black and mulatto colour." In his mid-century travels through Georgia, William Logan commented "that through the Counties of Kent & Sussex you see more Mulattos than of any other color."[72] Rather than being a recognition of the reproductive mixing of specific continentally divided heritages, "mulatto" could be a visually determined category that allowed colonists to sidestep the implicit violence of sexual intermingling under a race-based slave system. Its use meant that colonists could avoid explicitly mentioning European heritage in descriptions of enslaved people.

People could appear to be mulattoes without being labeled as a mulatto person, reiterating its use as a judgment of appearance. Guy was described as a "Negroe Man Slave" who had a complexion "much like a Mulatto." Ned was also described as a Negro who looked "much like a Mulattoe." On occasion, people of European descent were said to be mistaken for mulatto.

George Berry, an apprentice, "has often been taken for a Mulatto." English servant John Putt apparently "look[ed] like a Mulatto."[73]

While technically a term marking life and familial history, mulatto was, in reality, an imposed judgment of who someone was. It was a levied status that subsumed the importance of one's own life history under an owner's or master's evaluation of appearance. Advertisers employed a circular argument: a person adjudged to have mulatto features was likely to be labeled mulatto, and once labeled mulatto, that person was primarily described in terms of the imagined standard of a mulatto appearance. Such presentations lay bare the ambiguous relationships between race, skin color, and ethnicity in colonial America.

People who were enslaved understood the various ways that freedom related to multiple heritages. One Virginia runaway was a "Mulatto Man Slave" named Dick, whom his owner thought would be "pretending he has served as a Mulatto 31 Years, agreeable to the Laws of this Colony."[74] The owner was undoubtedly referring to a version of the Virginia law, first enacted in 1705, that set a thirty-one-year term of service for any "bastard child" born of a "free christian white woman" and "a negro or mulatto.[75] Dick's mulatto status was a prerequisite to making this law seem applicable to him in the eyes of those who might encounter him. Slave owners understood the relationship between the category of mulatto and the likelihood of believable free status. One advertisement explicitly noted that a runaway, "though not a Mulatto, may attempt to pass for a free Woman."[76] A mulatto appearance was tied to the possibility of freedom under the law.

Native American heritage could also be seen to threaten the legitimacy of enslavement.[77] Accordingly, advertisers sought to minimize or negate Native American lineage. In almost every advertisement about a Native American runaway, his or her specific heritage was replaced with a generic reference to Indian-ness: colonists were far more likely to note that a runaway escaped near a creek than was Creek, for example.[78] This imposed a European-created categorization in place of recognition of political membership. Colonists certainly were familiar with a variety of Native American communities: newspapers regularly reported on treaties with the Mingo and Delaware or noted trade with Cherokee, Catawba, or Creek Indians.[79] Yet Jacob, Joe, Mary, and Kate were all described just as "Indian," with no kinship or tribal lineage mentioned.[80] All four runaways were servants, not slaves, which points to the second pattern in descriptions of people of Native American descent: free runaways were much more likely to be identified solely as Indian than were enslaved people. Almost two-thirds of those identified as Indian were runaway servants in the advertisements I analyzed. There were a few enslaved people identified just as Indians: Wan was described as an "Indian slave," as was a woman who called herself Frances, and a man named Tonty. But advertisers more commonly mentioned indigenous heritage as an explanation for mulatto categorization. Sam, a "*Mulatto* Fellow," was said to be "of the Indian Breed." Harry was a Virginia-born slave who was a "dark *mulatto* . . . of the *Indian* breed," and an unnamed woman was "between the Indian and Mulatto breed."[81] By reducing Native American heritage to a "breed" of mulatto status, advertisers not only gave precedence to the continued presumption that African descent equaled slave status; they replaced any language of kinship with that of chattel. The "Indian breed," reminiscent of animal husbandry, did not have a European parallel: there was no "German breed" or "French breed" of runaways.

In many advertisements, Indian heritage was purposefully minimized, making Native American status into an imposed evaluation more than a self-identity. This approach to Native American status is visible in modifications made to an advertisement for a runaway slave in the 1775 *Virginia Gazette*. In January, Henry Hardaway ran an advertisement for two slaves. One was a "white Mulatto Woman Slave named Phebe." Two months later, his property apparently still on the run, Henry advertised again for Phebe's return with a description of her as "a remarkable white Indian Woman."[82] Without the subsequent advertisement, there would have been no public mention of Phebe's indigenous heritage. Instead, readers would likely assume that Phebe was of European and African heritage. This was not the only time Native American status made a belated entry: Peter Simmons identified Mary, an indentured servant, as "a young mulatto wench" and a "mulatto maid servant" whose mother was "an Indian wench" in April 1771. When Mary Simmons reran an advertisement for the missing servant in early 1772, she identified Mary as "a young mulatto or mustee WENCH," more directly signifying Mary's Native American heritage.[83] Yet Mary was renamed as *either* mulatto or mustee, the two alternatives marking the fluidity of such imposed categorizations.

Native American heritage was further minimized in descriptions that mentioned Indian features rather than outright identifying someone as an Indian. A "Mulatto Man Slave" named Sylvanus was said to be "of an Indian Look." A runaway in Virginia was described as being "a Negro man" with "much the appearance of an Indian." Molly had "a prominent Nose, and by her Complexion would pass for one of the Indian Race," but was not identified as an Indian person.[84] Advertisers seemed to go out of their way to provide information about people seeming Native American-ish instead of outright identifying their enslaved laborers as Indians. This continued the association of Negro and mulatto status with slavery by discursively avoiding the possibility that their slaves might be freeborn Indians.

Public erasure of Native Americans' ancestry was a tool of enslavement. Recent scholarship has shown the underrecognized overlap of Native American and African American communities, families, and racially constructed identities in early America. As historian Honor Sachs writes, Anglo-American slave owners had a vested interest in tailoring descriptions to emphasize African heritage: "Legally free as Indians, they became socially defined as black."[85] Advertisers consistently minimized Native American descent in favor of African descent for enslaved runaways who might have been able to claim Native American status. One newspaper described a runaway as "Negroe man, half Indian," while another described the same person as "Mulattow Slave, half Indian."[86] Despite needing two halves to add up to a whole, these men were described only as half Indian, not as half Negro or as mulatto. And when the man was labeled as "Mulattow," it was a modifier of "slave" to ensure that the absence of "Negro" did not undermine his enslaved status. His Indian heritage did not change his fundamental identity as an enslavable person of African descent.

Advertisers went to great lengths to avoid stating that a runaway was Native American. James was labeled a Negro slave who could "easily pass for an Indian." A "Mulatto Man Slave" who ran away from Maryland in the 1760s "resembles an Indian, as his Father was one." The writer of this advertisement used convoluted language to avoid saying that this slave was also Indian. An advertisement for a runaway slave named Aminta noted that she "has much the Look of an Indian, and is so, her Mother having been" one.[87] The convoluted text necessary to acknowledge that an enslaved person was of indigenous descent reflects European colonists' uneasiness with linking Native American ancestry to racial slavery.

Many of these Indian-like mulatto people might have been instead identified as mustee. Other runaways certainly were, including "A mustee wench named BETTY" and a "mustee fellow" named Bob.[88] However, "mustee" was not a widely used term. Historian Peter Wood may have been one of the first scholars to identify the use of "mustee" in South Carolina as a marker of combined Native American and (usually) African heritage.[89] Yet runaway advertisements in New York, Pennsylvania, and Virginia newspapers almost never used "mustee"; almost all mentions of "mustee" runaways appeared in South Carolina or Georgia papers that were published where Catawba, Creek, Cusabo, Yamasee, Yusi, and other Indian communities lived.[90] The categorization of "mustee" sidestepped Native American heritage among the enslaved: as Joyce Chaplin concludes, the term served to make "Indian slaves and Indian slavery invisible (to whites)."[91]

The intertwined uses of "mustee," "mulatto," and "negro" are a reminder that these terms were external evaluations, not reflections of any necessary bodily feature or specific national heritage. Tony was "a Mulatto or Mustee Slave . . . with long stiff black Hair, and greatly the Looks and Colour of an Indian." Cambridge, Jenny, Saunders, and David Jennings were all described dually as "Negro" and "Mustee."[92] This erasure of Native American heritage seems to have worked: both modern dictionaries and the *OED* define "mustee" simply as mixed race, not as including Native American heritage.[93]

This obfuscation of Native American background reflects slaveholders' fears that people of identified African descent might portray themselves as Indians as a means to claim freedom. Jacob was a "Mulattoe Fellow" who "had an Indian Father, pretends to be free." David, identified as a "Mulatto Slave" who "says he is of the Indian Breed," was supposed to have gone to the Virginia General Court "to sue for his Freedom" in 1773. A "dark Mulatto man slave" named Bob Colemand was said to claim his freedom "under pretence of being of an Indian extraction."[94] Labeling someone mulatto replaced their indigenous heritage with an imposed ethnic identifier that better conformed to a binary system of racial slavery.

When Simon Flowers was brought to a South Carolina workhouse, he clearly knew the importance of Native American heritage for his future claims of freedom. His jailer noted Simon, "an Indian or Mustee fellow . . . says he is free, (but has nothing to prove it)." Despite the conclusion that Simon had no proof, he had plenty of details of his own life history: he said that "his father and mother were Indians, named Tom and Betty Flowers, his father dead, but his mother alive, has two brothers Ben and Wall, they all live on Santee," and each of them had matching tattoos on their cheeks, which "his father did to all his children when they were small."[95] Simon attempted to use details of his family, his Santee heritage, and cultural body markings to document his freeborn status, but his life history was little match for a system that privileged external classifications of presumably enslaved bodies. The distinction between African and Indian status was not just one of racial or visual identification—it had momentous material consequences for an individual's chances at freedom.

Undoubtedly other runaways identified as Negro or mulatto were of Native American descent as well. It is not a stretch to wonder if Tom, identified as a "Negroe Man" who "speaks French-Indian well" and had a scar "which he says were done by an Arrow," was of Native American descent. Likewise for a "Negro Boy" who said "that he is free, and was born in the Indian town on Pamunkey river." This boy's birthplace was not taken as determinative of his heritage the way it would for a person born in Dublin or Bristol. Instead, his classification as "Negro" reduced a claim of Pamunkey descent to a location instead of a heritage. In another instance, an advertisement for a military deserter named John Chowen noted that he was "a molatto but calls himself Indian."[96] Even when they were free, people of Native American descent did not have the freedom to define their own public identities.

Thus, namings of both individuals and categories served to police an array of boundaries in colonial society. Runaways of multiple heritages were labeled with imposed terms like "mulatto" and "mustee." Native American and African heritages were geographically unmoored in an attempt to make bodies match a European-founded system of race-based enslavement. These kinds of imposed terms publicly erased the life histories of people of non-European descent, recasting them into categories that set heritage as externally temporal rather than geographically experiential.

*   *   *

Ebeneezer Cooke's eighteenth-century poem on Bacon's Rebellion described fighters as "*Staffordians, Indians,* and *new Negroes.*"[97] Englishmen were described by the West Midland county from which they were meant to originate, while African- and Native American–descended people were identified with imposed terms that had no geographic or national specificity. Negroes were only modified by their newness, a temporal reference to their status as a commodity.

Like Cooke, colonists relied on numerous assumptions and categorizations as shorthand identifiers of missing persons. People of European descent were notable for their variability, with a wide range of national heritages setting them as members in an imperial world of geographic and national polities. Colonists used "Negro," on the other hand, as if it were a stable category that was meant to exclusively overlap with enslavement. It was not marked by mention of specific origins but rather modified primarily by whether people had been kidnapped or born into slavery. Familial legacies—let alone patrilineal lineage—could not matter under a system of perpetual, inheritable enslavement. Native Americans' kinship identities would also be purposefully minimized once they entered Anglo-American labor systems. This effectively decreased the public presence of people of Native American descent, and restricted the image of enslavement to people who could be labeled as Negro or mulatto.

Allyson Hobbs's book on the history of racial passing repeats David Waldstreicher's analysis that in the eighteenth century, "to be white was not necessarily to be free; to be black was not necessarily to be a slave; and to be mulatto or racially mixed was not necessarily to be either of these."[98] Both scholars rightly point to the fluid racial intermixture in the eighteenth century and colonial attempts to mark freedom through racialized bodily forms. But they do so using potentially anachronistic terms. "White" and "black" may have been occasionally employed to compare groups, but they were not the common terms used to describe individuals who were being slotted into racial categories. Advertisers supported the fiction that race and labor status were necessarily one and the same by making some bodies more publicly malleable than others and by substituting externally imposed identities for the lineage, heritage, and self-identities of the people they described. Rather than an automatic opposition of whiteness versus blackness, descriptions of missing persons reveal the struggle to separate individuals of African descent from claims of freedom and the heritages that might accompany free status.

As we will see in Chapter 5, the negation of personal life histories in public descriptions of enslaved people left space for a backstory that instead emphasized the life experiences that physically marked their bodies. Advertisers presented African-descended people as identifiable by the damage done to them. Slavery literally molded bodies, providing a history to people whose lives had been taken over by the violence of enslavement.

CHAPTER 5

Written by and on the Body

Racialization of Affects and Effects

In 1751, Sarah Willmore ran away from her servitude in Westmoreland County, Virginia. Sarah was a woman with an "impudent Look" and a "remarkable Blemish near her fingers," who spoke with "a little of the *Irish* Brogue, but denies that Country." When she was last seen, Sarah had been wearing a dark-colored old gown that was stained with tar, a "blue quilted Coat lin'd with Yellow, and a pretty good furr'd Hat" but also carried an array of stolen clothes with her, including a purple calico gown, a blue-ribboned gown, and a coat with black glass buttons.[1] In 1768, a man named Ned escaped enslavement in North Carolina. He apparently had "a bold look," had "very good sense," and spoke "good English." While his enslaver, James Barnes, could not describe Ned's clothing, James did note that one of Ned's "under fore teeth" had fallen out and that he was "branded on the inside of his right thigh B," "branded on the left" the same, and branded on his "left breast IL."[2]

At first glance, these two advertisements may seem to simply offer an array of quirky descriptors, ranging from affect to language skills, and from attire to bodily damage and scarring. But a close reading of thousands of similar portrayals reveals that advertisers offered such details as a way to transform actions into corporeal significance. By predicting what missing bodies would do and explaining why bodies had been marked, advertisers translated expectations into a raced reality. Modern readers might view affects as an indication of a changeable attitude, but colonists saw them as a reflection of the workings of passions, humoral balances, or innate nature. When understood within the humoral framework that linked behavior and character to bodily workings, it makes sense that advertisers tried to show readers who their missing laborers were, not just how their corporeal features were shaped. Similarly, descriptions of clothing could serve as evidence of a presumed identity, an imposed status marker, or a commentary on a runaway's aspirations. In particular, they reinscribed cultural beliefs about racialized labor status. Discussions of language skills were built on raced assumptions about what details mattered about which laboring bodies. Finally, life histories were differentially marked on bodies through descriptions of scars and condition of teeth. Beyond what was necessary to recognize a scar, burn, or bodily abnormality, advertisers most often constructed experiential histories for people of African descent who had been forcibly separated from their pasts. The particularly evaluative nature of these descriptors—there was no reproducible measure for what constituted speaking "good" English or an "impudent" look—required that advertisers impose their beliefs on the bodies of absent laborers. Advertisements underscored racial divisions by subjecting African-descended people to external evaluation while portraying European-descended people's appearance as an expression of their internal world.

Comportment and Behavior as Bodily Description

Descriptions of runaways frequently included information about their behavior or character. Advertisers proclaimed if missing persons were surly or mannerly, impudent or artful, saucy or lively, smooth tongued or shy. These emotional states could be expressed through the look runaways had on their faces. In a world where temperament and physicality were necessarily intertwined, one's outward expression conveyed more than a feeling of the moment: demeanor revealed a permanent part of someone's identity and a useful means of recognition. Such character-driven commentaries reflected the nature, rather than the ephemeral attitude, of missing persons. With the opportunity to evaluate character came racially divided results: people of African descent were more likely to be described with having bad character traits (e.g., being a thief), while people of European descent were described by the wrong deeds they committed (e.g., stealing a horse). Intertwined racial and labor categorizations also corresponded to the portrayal of a runaway's language skills. Advertisers specified European-descended servants' varied language abilities while more often noting only whether and how well African-descended laborers spoke English.

About one in ten advertisements commented on a person's demeanor, often in terms of the person's countenance. Runaways were described as having agreeable, austere, bold, cheerful, earnest, good, mild, pleasant, sharp, sour, sprightly, subtle, and surly countenances, for example.[3] Advertisers related behaviors to facial expressions as a way to link (often undesirable) actions to a physical appearance. Ann Wilson had "a sour Countenance" and was "much given to Scolding." Peter was of a bold countenance and "a great Rogue." An enslaved woman had a "very impertinent countenance and was known to sing indecent songs when drunk."[4] How someone behaved was expected to be permanently on display because temperament and behavior were part of an individual's constitutional makeup, not just a temporary reaction to circumstance.

In a variation on countenance, people's "look"—how they seemed, how they behaved, how they felt—made repeated appearances in runaways' descriptions. As one advertiser described Isaac, a missing slave, his "countenance and disposition are altogether Indian."[5] Who one was could be visible not just via corporeal features but through a physical manifestation of one's disposition. More commonly, a look conveyed the advertiser's interpretation of what we might call the inner psyche of an individual. Runaway servant John Clark "looks shy and shameful," and John Ewin "looks remarkably dull and stupid." John Gallup, an apprentice, and Aesop, a slave, both had a "guilty Look."[6] How people might behave was visible in their looks—whether they were smart or dumb, shy or bold, innocent or guilty.

Because advertisers converted behavior that they disliked in their laborers into a description of their appearance, it may not be surprising that missing laborers were frequently considered too bold: by running away, they had already failed at their masters' version of appropriate submission. Unwarranted boldness appeared repeatedly in descriptions of looks, behavior, and speaking style. A fifteen-year-old named Ralph had "a bold, audacious countenance." Edmund Cooper and James M'Lane each had "a bold countenance," while Mary Smith was "a bold looking girl." In other cases, advertisers offered telling behavioral examples that correlated to fugitives' bold looks. Robert Shaw "appears bold, and talks much." Martha Murrey, a servant in Chester County, Pennsylvania, was described as having "a bold look, and will tell lies with great assurance."[7] Such descriptions reflected the shared beliefs that appearance, behavior, and character were intertwined and visible—at least on some bodies.

Runaways' facial reflection of their presumed emotional state was most noted on European-descended faces: more than three times as many advertisements for European-descended people discussed their "look" than did advertisements for people who were described as Negro or mulatto.[8] This was also the case for "bold" appearances, specifically: African-descended runaways account for only 2 percent of seventy *Pennsylvania Gazette* advertisements that mentioned boldness from 1750 to 1775. And in the pre-1776 *Geography of Slavery in Virginia* collection of advertisements for runaways, less than 1 percent of African-descended runaways were described as "bold."[9] This certainly should not be taken as evidence that enslaved runaways were less bold than other laborers. If behaving in a way that might be interpreted as "bold" had more consequences for an enslaved person than it would for a servant, enslaved people may have been careful in their public expressions. Or perhaps advertisers were unwilling to describe their chattel as bold in print because it could be seen to reflect negatively on their mastery. Slave owners might not as frequently note the expression of internal psyches on the faces of their human property. This lack of attention to reading character from facial expression paralleled the lack of attention to reading African-descended bodies humorally.

Boldness was also gendered in its application: women, particularly of European descent, were disproportionately described as bold. For instance, more than one-quarter of the seventy *Pennsylvania Gazette* runaway advertisements that mentioned boldness were for female runaways, which was at least double the rate of the newspaper's overall advertisements for women.[10] Women's boldness was repeatedly tied to their inappropriate speech in particular. Ann Leeson had a "bold countenance" and was sometimes "remarkably abusive with her tongue."[11] Through such references to women's boldness, their conduct and appearance were merged into a visible failure of gendered behavioral standards.

Of all affect descriptions, a "down look" was used the most often, appearing in about 2 percent of all advertisements and accounting for about 60 percent of affect mentions. For instance, more than a dozen runaways named Thomas or Tom were said to have down looks when they ran away from slavery and servitude.[12] Historians have interpreted a down look as a literal looking down, often as commentaries on slaves' submissiveness or deference.[13] But setting the phrase in terms of the visibility of a range of emotions on the face leads to an alternative interpretation. Contemporary dictionaries defined a "look" as "the air of the face; mien," suggesting it

Table 1. Dictionary Definitions of a "Down Look" as a Reflection of Character

Language	Definition	Translation of Definition
French	"Un regard morne, triste"	A glum or drab look, melancholy or sad
Latin	"Tristis ac severus vultus"	Sorrowful and serious look
	"Vultus demissus, tristis, moestus"	Looking down, sorrowful, sad
Dutch	"Een neérgeslaagen gezigt"	A dejected countenance
English	"Having a dejected countenance, sullen, melancholy"	

Sources: Abel Boyer, *The Royal Dictionary Abridged . . . : French and English. English and French . . .* (London: Messieurs Innys, Brotherton, Meadows, 1755), "A Down-Look"; Robert Ainsworth, *Thesaurus Linguae Latinae Compendiarius: Designed Chiefly for the Use of the British Nations: In Two Volumes . . .* (London: Mount et al., [1752]), 1: "Down Look"; John Holtrop, *A New English and Dutch Dictionary . . .* (Dordrecht and Amsterdam: A. Blussé en Zoon, 1789), 1:227; Thomas Sheridan, *A Complete Dictionary of the English Language: Both with Regard to Sound and Meaning . . . To Which Is Prefixed a Prosodial Grammar* (London: C. Dilly, 1789), "Downlooked."

related to a person's character or demeanor, not the physical act of looking in a direction.[14] Table 1 offers several eighteenth-century dictionary definitions and translations that confirm that a down look likely signaled a reflection of internal emotions and character, rather than just a tendency to avoid meeting someone's eyes. An English-French dictionary combined the two ideas with a definition of "a down look'd Man" as "Un homme morne, ou qui a le regard morne, qui va la tete baissee" (roughly translated: a gloomy or dismal man who consequently hangs his head).[15] Thus when a British sermon referred to people with "a Down Look, and a Sad Countenance," it was likely explaining the physical effects of sadness, not just a tendency to stare at the ground.[16]

Unlike some of the findings on nineteenth-century slaves, a down look was far more often used to describe a runaway of European descent (who accounted for about 70 percent of down looks). For colonial advertisers, a down look could be an acknowledgment of the internal world of their laborers. For historians, recalibrating the meaning of a down look offers the opportunity to recognize that laborers' lives and expressions were more than a monolithic reaction to fear of mastery. Perhaps people were expressing depression rather than submission with their "down" looks. We could certainly imagine that laborers had plenty of reasons to appear despondent and despairing—and people who tried to escape servitude and bondage may have had more reasons than most. Still, humoral interpretations more easily connected behavior to European-descended people's physical appearance.

The phrase "ill looking" offers another reminder that in colonial American worldviews, illness was not just a reference to physical disease or disability. Robert Rouse was "ill looking" and Patrick Burn was "very ill looking." So were Thomas Kelly, Thomas Manahan, Thomas McCormick, and Thomas Taylor. These might seem to be run-of-the-mill statements on physical sickness, but the description of William Hamilton as a "stout, lusty, ill looking Fellow" and William Johnston as a "lusty, well set, ill looking" man might give us pause.[17] Why would men who are ill be described as lusty, stout, and well set—all words that conveyed health? The answer seems to be found beyond the presumed relationship between physical appearance and health: in the early modern period, "ill looking" was understood in opposition to "good looking," not as a description of sickness.[18] Accordingly, in his eighteenth-century novel A New Voyage round the World, Daniel Defoe described Asian people as "strange, ugly, ill-looking fellows." So when the master of runaway convict servant Francis Richard described him as "very well made" and "very ill down looking," these were not contradictory descriptors.[19] Francis could be strong and healthy while appearing unpleasant looking and unhappy. Moreover, as with other humoral readings of bodily appearance, an ill look was applied virtually exclusively to European-descended bodies.[20]

In contrast, evaluative descriptions of people as deceitful overwhelmingly focused on runaways of African descent. African-descended people's misbehavior was often expressed in terms of their nature rather than their specific acts of wrongdoing. Peter was said to be a "cunning artful fellow" and Jacob was "a sly artful fellow," while Violet was "remarkably artful."[21] Overall, African-descended runaways were three times as likely to be called artful as were European-descended runaways. Even though almost half of what we might classify as character commentaries were made about European-descended runaways, less than one-fifth of deceitful categorizations were about them. In contrast, advertisements for people of European descent might focus on individual crimes they had committed. Thomas Plendible had previously been under suspicion of counterfeiting, and Thomas Douglas allegedly robbed members of his regiment. In contrast,

Moll was just described as a "notorious thief and liar," and Harry was a "sly thief."[22]

Perhaps African-descended people had reason to appear deceitful: slavery, a system of vast power inequities, privileged the judgments and evaluations of masters in ways far beyond what indentured servants likely had to contend with. But advertisers could have just chosen to list the kinds of supposed trickery practiced by their African-descended laborers rather than putting forth judgments on their deceitful character. In so doing, slave owners made personal descriptions into a literal display of their power to define the very nature of the people they owned.

Commentaries on runaways' speech patterns, appearing in about one-quarter of advertisements, reveal another means through which descriptions of runaways' behavior were tied to status. Accents were noted primarily about European-descended, and especially British, runaways. Reflecting the prevalence of Irish servants, most specifications were about Irish accents, otherwise known as speaking with "much of the Brogue." Advertisers sometimes recognized distinctions within British accents: John Purday, identified as Irish, was "a little inclined to the Scotch Accent," presumably marking him as Scots-Irish. Abraham White was "born near Manchester in England, and speaks much with that dialect."[23] Likely reflecting advertisers' expectations that Anglo-American colonists could most easily distinguish among British accents, such advertisements offered detailed evaluative gradations about the speech of many British runaways.

Advertisers also noted laborers who spoke European languages other than English: Dutch, French, German, Italian, Portuguese, Spanish, and Welsh speakers all appeared in advertisements. It may not seem surprising that people in the mobile transatlantic world had knowledge of multiple languages. But it may be surprising that a slight majority of the people noted to speak languages other than English were of African descent. Phoebe spoke French; Sarah spoke Dutch; Harry spoke "Scotch"; and Hercules spoke German. Other African-descended people spoke multiple European languages: Bridgee spoke Spanish and Portuguese; an unnamed slave spoke Dutch and French; and Will spoke French and Spanish.[24] The multinational slave trade created opportunities for its human commodities to learn languages that reflected their geographic pathways and associations with a range of European heritages. Advertisers sometimes noted when European-descended servants spoke a language other than English as well, but these were rare occurrences in comparison to mentions of their nationalities. Moreover, additional language skills often appeared *alongside* the runaway's national identity. Richard Crawford was Irish but could speak French and Dutch. Thomas Gland was Irish and could speak an Indian language, while Welshman Thomas Jones could speak several unspecified languages.[25]

These notations of language skills served different purposes: for European people who were nationally identified, knowledge of a language beyond their own was a piece of information that could prevent them from disguising themselves with another national heritage. For people of African descent, listings of European language skills were often the only descriptor of their life histories and *substituted* for national identifiers that would remain unstated. London spoke "very good French, and broken English," so readers might infer that he had grown up in a French colony—but he was certainly not identified as a French person. Lewis spoke "bad English" but "good French and Spanish"—perhaps he had lived on multiple Caribbean Islands or in imperially contested territories, but those details went unmentioned. Colonists understood the tie of origins to linguistic skills: Nat's master noted that his slave was "not a Virginia born Fellow, though he speaks very plain."[26] Language and place of origin were two means of identifying an individual's heritage.

Thus the languages listed for people of African descent substituted a description of behavior for a heritage. The multilingual abilities of people of African descent replaced national ties while still leaving the geographically unmoored classifications of Negro or mulatto intact. Lewis and London and the scores of other people of African descent who had mastered various European languages could be identified by their exceptional skill, not for the national or geographic heritage that skill might signal. As long as European heritage equaled freedom, people of African descent would be described with features and behaviors rather than national identifiers.

At the same time, colonial advertisers showed virtually no interest in or knowledge of any runaways' African-language skills. There was no discussion of Angolan or Igbo accents, or Mandingo, Fula, or Wolof languages. Instead of noting skill in African languages, advertisers focused on how effectively African-descended runaways spoke English. Almost 70 percent of the runaways described specifically as speaking bad English, broken English, little English, or no English were people of African descent. For example, Aberdeen, Bacchus, Chloe, Derry, Emanual, and Friday were all described as lacking English language skills.[27] Many of the enslaved people

who apparently could not adequately speak English were atypically identified by an African place of origin or as "new Negroes," suggesting that
they were relatively recent arrivals and highlighting the connection between
speech and nationality. And as Harriet Jacobs's autobiography made clear
in the nineteenth century, enslaved people might also feign a lack of understanding as a form of resistance to slavery.[28]

This was not the only area where speaking deficiencies were noted: well
over three-quarters of people who were described as stammering or stuttering were of African descent. A man identified as Boston was "Stammering
in his Speech." There was some recognition that stammering could be a
reaction to a specific situation: a thirty-six-year-old man named Pompey
apparently stammered "when under any apprehension or fear"; Cyrus was
said to stammer "when frighted or confused"; and Ned did so when he
was surprised.[29] Scholars have offered a variety of explanations for enslaved
people's speech impediments: Were enslaved people stuttering out of fear?
As an effect of the trauma of slavery? As a purposeful avoidance tactic to
circumvent racial oppression? It may also be that slave owners saw a reason
to describe their chattel as stammerers. People who stuttered were, to colonial minds, unable to competently express thoughts; it was not a far leap to
the belief that they did not have thoughts worth expressing.[30]

In contrast, the majority of runaways described as talkative were of
European descent. Many were described as talking too much when under
the influence of alcohol. Joseph Dealy was "apt to get in Liquor, and then
very talkative." An unnamed English woman "loves strong drink and is a
great talker." Thomas Philips was not only talkative but "addicted to Swear-
ing and Drinking."[31] Like the commentaries on European-descended servants' boldness in speech, notations of talkativeness were comments on
inappropriate behavior. Unlike the stammering mentioned more often
about African-descended runaways, talkativeness described willful misbehavior of European-descended servants. For advertisers, runaway servants'
problem was not that they had nothing to say or could not speak, it was
that they did not limit their speech appropriately.

Fashioning: Clothing and Hairstyle

Unlike many somatic features, clothing and hairstyles could be relatively
easily modified. Runaways could put on a new outfit, don a wig, cut their

hair, or change their hairstyle. Yet both were still regularly used to identify missing persons because who a laborer was could be conveyed by the stylings others ascribed to them. Descriptions of fashioned exteriors offered the most detail about European-descended men, with far fewer descriptive offerings about European-descended women's and African-descended people's clothing and hairstyles. Recounting a runaway's clothing and hairstyles effectively delineated an individual's class and sex, race and status.

Mentions of clothing were common: more than two-thirds of advertisements gave details of the clothing runaways "had on and carried with" them.[32] Clothing descriptions were so ubiquitous that textile scholars have relied on these advertisements as a major research source, and historians have described clothing as an extension of runaways' status and corporeal appearance.[33] Colonial readers, too, expected to see a description of a runaway's attire—so much so that advertisers used limited advertisement space to note when they could "give no particular description of their clothes." Advertisers also explained that runaways might have an array of clothing to choose from: Ann Broughton took "different Kinds of womens Apparel" with her when she ran from her master. Even when escaped laborers did not leave with a change of clothes, masters assumed that they would "change [at] the first Opportunity."[34] It is unclear how easy it might have been to acquire new clothing: runaways did not regularly have access to unknown outfits, and there were likely few opportunities to purchase ready-made clothing, even if they could afford it, that would not lead to suspicion. This was likely why runaways like William Hood "stole and took with him a new suit of cloaths" when he escaped servitude.[35]

Despite its changeability, clothing was a mainstay of runaway advertisements. Indeed, clothing color, style, trim, and state of wear could take up as much, if not more, space than descriptions of a runaway's physical features. The entire advertisement for the return of Valentine Strong contained seven lines of description. Three of them detailed his clothing. Philis was described as "a Negro Wench" with "a likely smooth handsome Face, but not very black one." A mere dozen words described her corporeal appearance while more than three dozen described the clothing she "had on and carried away with her," including a striped homespun coat; a second coat with dark quilting on one side and coarse red felt on the other; striped gowns; blue and white stockings; a white apron and stockings; and leather shoes with heels. Runaway Irish servant Mary Heany was described as "short and thick." The remainder of the advertisement focused on her

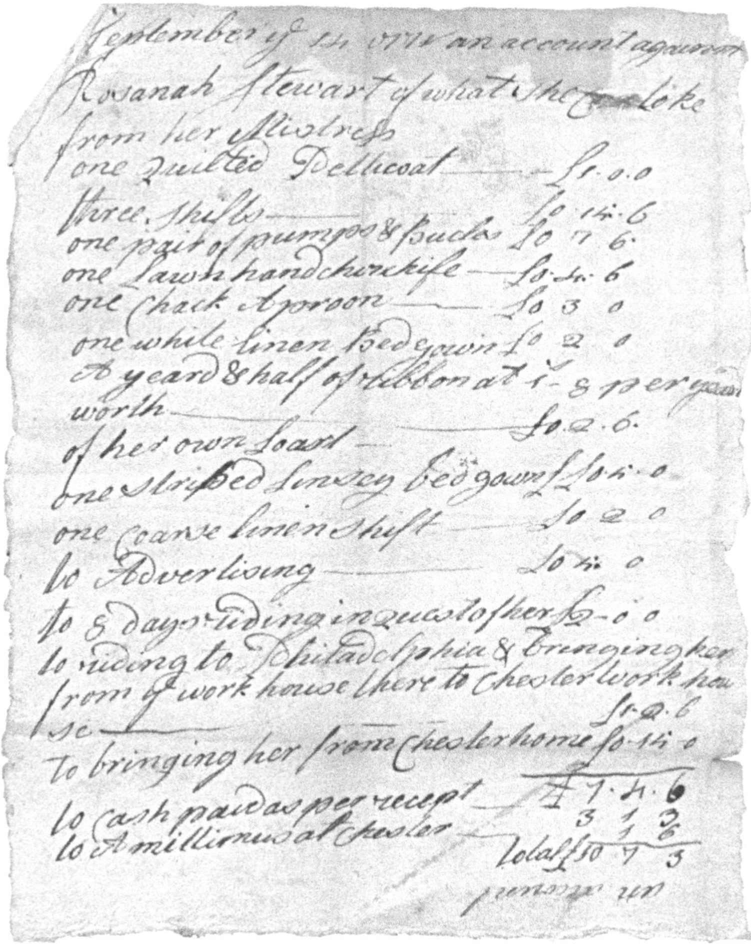
September ye 14 1771 an account against
Rosanah Stewart of what she toke
from her Mistress
one Quilted Petticoat — £1.0.0
three Shifts — £0 14 6
one pair of pumps & buckles £0 7 6
one Lawn handcherchife — £0 4 6
one Chack Aproon — £0 3 0
one white linen Bedgown £0 2 0
A yeard & half of ribbon at 1-8 per yard
worth — £0.2.6
of her own board —
one striped linsey bed gown £0 4 0
one coarse linen shift £0 2 0
to Advertising — £0 4 0
to 8 days riding in quest of her £2-0-0
to riding to Philadelphia & bringing her
from ye work house there to Chester work hou
se — £1.2.6
To bringing her from Chester home £0.14.0
£7.4.6
to cash paid as per receipt 3 1 3
to A millimus at Chester — 1 6
Total £10 7 3

Figure 3. Rosanah Stewart's master offered a list of clothing that she allegedly took from her mistress in his accounting of what Rosanah's departure had cost. In newspaper advertisements, advertisers also regularly detailed the clothing that runaways had with them. Petition of Thomas Whiteside against his servant, August 25, 1772, Folder 93, Chester County Court of Quarter Sessions, Indentured Servant and Apprentice Records, Chester County Archives.

"lightish coloured Jacket, an old black Quilt, brownish striped Petticoat, blue Yarn Stockings, and Neate Leather Shoes, with Buckles in them."[36] Advertisers might reproduce far more details about clothing than about the runaways wearing them.

Focused quantitative analyses of runaway descriptions in several newspapers confirm that advertisers used more words to describe clothing than other features of an individual's appearance. For instance, in over one hundred runaway advertisements published in one year in the *Pennsylvania Gazette*, advertisers used an average of thirty-eight words to describe clothing and thirty-two words to describe all other aspects of runaways' appearances.[37] This gap of about six words was fairly consistent across race and sex divisions. Still, European-descended runaways' clothing received the most attention. First, advertisers described the clothing of more than three-quarters of European-descended but only about two-thirds of African-descended runaways. Second, advertisers offered more overall detail about European-descended runaways' clothing. In the one hundred *Pennsylvania Gazette* advertisements, European-descended men averaged thirty-nine words about their clothing, compared to thirty-six for African-descended men.[38]

A similar evaluation of a year of the *Virginia Gazette* suggests that this difference in level of detail was even more pronounced in southern advertisements. Advertisers used an average of only twenty words to describe African-descended slaves' clothing, as compared to twenty-nine words to identify the clothing of European-descended servants.[39] South Carolina newspapers focused even less on runaway slaves' clothing. While there are not enough European-descended runaways to offer a direct comparison, a year of advertisements in the *South Carolina Gazette* shows that almost half of enslaved runaways' clothing went undescribed, leaving an average of only five descriptive words per advertisement.[40] Unlike in other colonies, many of these runaways were described after they had been seized and confined in a workhouse, so one could imagine that detailed clothing descriptions would be a particularly helpful way for an owner to recognize his property. But it appeared that the more widespread slavery was in a given colony, the less advertisers focused on individual features such as clothing. It may be that South Carolina slaves were dressed in remarkably similar outfits, in part because South Carolina enforced sumptuary laws that dictated what a slave could wear. A 1735 act noted that because many bondpeople "wear clothes much above the condition of slaves, for the procuring whereof they use sinister and evil methods," a strict dress code, including "negro cloth" and other coarse fabrics, would be enforced.[41] When slaves had to wear set attire, details of that clothing became less useful for the purposes of identification.

Beyond sumptuary laws, the style, fabrication, and condition of clothing signaled the wearer's status; what people wore conveyed who they were supposed to be. Laborers not only wore fewer fashionable details and trimmings than more elite colonists, the fabric used for their clothes was less refined—ruffled dress shirts and fine silk stockings were considered far too delicate for laborers. Slaves and servants would likely be dressed in osnaburg (a coarse, often undyed linen) or homespun fabric. Advertisements specified the degree of wear of runaways' attire. Many descriptions signaled the "half worn" or "old" state of clothing. Runaways might be wearing an "old light coloured Coat, much patched and darned," "leather breeches, very old and greasy," perhaps a "ragged shirt" or a "broad cloath coat about half worn."[42] By signaling the penurious status of runaways, worn-out clothing could distinguish them from other travelers or cast doubt on the life and occupation they might claim.

For enslaved people, advertisers might use an inverted shorthand to describe clothing by those who wore it. A Virginia advertisement for Stepney noted that he had both "a Sailor's and Negroe's Dress" with him, assuming that readers would recognize the uniforms of both maritime work and slavery. Two slaves who ran away from Richard Randolph carried "cloaths of the best kind that are given to Negroes that work in the ground." Quash ran away with "sundry other Clothes usual for Negroes to wear."[43] By the nineteenth century, "negro cloth" would be a common phrase. But in the colonial period, it was still an uncommon colloquialism outside of the Deep South. There were almost no mentions of "negro cloth" in advertisements for runaways in northern newspapers, and only a few Virginia advertisements noted that a runaway slave wore "common Negro Clothes."[44] In contrast, many hundreds of descriptions of missing slaves in South Carolina and Georgia referred to their clothing as "negro cloth."[45] Fugitive South Carolinian husband and wife Tony and Esy "had on white negro cloth Clothing," while Caesar and Bond wore "blue negro cloth jackets and breeches" when they ran from a Charleston plantation, and Dick was wearing an old "negro cloth jacket" when he was brought to the South Carolina workhouse.[46] South Carolina newspapers also advertised "NEGRO Cloth" for sale, confirming that the fabric had become so closely associated with enslaved people it had been named according to those in the colony who were expected to wear it.[47]

For people of African and Native American descent, in particular, such regimented European-style clothing could be a fundamental remaking of their externalized identity. Indentured servants of European descent might wear leather breeches of differing quality or degree of wear from those worn by their masters, but they would have been used to such European-based clothing styles. For enslaved Africans and Native Americans, however, their re-dressing in Western clothing could remove them further from their own heritages and cultural traditions.[48] In that sense, even the generic "negro clothing" of osnaburg or other coarse linen was an imposition that re-created the wearer in the image of a slave.

With clothing associated to particular identities and occupations, a change of clothes could provide a means for runaways to attempt to transcend their laboring status. Many colonies had long histories of sumptuary laws that were aimed at policing status.[49] Advertisers might note when runaways wore clothing that made them appear above their station. In particular, clothing could be a sign of freedom, allowing individuals to recast their visible status. Catherine Lefferty's master noted that she was "well dres'd," which allowed the others she ran away with to "pass for her Relations and servants." Parker Hare noted that his "Negro woman" named Amy "had when she went away silver buckles, and change of apparel, which makes her appear more like a free woman." Sarah Wilson, an escaped convict servant, apparently decided to aim for the highest possible perch with her attire: her master believed that she was pretending to be the British king's sister and so had "marked her cloaths with a crown and a B."[50] While most servants would find trying to pass as a free colonist more effective than passing for royalty, the same principle was in effect: clothing helped define who one was perceived to be.

The overlap between who someone was and how they dressed was clear in the use of the term "genteel" in advertisements. Suggesting the station of the gentry, of being polite, well-dressed, or elegant, "gentry" was not a term that one automatically associated with laborers.[51] An exceptionally long advertisement for a runaway "Mulatto Servant Man" spent ten lines detailing the clothing he took with him and his propensity "to dress very neat and genteel." Simon Pugh was said to be "capable of making a genteel Appearance." For servants, "genteel" suggested a contrived appearance. Runaway Arthur McDonnald "went genteel," wearing a fine hat, thick coat,

linen jacket, and white stockings. Seventeen-year-old convict servant Arun-
dale Carnes, "if drest would make a genteel enough appearance." Appearing
genteel contradicted laboring status. William Dury would "dress genteel,
and on that account may not be suspected for a runaway."[52] Genteel runaways were notable because their external appearance contradicted their
imposed classification as laborers.

Slave owners, in particular, seemed less concerned about "genteel" dis-
guises; they instead feared that their runaways would use attire to appear
to be free Native Americans. Appearance was directly associated with free
status; looking like an Indian meant matching a culture outside of an
Anglo-American slave system.[53] Nicholas Everson cautioned *Pennsylvania
Gazette* readers that a "mulatto Negroe, named Tom," had plans "to make
him[self] Indian stockings . . . get a blanket, to pass for an Indian," and live
with the Susquehannock. Jehu was a "Molattoe slave" who "looks much
like an Indian," since he had "a striped Indian match coat with him," and
so might join an Indian community to try to "pass for a free Molattoe." In
a particularly detailed advertisement, a man named Jem who was identified
as mulatto had left wearing a "Cotton Jacket, brown Roll Trowsers, and old
Shoes" but had since been seen wearing "an Indian Matchcoat," so his
master believed that he planned to "pass for an Indian" and "a free Man."[54]
Just as advertisers minimized Native American heritage to reduce the possibility of free status, they were concerned that supposed Indian-style clothing could undercut the assumptions that mapped African heritage to
enslavement.

Clothing was also central to one's sex identification. Even with the most
minimal detail, clothing effectively signaled sex. Gendered sartorial expectations implicitly affirmed the brief references to an individual's sex common
in advertisements (man or fellow; woman or wench). Male runaways had
their jacket, breeches/trousers, shirts, and hats described. Female runaways
were commonly described by their shifts, gowns, petticoats, aprons, and
jackets. As with personal names, notation of the clothing a runaway wore
implicitly described the kind of body that a reader might expect to encounter. Advertisers feared wrong-sexed clothing as a means of disguise. When
Elizabeth Beaver ran away, her owner took care to note that "I imagine she
now wears a man's hat," since her male accomplice had taken two with
him. Hannah Wilson was believed to have "dress'd herself in a Sailor's
Apparel, in Order to go to London."[55] Advertisers might assume a utilitar-
ian basis for dressing in men's clothes, but some women's bids for freedom

may also have included a desire to dress and live as men. Margaret Grant, a runaway servant, was believed to have "since disguised herself in a suit of mens blue cloth clothes." A person who appeared to be David Currie's missing servant was "a Woman in Mens Cloaths" who claimed to be a doctor named Charles Hamilton.[56] Because clothing was a crucial factor in how others adjudged a runaway's assigned sex, it was a powerful tool of disguise and reformulation.

Like clothing, hairstyles implicitly signaled assigned sex. However, such stylings were less frequently mentioned in advertisements for runaway laborers. By the Revolutionary era, specific hairstyles could signal virtue, status, and even political affiliation.[57] Given the time and effort necessary for fashionable coiffure, elaborate hairstylings could have been more accessible for higher classes. One of the most well-known men's hairdos, the elaborate fashion of the "Macaroni," included "hair dress'd high . . . Five pounds of hair they wear behind." Hairdos mattered to one's reception by others. Quaker diarist Sally Wister fretted that her "*auburn ringlets* were much dishevell'd" so she did not merit the "honor" of a bow from a passing brigadier general.[58] Alternatively, unkempt hair could signal a lack of civilized or class status. William Byrd's description of a hermit and "wanton Female" who lived together referred repeatedly to their slovenly hair. His "Length of Beard" and her "Length of Hair" that "dangled behind quite down to her Rump" were offered as evidence of their living in a state of nature like "east Indian Pigmies." Their uncontrolled hair was the prime physical evidence of how "wild" and "dirty" they were.[59] As part of an individual's self-presentation, hair was a public marker of who people were and how others were expected to view them.

While women's and men's hair color seemed to be described in similar proportions, European-descended male runaways' hairstyles were more frequently noted. It may have been that the predominantly male advertisement writers were not particularly attentive to exact variations in women's hairstyles. Perhaps their greater familiarity with European-descended men's coiffure led them to offer more details about what they knew. Plus, a basic feature of European-descended men's hairstyles was easy to describe: whether or not the runaway wore a wig. Adam Algrey, a German runaway, was described as a man who "wears his own hair," when he ran away in 1756, and Tobias Chop, a Frenchman, ran "with his own brown hair" a year later. Numerous other male servants wore cut wigs, bob wigs, or old wigs. Other commentaries described how male servants wore their hair: tied, in a "club," or in a queue, or as one particularly colorful advertisement explained, "wears his hair somewhat like the lock of a wolftail."[60] These advertisements recounted the choices of European-descended men who had, at least to some degree, self-fashioned their appearance with wigs and hairstyle options. Even though hair could be changed and wigs could be removed, advertisers noted these specific styling choices as part of the individualized image of European-descended men.

Overall, European men's hairstyle or length was mentioned in advertisements at least four times as often as that of European-descended women or African-descended women and men. Irish runaway Alexander Steel had long hair, "sometimes plaited with a black ribbon," and James Drummond wore his hair "sometimes curled and sometimes straight." Charles Cada had hair that was "thick, newly cut on the top of his head," Morrish Welsh had hair "cut off his forehead," William Evans had "the hair cut off the crown of his head," and numerous men had their hair described as cut short.[61] These haircuts were one of the many details of self-presentation accorded weight in European-descended men's descriptions.

European-descended women's hairstyles appeared in only a few percent of their advertisements. Advertisers mostly commented on whether women had short or long hair and whether it might be curled or tied back rather than any more detailed style descriptions.[62] On occasion, advertisers would describe a woman's hairstyle to mark health or abnormality: Alice Briscoe had "a bald Place" on her head, and Betty Slone's "hair is very thin, by a spell of sickness that she had."[63] Despite the rising fashion of high rolls and vertically enhanced hair height, there appeared to be virtually no commentary on these kinds of elite hairstyles for runaway servant women. It did not seem to be the case that women's specific hairstyles were too changeable to comment on; the few instances where advertisers openly mused that their runaways might cut off their hair all involved men.[64]

Unlike the findings of studies that focus on later time periods, only a few percent of runaways identified as Negro had their hairstyle described in any way in these colonial advertisements.[65] Advertisers rarely commented on African-descended runaways' hairstyles. The wide range of runaways identified as Negro could certainly have been productively distinguished from one another through hairstyle specifics. Enslaved people wore relatively homogeneous clothing, but advertisers still described what their missing laborers had last been wearing. A particularly detailed description of Joe (alias Dick), a "salt water Negroe man," was one exception. Joe had "the crown of his head shaved, with a ridge of wool left all round and a foretop, which he turns back." A few other African-descended people had less lavish descriptions of atypical, but not necessarily culturally African, hairstyles. One African-descended runaway who had been born in New England wore her hair "combed over a large roll," perhaps suggesting that she was following Euro-American women's fashion rather than West African customs. The hairstyle of an enslaved man named Gilbert Morris merited mention likely because he "combs it back like a woman." David's "very high and well combed" hair was noted by his enslaver because, "as he wants to be free, I imagine he will cut it off, and get a Wig to alter and disguise himself."[66] These descriptions of the hairstyles of African-descended people were notable as an exceptionality that might disguise their labor status.

In fact, descriptions of African-descended men's hairstyles were mentioned largely for runaways who already were marked as distinct from the overarching categorization of Negro. People identified as mulatto or mustee were most likely to have their hairstyle described: more than six times as often as people just described as "Negro." Men described as mulatto wore their hair "cut pretty short on top," "cut off on top of head, long at sides," or in "two Crowns on top of his head."[67] Other people identified as mulatto wore their hair tied, combed back, clubbed, or curled "handsomely." In an exceptionally detailed advertisement, Frank, a "mustee" man, wore his hair "in the maccaroni taste" with side locks and a queue, but "when too lazy to comb, ties his head with a handkerchief."[68] Many of the hairstyle descriptions offered about people of African descent were similar to those about European-descended men, reaffirming that advertisers had a narrow sense of what hairdos were worth noticing and documenting. Frank's advertisement, in particular, suggests the ways that people of African descent might pay attention to fashion and self-fashioning, even if colonial advertisers rarely noted their efforts. Frank's multiple hairstyles were likely documented because he was reputed to pass for a freeman—and his fashionable hairstyle was a way to mark that free status.

Advertisements likewise offered almost no descriptions of traditional Native American hairstyles. While colonists' travel narratives often referred to Native Americans' hairdos to distinguish Native American from European cultural norms, advertisements almost never mentioned Native American hairstylings. It may be that Native American–descended servants and slaves no longer wore the hairstyles of their heritages, whether by choice or at the insistence of their masters. Advertisements did not portray "traditional" Native American garb and styling as compatible with being an indentured servant or slave.

Because an individual's hairstyle and clothing could be means of self-expression or of community, cultural, and class belonging, advertisers could offer descriptions of these features as much to categorize as to detail. Descriptions of external fashionings did not simply oppose one another along racial lines. Instead, they created European-descended specifications (particularly for men) in contrast to more monolithic categorization of people of non-European descent. Colonists used descriptions of hair and clothing to mark sex, erase indigenous practices, and warn against claims of freedom. Advertisers only occasionally described their laborers of African and Native American descent in terms of any self-styled presentation that referenced other lives and cultures. Instead, advertisements' focus on hair and clothing descriptions reified the relationship between heritage and appearance.

Scars and Dentition: Writing Malleable Identities

When a teenaged George Washington wrote down etiquette guidelines, his rule #71 was: "Gaze not on the marks or blemishes of Others and ask not how they came. What you may Speak in Secret to your Friend deliver not before others."[69] Mannerly social behavior dictated that one should not publicly speak about how people of a certain status had received their injuries or blemishes. Where elites could apparently keep their own counsel on traumatic events, advertisers' focus on the damage life had left on laborers' bodies allowed them to create imagined meanings and histories out of these marks, particularly for those who had been forcibly separated from their heritage and culture. In particular, explanations of bodily damage envisioned that African-descended people's bodies were bendable to external forces.

There has been significant modern scholarship on the cultural work done by scarred and marked bodies. Literary scholar of race Carol Henderson argues that scars turn the body into a "walking text." Feminist literary scholar Jennifer Putzi argues that white men's superiority could be delineated through the marking of women's and non-white men's bodies. Readers of Toni Morrison's description of a "chokecherry tree" on Sethe's back in *Beloved*, or viewers of the 1863 photograph of Gordon (aka Peter), a Louisiana slave with a back blanketed by horrific keloid scars of whippings, cannot doubt the use of scars as a sign of enslavement. Indeed, Henderson suggests that African-descended bodies were Americanized through the scarification of enslavement: country marks being replaced with the masters' brandings and whip marks became the "*signatures* of slavery."[70]

In colonial advertisements for missing persons, mention of scars was far less common for European-descended than for African-descended bodies. More than twice as many advertisements for African-descended runaways mentioned bodily scars. Some of this disparity was due to the ritual scarification practices of African runaways. Even without counting ritual markings, however, advertisements for African-descended runaways still mentioned scars almost twice as often as did advertisements for European-descended runaways.

We might assume that the horrific conditions of slavery would more often lead to permanent scars. But even if that were true, it is not the case that advertisers reported all marks on all bodies with equal frequency. Discussions of European- and African-descended injuries at the time they ran away were consistently within a few percentage points of one another. While many African-descended people may have done more dangerous labor under the harsh conditions of slavery, European-descended servant runaways also were injured in the course of their daily lives. Welshman William Thomas's big toe had recently been crushed; and Richard Humphrey and James McFall both had black eyes when they ran away. Others had open wounds: Robert Kilby had "a new cut upon the fore-finger of his right hand"; William Gill, a deserter, had a "cut on his left cheek"; and Elizabeth Wilson had "her right hand sore by a cut." Enslaved runaway Carolina had "the mark of a large wound on one of his arms"; Joseph had "a cut across his left ear"; and Ned had a crushed finger.[71]

Enslavers used permanent marks on the bodies of their chattel to tell a version of that person's life story, whether referencing accidental injuries or mutilations imposed by those who enforced their enslavement. These kinds of narrative histories made scars into visible symbols of an event or experience. Mentions of scars on African-descended bodies were much more likely to explain how the injury occurred. This may mirror the way that slave traders described slaves they were selling, where a story could

> RUN away, on the firſt of September laſt, from the Subſcriber, living near Tuckahoe Bridge, in Queen Ann's County, Maryland, a Negroe Wench, Country born, named Nann, of a very b'ack Complexion, between 28 and 29 Years old, hath a very ready and deceiving Tongue, ſhe is about 5 Feet 5 Inches high, hath loſt ſome of her Fore-teeth, which were kicked out by a Horſe, has two large Scars on one of her Arms below the Elbow, occaſioned by a Burn, and three Scars on one of her Knees, by the Kick of a Horſe; had on, when ſhe went away, a ſtamped Cotton Gown, and home ſpun Petticoat. It is ſuppoſed ſhe hath a Paſs. Whoever takes up ſaid Wench, and brings her home, or ſecures her, ſo as her Maſter may get her again, ſhall receive Forty Shillings Reward, paid by   JOHN HALL.

Figure 4. This particularly detailed ad for Nann, "a Negroe Wench, Country born," contains descriptors characteristically used to describe runaways of African descent, including a focus on the cause of scars, mention of damaged teeth, and a commentary on character. A comparison to Charlotte Anne Aston's description (Figure 2, on p. 87) in the same newspaper issue shows some of the subtle differences between the descriptions of African-descended and European-descended runaways. *Pennsylvania Gazette* February 14, 1765, p. 1. Library Company of Philadelphia.

make the scar or injury evidence of a past occurrence, not a current problem. Less than 20 percent of advertisements for European-descended runaways explained the origin of a scar, compared to more than half of African-descended runaways' advertisements. A deserter named Josiah Wood had "three scars on his Right Hand," while runaway servant Elizabeth Smith had several scars on her chin and arms. Runaway servant Elizabeth Campbell "has a Scar on her Forehead," as did John Maylam.[72] No mention was made of any of the causes of these marks or the circumstances or time frame in which these European-descended runaway servants received these permanent marks. In contrast, colonists regularly described the circumstances that had led to scarring on African-descended bodies. A slave named Betty had a scar on her breast "occasioned by a stroke from her overseer." Nann had "three Scars on one of her Knees, by the Kick of a Horse" (Figure 4). Will had a deformed finger due to an injury he received as a child, and Peter had lost his right eye "by the bursting of a Gun."[73]

Commentaries on specific kinds of scars also turned bodily appearance into a narrative of personal history for people of African descent, presenting their bodies as a sum of their life experiences. For instance, when discussing burn marks on European-descended bodies, writers were far more likely to omit any explanation of how burns had happened. John Leacroft, a run-away servant, apparently had the "mark of a burn on one of his hands" when he ran away in South Carolina; Ann Smith was "marked on her Fore-head with a Burn or Scald near her Hair."[74] Only about one in six of the burns noted on European-descended bodies included a story, compared to more than one in three burns on African-descended bodies. Ned, a runaway slave, had a large scar on his hand, "occasioned by its being burnt when he was a child"; Sam had burns on his torso from "sleeping too near a fire"; and Brumall had burns on his arms from "melted cinders flying on them when at work." Even when advertisers did not mention the specific cause of a burn on their slaves, they often noted, as with Ned, the time frame when the burn had occurred. Daniel and Jemmy were both scarred by burns received "when young"; Bob's thumb had been burned off in child-hood; and Jude had "one of her feet scalded some time ago."[75]

Ritual scarification marked people of African descent in terms of their foreign or domestic relationship to enslavement. Some scars clearly empha-sized the African heritage and transatlantic journey that enslaved people had taken. Coak's scars were ritually made: they were described as "3 remarkable spots on the upper part of each cheek, near his eyes, supposed to be marks made in the Negroe country." The advertisement for Tom, a runaway slave, described the "figure of a Deer pricked on his Belly after the Fashion of the Guinea Negroes." Unlike these specific details, most advertisements used the shorthand of "country" or "Negro" marks to explain ritualistic scarification. Dick had "his country marks on his right arm," Jasper had "his country marks down his temples," Phebe had "three or four large Negroe Scars up and down her Forehead," and a description of Jack just noted "the usual Negro cuts on his cheeks."[76] Such scars on African-descended bodies offered up a reminder of a generic African heri-tage and provided a way to again mark African slaves with an imagined history outside the bounds of colonial American settlements. But they only rarely included the details of the marks or the specific cultural meanings, instead noting them only in terms of their Negro-ness. Conversely, John Gwin, an Irish runaway, had a mark on his forehead "like a half moon," and James Sampson, a sandy-complexioned sailor, had a tattoo "on both Breasts and Arms, a Man and Woman, with blue."[77] Barring a few excep-tions, advertisers did not offer such details of "country marks" as a precise means of identification of African-descended runaways.

Other kinds of marks set people of African descent apart by displaying assumed misdeeds on their bodies. Advertisements noted whipping scars on the bodies of people of non-European descent. Hannah had "many scars on her back, occasioned by whipping," Boston was "scarified by Whipping," and Limerick was "very much marked on the back &c by severe whipping." One unnamed runaway slave was "marked under the wasteband of his breeches," perhaps by whip or branding.[78] These marks were only useful identifiers if a newspaper reader would be able to strip off suspected runaways' clothing—a circumstance undoubtedly more likely for African-descended people than European-descended ones. The mention of scars that were not immediately visible to any passerby reflected a sense of entitlement to African-descended bodies and reinforced the image of runaway slaves as having been visually transformed by enslavement.

As with burns and other scars, advertisers repeatedly made explicit the reasons behind African-descended people's whipping scars. Jack, labeled a mulatto slave, had scars on his back, "occasioned by a Whip for his Villainy." A man alternatively named Jupiter or Gibb had whip marks on his back from "having been tried [at Sussex] for stirring up the Negroes to an insurrection." In other cases, advertisers did not let a lack of information hinder their attempt to narrate enslaved people's misdeeds through their bodies: Jenny had a "small scar on one of her cheeks which seems to have been occasioned by the stroke of a whip."[79] Advertisers were not explaining a corporeal feature by listing the misdeed behind the whip marks. Instead, descriptions of whipping scars publicized the enslaver's interpretation of a runaway's history of misdeeds. Through state-sponsored physical mutilation, African-descended bodies became morality tales about the consequences of misbehavior, rather than people who were injured or suffering.

When describing the corporal punishment of European-descended bodies, advertisers seemed more likely to note crimes and punishments, not resulting scars. Alice McCarty, an Irish servant, had apparently "been several times whipped in the workhouse, in Philadelphia, and whipped for theft at the public post," but any resulting scars went unmentioned. William Springate, a runaway convict servant, might have been likely to have whipping scars, especially since he was described as being "much addicted to drinking and thieving." But only the current injury from "a severe whipping given him lately for breaking into a house" was mentioned in his advertisement.[80] When two convict servant men ran away from Virginia in 1773, their owner offered lengthy descriptions, but rather than detailing injuries or scars, he instead noted that both men's backs "must still be sore" from a whipping they had received a few days before their departure.[81] The servants' feelings of soreness apparently took precedence over notation of scars or specific injuries that whipping might have caused.

The eighteenth-century decline in corporal punishment for free people made enslaved bodies exceptional in their marks of branding, whipping, and mutilation.[82] Courts regularly sentenced enslaved people to stomach-churning mutilations. In South Carolina in 1754, a thirteen-year-old enslaved boy named Jonas was given forty lashes and branded three times "in the Forehead with the Letter R with a Red hot Iron"; petitioners asked that the court remit the additional sentence of "the slitting of nostrils and cutting of [Jonas's] right ear." An enslaved man named Tom was branded on the cheek and had his ears cut off as punishment for a non-capital crime. Cyrus was "tried for his Life and burnt in the Hand." Southern courts might even instruct that the bodies of executed enslaved men be displayed postmortem.[83]

On top of punitive markings, people of African and Native American descent were the only runaways noted to have brands purposefully marked on their bodies, just like other valuable chattel. An advertisement for a "young Negro fellow named *Donas*" who was "branded LD on his cheek" appeared alongside advertisements for horses branded TN, CPL, CH, and IE. Such brands—on horses and humans—expressly marked permanent ownership. Guy was "branded on the cheeks HUP," presumably to mark him as property of his master, Hardin Perkins.[84] I found no runaways of European descent who were described as having a brand on their bodies, despite a history of corporal punishment that included branding in earlier colonial eras and in military courts.

While many slaves may have been branded, the mention of brands seemed to be more prevalent in advertisements that mention the possibility of a runaway claiming freedom. Charles, a slave of the "Indian breed," "was branded by his late Master (Robert Temple) with the letters R and T, one on each Cheek." Annas, a "white mulatto wench," who ran away from Edward Rutland, was "branded on the right cheek E, and on the left R." A "Mulatto Man Slave" named Aaron had unsuccessfully sued Henry Randolph for his freedom before he ran away; perhaps the "IR" branded on his cheek referred to Isham Randolph, the Virginia planter (and grandfather to Thomas Jefferson).[85] Such brands mutilated enslaved people as a way to force their bodies to reveal the permanence of their status as property.

While most people with brands were enslaved, freedom did not remove such burn marks from people of African descent. Peter Holmes, described as a "free negro" indentured servant, was "branded on his cheek with the letter R, which is covered by whiskers." A "Negro" man who insisted that he was free "had an obscure brand on his right cheek."[86] Punishments that may have been meted out under slavery did not disappear with freedom; the notations of marked African-descended bodies remained a salient feature to advertisers.

Similar patterns occurred in descriptions of runaways' teeth. The condition of enslaved people's teeth seemed to be particularly emphasized in the advertisements for African-descended runaways. Only 25 percent of the almost two hundred comments on runaways' teeth were about people of European descent. Twice as many African-descended as European-descended runaways' advertisements included descriptions of teeth. Scholars have shown the centrality of the examination of mouths in nineteenth-century slave sales, using the health of teeth as a proxy for bodily health.[87] Not only were European-descended teeth much less frequently mentioned, but advertisers' comments on them differed significantly. Nearly 30 percent of the descriptions of European-descended teeth noted tooth peculiarities rather than loss or damage: William Hopkins had "short fore teeth," John Shee's front teeth were "wide apart," and Robert Caten's "upper Teeth . . . ride over each other." John Young had "his upper teeth bending outwards very much." In even more detail, Claudius Smith, who broke out of jail, apparently had "short white teeth, and seldom shows them but when he laughs," while William Furbush, an apprentice, had "large Teeth, which appear when speaking."[88] This variety of commentary on European-descended runaways used teeth as another specific feature to detail.

Comments on unique dentition, as opposed to damage or loss, accounted for only about 15 percent of teeth descriptions offered for African-descended people. In some cases, newly arrived Africans had had their teeth ritually filed, marking another category of incompatibility with European-descended runaways.[89] Generally, however, advertisements contained commentaries on African-descended runaways' missing and damaged teeth. Runaway slave Guy had "lost two of his lower fore-teeth" and Tom was missing some "of his upper fore Teeth," as were Ned, Cyrus, Dick, and Moll. Jude's teeth were "a little bit rotten," John's teeth were described as simply "bad," and George's top teeth were "a good deal worn."[90] All of these slaves were described through the details of the damage done to their teeth, leaving readers to imagine how their life histories may have led to such loss and destruction.

As with scars, advertisers repeatedly provided direct explanations for the damage to an African-descended runaway's teeth. The advertisement describing Charles, a Virginia fugitive slave, not only mentioned his broken teeth but specified that they had been broken off by a cow in Africa. Ned apparently lost his teeth through a beating. Nann "hath lost some of her Fore teeth which were kicked out by a Horse."[91] Knowing that teeth had been lost through a beating or a run-in with domestic animals would likely not help someone identify a missing slave. But it did allow owners to emphasize the salience of external impacts on their chattel, making their bodies notable for their surface markings rather than their internal individualities.

The teeth of commodified human beings received attention because they were seen to represent the potential health and labor value of that individual. Describing what had damaged their chattel was a way of entering owner-determined life histories into physical descriptions. This naturalized the experience of enslavement into bodily description, leaving free people as, literally, more often free of permanent marks and damage from their pasts. African-descended bodies were made impressionable, an ideal feature for the people whom colonial Americans expected to be slaves.

*   *   *

At first glance, this chapter's opening descriptions of runaway servant Sarah and runaway slave Ned appear to be a collection of individual facts about each runaway. But when compared to each other, they highlight the racialized meanings to which individual features, behaviors, and attributes could be put. Both runaways' less-than-desirable "looks" were described, but Sarah, like many other female runaways, was criticized for her boldness, while Ned, like many other African-descended runaways, was characterized by his supposed impudence. Sarah had an Irish accent that she might try to hide, while Ned's possible native language went unmentioned; readers would only be told about his English proficiency. Readers would also learn many details about Sarah's theft of clothing, while Ned's master would instead focus on his own judgment of Ned having good sense despite his impertinence. Sarah had a blemish of indeterminate origins, while Ned's missing teeth and multiple brandings clearly marked his labor status. The

Bs burned into Ned's flesh could have stood for burglary, but given their locations on his inner thighs, they may have literally marked him as the property of James Barnes. The "IL" burned into his chest undoubtedly was a previous owner's imprint, turning Ned's body into a visible history of enslavement.

In such newspaper advertisements, public recognition of African-descended people's geographic and national belonging was replaced with an exegesis of the damages their bodies had survived. By racializing affect or language skills, advertisers linked people's behavior to their presumed identities. Descriptions that interpreted a runaway's internal world were more commonly applied to European-descended runaways, using broad humoral understandings of bodily appearance to connect behavior to physical features. In contrast, the external marks others had left on bodies more often filled African-descended runaways' descriptions. Such selective interpretations, not innate and essential corporeal differences, made race into a physical reality.

Epilogue

Racism is rendered as the innocent daughter of Mother
Nature, and one is left to deplore the Middle Passage or the
Trail of Tears the way one deplores an earthquake, a
tornado, or any other phenomenon that can be cast as
beyond the handiwork of men.
— Ta-Nehisi Coates, *Between the World and Me*

The stories we tell have consequences, and the harm that
some stories produce goes beyond their individual context.
— Open letter from Indigenous Women Scholars,
Indian Country Today, July 7, 2015

Both of these quotations reflect the history of the daily instantiation of race
onto individual bodies on which this book has focused. The past is very
much present in modern race relations. Racism continues to rely on an
unproblematized naturalization of bodies that harkens back centuries. As
Ta-Nehisi Coates writes, it arose out of historically specific circumstances
to serve particular material purposes and remains vibrantly, violently alive
in the American cultural consciousness. The letter signed by a dozen indigenous women scholars emphasizes the consequences of the narratives we tell
for our racialized present. Responding to a controversy over personal and
public identity, they called for a reckoning of the "deeply ingrained notions
of race" that continue to carry measureable consequences in the twenty-
first century.[1]

As the late historian Thelma Foote noted, the ostensible purpose of
advertisements for runaways was to "conjure a visual image of the body of
each advertised fugitive in the minds of the townspeople."[2] Creating a visual
image relied on shared cultural scripts, norms, and assumptions and, as
such, reinscribed the categories of hierarchical personhood that structured

colonial American society. Colonists created identities through bodily descriptions that naturalized race as a reflection of corporeal reality. Philosopher George Yancy labels the assumptions contained within the white gaze on black bodies as the "bodily perceptual practices" that are central to ongoing racism.[3] The stories a society tells have the power to mark whose bodies can be possessed, whose are available for others to name and label, and whose are afforded the privilege of individual recognition and self-identification.

There are all too many examples of the poisoned fruits of race-making in twenty-first-century America, where racism continues to rely on the assumed-to-be-natural binaries of skin color that grew out of colonial interpretations of bodily difference. For example, in summer 2008, the *Los Angeles Times* ran an article about the fallibility of DNA identification. It showcased two felons with "remarkably similar genetic profiles" and noted that the odds of unrelated people sharing such markers were extremely low. This DNA profile was likely in error, the authors concluded, because "the mug shots of the two felons suggested that they were not related: One was black, the other white."[4] The felons' blackness or whiteness was not only assumed, it was used as a self-evident exclusionary categorization that made close familial relations impossible. Readers were meant to "know" that once categorized, black and white bodies could not be biologically related.

Or we might turn to the modern media's fascination with other stories of seemingly impossible racial identities. In 2011, CNN ran a headline of "Surprise! You're African-American!" with the news anchor asking viewers, "Does this man look black or white to you? Wait until you hear his answer." Likewise, a perennial media favorite seems to be of a set of twins who appear to be "Black and White."[5] These stories carry the ghosts of colonists' need to decide the heritage of others, turning black identity over to observers for determination. They are also strongly reminiscent of eighteenth-century newspaper stories that marveled at the birth of twin babies who seemed to be of different racial heritages.[6] Interest in these kinds of stories of seeming racial impossibility has survived seismic shifts in scientific thought, from geohumoralism to Darwinian evolution, and from Mendelian genetics to genome mapping. These stories of exceptionality only make sense because of daily creation of racial meaning through corporeal appearance. Race can be seemingly self-evident because people produced its meaning in innumerable commentaries, classifications, and interactions over centuries.

Scholars across disciplines have documented the ongoing assumptions made through visual judgments of race. One large-scale study found that people who were not perceived as black by interviewers had a lower likelihood of arrest than those who were perceived as black, regardless of their racial self-identity. As one of the study's authors summarized, "The odds of arrest are related to what others see."[7] A study of 23,000 death certificates found that "the cause of somebody's death becomes part of the information used by people to racially classify the decedent."[8] "Experts" linked causes of death to what they believed someone's race to be. People who died from cirrhosis were more likely to be labeled as American Indians, and murder victims were more likely to be labeled as Black on their death certificates. Supposedly objective data thus continue to naturalize racist beliefs, creating a cycle of racism that feeds itself.

Deconstructing the supposed naturalness of appearance is crucial because perceptions of racialized appearance continue to have lethal consequences. First rising to mainstream awareness in 2014, the killings of black and brown people galvanized Black Lives Matter activists who were intent on reforming the criminal justice system. In the aftermath of a series of devastating killings of African Americans (and, less publicized, Native Americans) by law enforcement officers and others who were not found legally culpable, the role of whites' interpretations of black bodies became front-page news.[9] Following a white supremacist's mass murder of African American churchgoers in 2015, public intellectual Jelani Cobb poignantly declared that "the existential question of who is black has been answered in the most concussive way possible: the nine men and women slain as they prayed last night at the Emanuel African Methodist Episcopal Church, in Charleston, South Carolina, were black."[10] The meanings ascribed to bodies of people of African and Native American descent are not just historic artifacts. They are formulations that continue to carry the weight of life and death.

To fully understand the violent national heritage that destroys black and brown bodies, we need to question the corporeal categorizations behind the foundations of American racism and their all too often unproblematized applications of black, white, and red. Popular culture still uses racial labels and binaries as if they are realities, grounded in discernable bodily features. Research that is predicated on "whiteness" and "blackness" proliferates. Studies that purport to show racial and racist attitudes, like much-critiqued studies of sex and sexuality, often rely on unexamined notions that assume that phenotype is readily apparent and easily classifiable by the eye of the beholder.[11]

There is an irony to the fact that American society continues to reify race in a time when body parts are surgically manipulated, when images of bodies are regularly retouched into more pleasing forms, and when computer scientists claim the ability to use mathematical algorithms as "beautification engines" on human faces.[12] Bodies are omnipresent, being offered to the world in social media selfies, as objects of state-sanctioned violence on dashboard cameras, and through a daily barrage of professionally produced popular culture. Despite all these material, technological, and ideological changes, however, some bodies continue to be categorized as more available for evaluation and destruction than others.

Historical antecedents of racism continue to hold sway in how we conceptualize the past as well. In 2015, the Broadway musical *Hamilton* launched to unprecedented acclaim. A prominent review of the production quoted historian H. W. Brands: a show focused on Alexander Hamilton is particularly important, he explained, because since the 1960s, biographies of great men have fallen out of favor for "the history of the voiceless and faceless."[13] In a familiar zero-sum game, Brands implicitly contrasts great white men with people who are, to him, literally indescribable. It is perhaps convenient to group the people whose names we have not bothered to note, whose faces do not grace paintings in museums and government buildings, and whose records are not preserved in ink or typescript as voiceless and faceless. But to do so is to continue the ideology that identity was a natural, unavoidable reality, unrelated to the meanings given to the physical bodies attached to those faces and names. Facelessness was neither random nor accidental. It was intentionally promoted, curated in the archive, and reinforced in innumerable scholarly projects.

Only by re-placing the physicality of bodies into historical analysis can we see how such constructed physicalities allowed for the development of the virulent racisms that, perhaps more than any other single ideology, continue to shape U.S. history. While the racial opposition of black and white had not yet achieved regular usage in the colonial eighteenth century, its arrival was augured by the assumptions and divisive descriptions proffered in daily colonial life. Colonists shunted Native American laborers into racial identities, replacing individuals' kinship with the misnomer of Indian and then sliding Indian into a sidelined descriptor of Negro slave status. Alienating Native Americans from their geographic homelands through descriptions of bodies erased centuries of national traditions and cleared the way for settler colonialism. The opening lines of historian Tiya Miles's novel capture this indigenous alienation from land through bodily categorization as well as any historical analysis: in the untended "graveyard on the outskirts of town," "Negroes were buried there, and Indians, too, and Indians who were mistaken for Negroes."[14]

We do not need to turn to fiction, however, to see examples of this ongoing reformulation of Native American heritage into African heritage. In 2008, the death of Mildred Loving (of the renowned *Loving v. Virginia* Supreme Court decision that struck down miscegenation laws) occasioned an obituary in the *New York Times*. The first words of the article are "Mildred Loving, a black woman." Not until the sixteenth paragraph do readers learn that "Mildred's mother was part Rappahannock Indian, and her father was part Cherokee. She preferred to think of herself as Indian rather than black."[15] Even in death, Mildred Loving's self-identity as Rappahannock and Cherokee was marginalized. With disturbing similarity to eighteenth-century runaway advertisements, in print, she would be labeled as black and her Native American heritage transformed into a personal preference rather than a public reality. The assumptions, characterizations, and evaluations that undergirded descriptions of physical appearance in colonial writings would send bodies to the (segregated) grave through both textual and physical violence.

Thus, to return to one of the original questions that inspired *Colonial Complexions*: black, white, and red were not mutually exclusive categories with fixed meanings in late colonial America. Text portrayals of individuals allowed colonists to write race indivisibly onto American bodies in ways we are just beginning to understand. These descriptions can serve to remind historians of the perils of imposing assumed categorizations on our subjects. Descriptive labels of racial identities were less about reflecting actual heritage than constructing a supposedly visual schema that would nurture and sustain a race-based labor system. Descriptions of bodies were no more transparent than bodies themselves.

Racial optics gained power by defining whose corporeality was ranked, destroyed, enslaved, or uplifted. By comparing the portrayal of African-descended, European-descended, and Native American–descended people, implicit patterns of corporeal identification are made visible. By publicly creating features of bodily appearance, advertisers were making race in daily life. Rethinking our anachronistic assumptions points to the ways that colonial interpretations of bodies have become the stories that continue to haunt us.

Advertisements for Runaways

Sources and Methodology

Advertisements for missing persons regularly appeared in colonial newspapers alongside advertisements for products, people, and real estate for sale; notices about missing or found livestock; or brief announcements about local happenings. Advertisements for missing servants had appeared in England since the seventeenth century, and advertisements for fugitive slaves would be an integral feature of U.S. newspapers until the Civil War.[1] One effect of advertisements for runaways was that people of African descent overwhelmingly appeared as commoditized bodies in colonial print. In the *Pennsylvania Gazette*, for instance, more than 95 percent of the mentions of the word "Negro" related to advertisements that offered either them for sale or a reward for their return.[2] People of European descent, on the other hand, appeared in advertisements in numerous roles: not only as runaways but also as the owners of other people, goods, properties, and services for sale.

In the 1730s, the *Pennsylvania Gazette* announced a charge of five shillings for an advertisement, and the newly founded *Virginia Gazette* offered to run advertisements the first week "for Three Shillings, and for Two Shillings per Week" after that. Figures 5A and 5B offer examples of the expenses associated with recovering a runaway, which included newspaper advertising costs. Advertisements were, as far as we can tell, usually written and edited by a varying combination of advertisers and editors. For example, in 1756, the *Pennsylvania Gazette* rejected an advertisement and offered to return the prospective advertiser's ten shillings because it was "not tho't proper to print." By the second half of the eighteenth century, newspaper advertisements were an economic boon for publishers, taking up close to

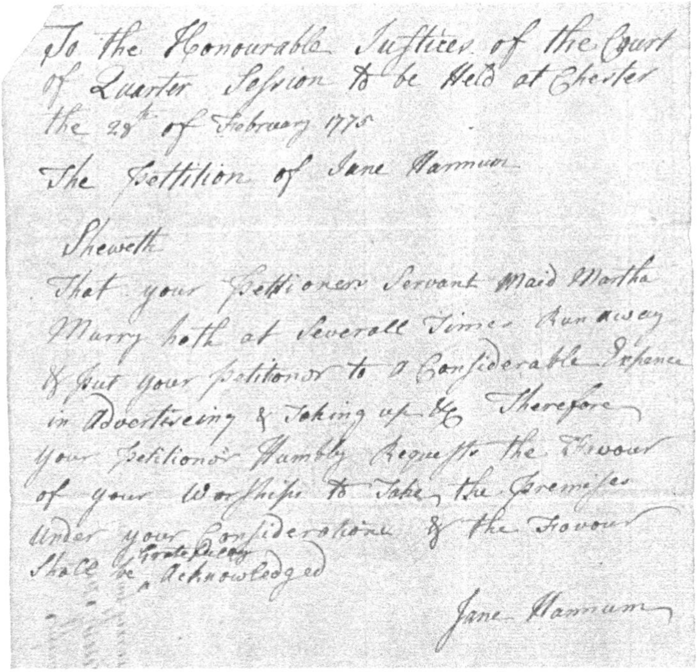

To the Honourable Justices of the Court of Quarter Session to be Held at Chester the 28th of February 1775

The Petition of Jane Hannum

Sheweth

That your Petitioners Servant Maid Martha Murry hath at severall Times Runaway & put your petitioner to a Considerable Expence in Advertiseing & Taking up &c Therefore your Petitioner Humbly Requests the Favour of your Worships to Take the Premises under your Consideration & the Favour shall be gratefully acknowledged

Jane Hannum

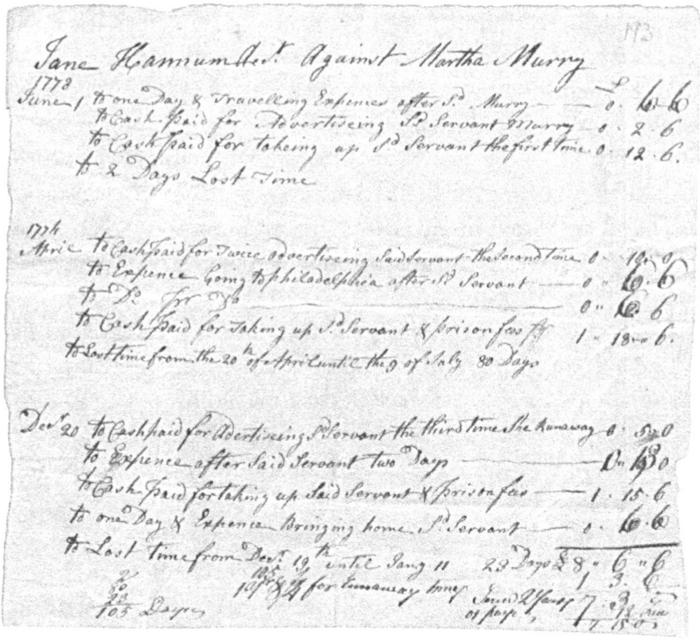

Jane Hannum Acct Against Martha Murry

1773
June 1 to one Day & Travelling Expenses after Sd Murry — 0 · 6 · 6
to Cash paid for Advertiseing Sd Servant Murry — 0 · 2 · 6
to Cash paid for taking up Sd Servant the first time 0 · 12 · 6
to 2 Days Lost Time

1774
Aprile to Cash paid for Twice advertiseing said Servant the Second time 0 · 13 · 0
to Expence Going to philadelphia after Sd Servant — 0 · 6 · 6
to Do for Do — 0 · 6 · 6
to Cash paid for Taking up Sd Servant & prison fees — 1 · 18 · 6
to Lost time from the 20th of Aprile untill the 9 of July 80 Days

Decr 20 to Cash paid for Advertising Sd Servant the third time She Runaway 0 · 5 · 0
to Expence after said Servant two Days — 0 · 6 · 0
to Cash paid for taking up said Servant & prison fees — 1 · 15 · 6
to one Day & Expence Bringing home Sd Servant — 0 · 6 · 6
to Lost Time from Decr 19th untill Jany 11 23 Days 8 · 6 · 6
185 & ½ for runaway time 105 Days 7 · 3 · 6

Figures 5A and 5B. Pennsylvanian Jane Hannum's petitions for reimbursement for the costs of recovering her runaway servant, Martha Murry, through extension of Martha's indenture. Costs included the "Considerable Expense" of "Cash paid for Advertising." Petition of Jane Hannum, February 28, 1775, Folder 104, Chester County Court of Quarter Sessions, Indentured Servant and Apprentice Records, Chester County Archives.

half the total print space and accounting for more than half the number of discrete items in colonial newspapers.[3]

Advertisements for runaways offer fertile research possibilities because they were ubiquitous throughout late colonial America. William Parks, the *Virginia Gazette*'s publisher, confidently assured readers that such advertisements "will probably be read by some Thousands of People" across colonies.[4] While Parks may have been exaggerating the reach of his *Gazette*, advertisers expected that their notices would be widely shared beyond those who purchased or read the newspaper. When John Lloyd advertised for a missing servant in the *Boston Evening-Post* in 1761, he added a postscript that "*inserting Advertisements in the several Newspapers is judged the most expeditious Method of spreading them far & near*," and he requested that "*if any Gentlemen will be so good, when they have read their Papers, to cut out this Advertisement and set it up in the most public Place, it will be esteemed as a Favour*."[5] Unlike the writings of elites that are sometimes a focus of intellectual histories, advertisements were not an individual's explicit or prescriptive thoughts on race, slavery, or servitude. Advertisers paid for publicity, attempting to describe missing laborers in ways that resonated with those who read or listened to their advertisements.

Despite their wide impact, advertisements for runaways are not the perfect sources: they focus on a subset of society and were constructed according to the genre's expectations. But any shortcomings are outweighed by what they do offer: advertisements for runaways are, to my knowledge, the only source in colonial America that offers an opportunity to aggregate thousands of parallel descriptions of physical appearance of enslaved and free people. Colonial-era personal writings were generally filled with reports of weather and daily activities, not lengthy musings on appearance. When diarists did comment on ill health or injury, details of physical effects were rarely mentioned. More importantly for a discussion of race-making, descriptions of individuals of non-European descent were largely absent from the private writings of European-descended women and men that make up the overwhelming majority of extant sources. Diarists might not even note the names of people of African and Indian descent, let alone any description of their appearance.[6] Likewise, local court records, generally a rich source for histories of the marginalized, rarely had reason to detail overall physical appearances. Even in rape cases, where signs of physical injury or relative size of assailant and victim might be imagined as particularly relevant to court proceedings, very little physical description of participants was recorded.[7] Prison records that might provide details about height, eye color, hair color, and complexion were a post-Revolutionary development, as was the kind of descriptions offered in the "Book of Negroes" which listed three thousand former slaves who were eligible to stay with the British military.[8] Thus colonial advertisements for missing persons offer a unique opportunity for large-scale analysis of public descriptions of individuals' appearances.[9]

As some of the only colonial sources with extensive details about common laborers, advertisements have a deep historiography associated with them. Thanks in part to compilations and, more recently, online searchable databases, extensive scholarship has focused on what runaway advertisements can reveal about slavery and enslaved people.[10] Somewhat less work has focused on runaway servants; in many cases, scholars have incorporated advertisements for runaway servants into their broader social histories.[11]

Social historians, intent on reconstructing material experiences, have sometimes tended to treat listings of physical features as objective representations rather than symbolically powerful choices. One study explains that the "physical traits" of runaways listed in advertisements were "more reliable than the owners' subjective assessments of their bondpeople," as if physical traits were not also owner assessed.[12] An excellent social history asserts that "runaway advertisements contained objective information about sex, race, height and age" that contrasted with "far more subjective descriptions" on other aspects of the runaway's life.[13] Even literary scholars who analyze the representation of bodies can see objectivity in runaway advertisements, taking for granted that "slavemasters who sought to reclaim their 'property' would list any distinguishing marks or characteristics that would make capture easier," rather than recognizing that advertisers wove their own visions of who their laborers should be into their descriptive choices.[14]

In order to analyze the descriptive contents of advertisements for runaways, I first gathered about four thousand advertisements for missing persons that appeared in more than two dozen newspapers published in eight colonies between 1750 and 1775 (Figures 7–8, on pp. 150–51).[15] Most of these advertisements were for missing servants and slaves; smaller numbers were for individuals who had escaped from jail, who had deserted from the military, or who had been put in a workhouse (Figure 10, on p. 152). This was not a random sample: I aimed for a geographic and chronologic variety of advertisements and made a concerted effort to include female runaways. Women, who are generally believed to have run away in lower numbers

than men, account for about 16 percent of the runaway advertisements I
collected (Figure 9, on p. 151).[16] Because people of Native American descent
were conspicuously underrepresented in runaway advertisements, even
with concerted efforts, they account for less than 2 percent of runaways I
identified (Figure 11, on p. 152). This makes their inclusion in various quantitative analyses difficult. Accordingly, I have been particularly attentive
to wider contemporary commentaries on Native American bodies, while
remaining cognizant of the different descriptors that may be used to reference groups versus individuals.

To aggregate the information offered in runaway descriptions, I identified and quantified more than two dozen possible categories for descriptive
statistical analysis. To determine the overall frequency of descriptive features, I then tabulated how many categories were filled for each individual.
For example, under this measurement system, Ann Kennedy, who was a (1)
female (2) Irish (3) servant with (4) dark hair, (5) gray eyes, and (6) brown
skin, who was (7) slender and (8) lively and whose (9) clothing was
described, had nine pieces of information about her. On the other hand,
Priscilla, who ran away the same year as Ann, was a (1) sixteen-year-old (2)
enslaved (3) Negro (4) woman, who had only four pieces of information
identifying her.[17]

This discretization of information allowed me to undertake statistical
analyses that show relationships between particular descriptors (were tall
people less likely to merit other descriptors?) and differences in the portrayal of groups (were African-descended people described in less detail
than European-descended people?).[18] Unless otherwise specified, any enu-
merated trends come from this corpus.

Overall, advertisements had more descriptive information about men
than women: male runaways averaged almost 20 percent more filled categories than did female runaways.[19] This is visible at the level of individual
advertisements as well: in 1768, an advertisement for "two servant men and
a Negro fellow" described each missing man: George Pitt was about five
feet five inches tall, had a brown complexion, smallpox scars, hair that was
short, black, and curly, and had a scar from being shot through the foot.
He was "much given to liquor, and has a very smooth tongue." Henry
Valentine, the second servant, was born in Leicestershire eighteen years
earlier and had been in the colonies for three years. He was about five feet
three inches, had short brown hair, and was "very well made." He had a
"fair countenance . . . and tho' a very great villain, has a very harmless,

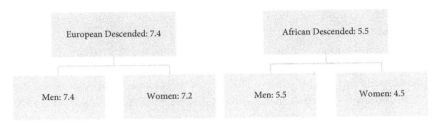

Figure 6. Average number of categories of detail for runaways by heritage and sex. Based on an analysis of 4,021 runaways. Runaway servants without a specific heritage listed were grouped into European descended. For a full discussion of the rationale for this grouping, see pp. 102–3.

inoffensive look." Jack, the third man, was described only as a "Negro fellow," six feet tall, "well made" with large feet, and formerly a slave in South Carolina.[20] Thus the European-descended men each had eleven categorizable pieces of information offered about their appearance compared to Jack's five.

Figure 6 also reveals that the biggest difference in the amount of detail was *within* the group of runaways identified as women. Many women of African descent were described with very few details about their appearance.[21] To offer a qualitative example: Peg, a "mulatto" runaway teenager, was described as "likely" and of middling height but with no other physical specifics. This was not because the writer did not have a good recollection of Peg. Despite her absent physical description, Peg's enslaver, Richard Hipkins, told readers that she had been brought up as a house servant, had never traveled far from home, and was apt to burst into tears when chastised. He added that she must have been "prevailed on to go off" because he saw no reason for her departure.[22] Richard clearly knew Peg well enough to have offered readers a physical description of her—but he did not detail her appearance beyond a mulatto designation, approximate age, size, and likeliness. Instead, he wrote an interpretation of Peg as the public version of his property—his relationship to her replaced her physical appearance once he had identified Peg by her African heritage.

After identifying possible patterns, I searched more widely through advertisements beyond the database I had constructed to test those patterns. For instance, once I became interested in how colonists understood a "yellow" or "fresh" complexion, I specifically looked for additional advertisements that discussed related terms. These additional documents are not included in any general statistics, but are used in various qualitative discussions. If I completed additional quantitative analysis (such as what percent of *Pennsylvania Gazette* advertisements mentioning mulatto runaways also noted a specific complexion), the corpus for these additional findings are specified in the text.

Colonial Complexions is greatly influenced by the rise of, and my own work in, digital humanities.[23] Recent work in computational and digital histories added to my interest in using the ephemera of weekly publications to write a cultural history that relied on quantitative analysis.[24] Additionally, the practical reality of my professional and personal life made extensive travel to East Coast archives difficult. Given that, I decided to work with multiple free and paywalled collections of colonial documents.[25] While I remain a stalwart advocate for the importance of archival study, I also believe that we can undertake productive historical research within the digital world. For example, being able to trace descriptive phrases in a dozen contemporary dictionaries and scores of eighteenth-century literary publications was particularly useful for gaining a sense of contemporary usages of many corporeal descriptors. Despite concerns about digital privilege (which documents become accessible and to whom?), this project would not have been possible without digitization and computational tools.

Graphic Overview
of Advertisements for Runaways

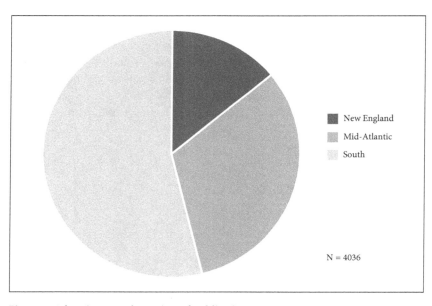

Figure 7. Advertisements by region of publication.

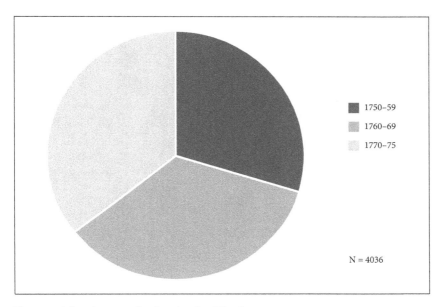

Figure 8. Advertisements by decade of publication.

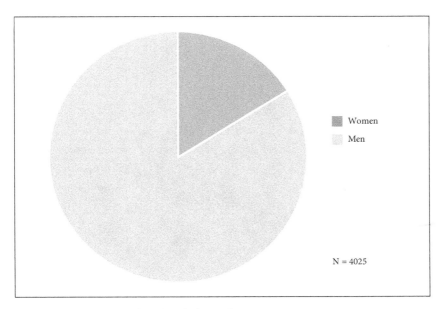

Figure 9. Advertisements by identified sex of runaways.

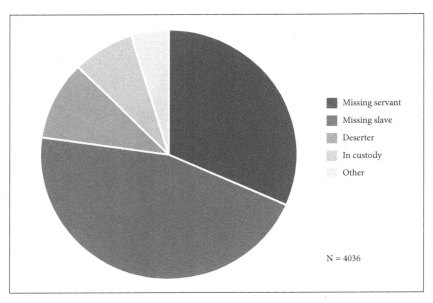

Figure 10. Reason for missing person advertisements. "Missing servant" includes indentured servants, apprentices, and convict servants. "Other" primarily includes warrants, jail escapes, and people accompanying runaways.

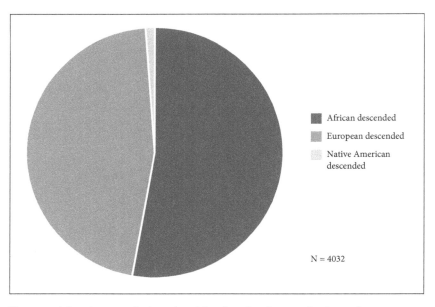

Figure 11. Advertisements by broad racial and national categorizations of runaways.

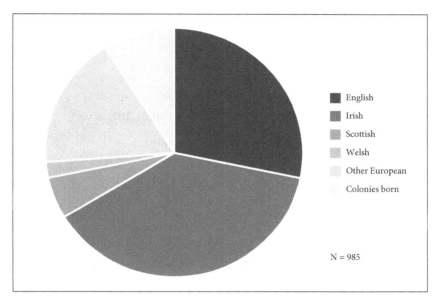

Figure 12. Nationalities listed for people of European descent.

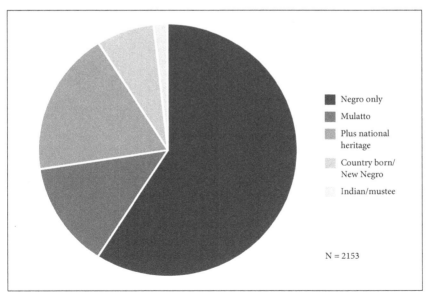

Figure 13. Identifiers listed for people of African descent and Native American descent. "Plus national heritage" refers to mention of a specific nationality or named community heritage. People who were categorized as "Mulatto" and "national heritage" or "Mulatto" and "Indian/mustee" are counted in both categories.

Newspapers with Advertisements
for Runaways (1750–75)

The newspapers listed here include those used for both quantitative findings and qualitative examples throughout the text.

Boston Chronicle
Boston Evening-Post
Boston Gazette
Boston News-Letter
Boston Post-Boy
Boston Post-Boy & Advertiser
Boston Weekly News-Letter
Connecticut Courant
Connecticut Gazette
Connecticut Journal
Connecticut Journal; and New-Haven Post-Boy
Essex Gazette
Essex Journal
Georgia Gazette
Maryland Gazette
Massachusetts Spy
New-England Chronicle
New-Hampshire Gazette
New-London Gazette
New-London Summary
New-York Evening Post
New-York Gazette

New-York Gazette, and Weekly Mercury
New-York Gazette, or Weekly Post-Boy
New-York Journal
New-York Mercury
New-York Weekly Journal
Newport Mercury
North-Carolina Magazine; or, Universal Intelligencer
Norwich Packet
Pennsylvania Chronicle
Pennsylvania Gazette
Pennsylvania Packet
Providence Gazette
Rivington's New-York Gazetteer
South-Carolina Gazette
South-Carolina Gazette; And Country Journal
Story & Humphreys's Pennsylvania Mercury
Virginia Gazette

NOTES

Introduction

1. For a call for scholars to complicate the association between skin color and race, see Clarence E. Walker, *Mongrel Nation: The America Begotten by Thomas Jefferson and Sally Hemings* (Charlottesville: University of Virginia Press, 2009), 30–31. For a broad intellectual history of anti-black ideologies, see Ibram X. Kendi, *Stamped from the Beginning: The Definitive History of Racist Ideas in America* (New York: Nation Books, 2016).

2. John Josselyn, *Account of Two Voyages to New-England* (London: G. Widdows, 1674), 124. On the stereotype of the goggle-eyed Jew, see Marie Mulvey Roberts, *Dangerous Bodies: Historicising the Gothic Corporeal* (Manchester: Manchester University Press, 2016), 154. Austrians were known by the royal Habsburg family's tendency toward a protruding lower jaw (prognathism), which may be what Josselyn referred to, rather than lip size per se. On a Bavarian's tendency to goiters, see "poke, n.1," *OED*, June 2016, http://www.oed.com/view/Entry/146699, #5a.

3. William Clarke, *Observations On the late and present Conduct of the French, with Regard to their Encroachments upon the British Colonies in North America. . . . To which is added, wrote by another Hand,* [Benjamin Franklin,] *Observations concerning the Increase of Mankind, Peopling of Countries, &etc.* (Boston: S. Kneeland, 1755), 14. The London republication used notably different categorizations, claiming that only Spaniards, Italians, and French were swarthy and that "the more northern Nations with the English" were white people, suggesting transatlantic differences in the meanings of whiteness. William Clarke, *Observations On the late and present Conduct of the French. . . .* (London: Reprinted for John Clarke, 1755), 53.

4. Irene Tucker, *The Moment of Racial Sight: A History* (Chicago: University of Chicago Press, 2012), 7; Joshua D. Rothman, " 'To Be Freed from Thate Curs and Let at Liberty': Interracial Adultery and Divorce in Antebellum Virginia," *Virginia Magazine of History and Biography* 106, no. 4 (Autumn 1998), image on p. 449.

5. Honor Sachs, " 'Freedom by a Judgment': The Legal History of an Afro-Indian Family," *Law and History Review* 30, no. 1 (February 2012): 196, in reference to the 1806 case of *Hudgins v. Wrights*; Walter Johnson, *Soul by Soul: Life Inside the Antebellum Slave Market* (Cambridge, Mass.: Harvard University Press, 1999), 139.

6. Barbara J. Fields, "Slavery, Race and Ideology in the United States of America," *New Left Review* 1, no. 181 (May/June 1990): 101. For expanded development of these ideas, see Karen E. Fields and Barbara J. Fields, *Racecraft: The Soul of Inequality in American Life* (London: Verso, 2014).

7. Allyson Hobbs, *A Chosen Exile: A History of Racial Passing in American Life* (Cambridge, Mass.: Harvard University Press, 2014), 25, italics in original. See also David J. Silverman, *Red Brethren: The Brothertown and Stockbridge Indians and the Problem of Race in Early America* (Ithaca, N.Y.: Cornell University Press, 2010), 6.

8. Roxann Wheeler, *The Complexion of Race: Categories of Difference in Eighteenth-Century British Culture* (Philadelphia: University of Pennsylvania Press, 2000), 2.

9. *Virginia Gazette*, July 20, 1769, July 27, 1769. For background on Augustine Smith, see Louise Pecquet du Bellet, *Some Prominent Virginia Families* (Baltimore: Genealogical Publishing Company, 1976), 10–13.

10. *Virginia Gazette* May 16, 1771.

11. Ibid.

12. *Virginia Gazette* July 23, 1772.

13. *Virginia Gazette* October 1, 1772; *Virginia Gazette* December 31, 1772. It is clear that these descriptions are for the same person based on the listed owners and additional details in the advertisement.

14. For example, Erica Armstrong Dunbar, *Never Caught: The Washingtons' Relentless Pursuit of Their Runaway Slave, Ona Judge* (New York: Atria/37 INK, 2017); Marisa J. Fuentes, *Dispossessed Lives: Enslaved Women, Violence, and the Archive* (Philadelphia: University of Pennsylvania Press, 2016), 13–45; Stephanie M. H. Camp, "'I Could Not Stay There': Enslaved Women, Truancy and the Geography of Everyday Forms of Resistance in the Antebellum Plantation South," *Slavery and Abolition* 23, no. 3 (December 2002): 1–20; John Hope Franklin and Loren Schweninger, *Runaway Slaves: Rebels on the Plantation* (New York: Oxford University Press, 2000).

15. For example, Michael P. Johnson, "Runaway Slaves and the Slave Communities in South Carolina, 1799 to 1830," *William and Mary Quarterly* 38, no. 3 (1981): 418–41; Johnson, *Soul by Soul*.

16. On archival choices, see Fuentes, *Dispossessed Lives*, 144–48; Ashley Glassburn Falzetti, "Archival Absence: The Burden of History," *Settler Colonial Studies* 5, no. 2 (Winter 2015): 128–44.

17. Kim F. Hall, *Things of Darkness: Economies of Race and Gender in Early Modern England* (Ithaca, N.Y.: Cornell University Press, 1995), 18. See also Holloway, *Private Bodies, Public Texts*, 7, 9, 14; Jennifer Putzi, *Identifying Marks: Race, Gender, and the Marked Body in Nineteenth-Century America* (Athens: University of Georgia Press, 2006), 2.

18. On the vulnerability of "women and black Americans" to "public unveiling," see Karla F. C. Holloway, *Private Bodies, Public Texts: Race, Gender, and a Cultural Bioethics* (Durham, N.C.: Duke University Press, 2011), 9. For the use of advertisements as objective descriptors, see Billy Smith, "Resisting Inequality: Black Women Who Stole Themselves in Eighteenth-Century America," in *Inequality in Early America*, edited by Carla Gardina Pestana and Sharon V. Salinger (Hanover, N.H.: University Press of New England, 1999), 136 (see also his contrast between owners' "subjective beliefs" and "material characteristics" of runaways on p. 137); Simon P. Newman, *Embodied History: The Lives of the Poor in Early Philadelphia* (Philadelphia: University of Pennsylvania Press, 2003), 95; Karen Sánchez-Eppler, *Touching Liberty: Abolition, Feminism, and the Politics of the Body* (Berkeley: University of California Press, 1993), 23.

19. For instance, Heather Kopelson, *Faithful Bodies: Performing Religion and Race in the Puritan Atlantic* (New York: New York University Press, 2014), 19–21; Silverman, *Red Brethren*, 9–10.

Chapter 1

1. Samuel Smith, *The History of the Colony of Nova-Caesaria, or New-Jersey* (Burlington: James Parker, [1765]), 2.

2. On European understandings of humoral complexion, see Valentin Groebner, "Complexio/Complexion: Categorizing Individual Natures, 1250–1600," in *The Moral Authority of Nature*, edited by Lorraine Daston and Fernando Vidal (Chicago: University of Chicago Press, 2004), 361–83.

3. James Egan, *Authorizing Experience: Refigurations of the Body Politic in Seventeenth-Century New England Writing* (Princeton, N.J.: Princeton University Press, 1999); Mary Elizabeth Fissell, *Vernacular Bodies: The Politics of Reproduction in Early Modern England* (New York: Oxford University Press, 2004), 144–45; Mark M. Smith, *Sensing the Past: Seeing, Hearing, Smelling, Tasting, and Touching in History* (Berkeley: University of California Press, 2007), 31.

4. Winthrop Jordan, *White over Black: American Attitudes Toward the Negro, 1550–1812* (Baltimore: Penguin Books, 1969), 216–28; Susan Scott Parrish, *American Curiosity: Cultures of Natural History in the Colonial British Atlantic World* (Chapel Hill: University of North Carolina Press, 2006), 8–9.

5. Hippocrates laid out the traditional understanding of the many ways that environment, seasons, and natural phenomena led to human bodily variations. Hippocrates, *On Airs, Waters, and Places*, translated by Francis Adams (London: Wyman and Sons, 1881). See also Rebecca Earle, *The Body of the Conquistador: Food, Race, and the Colonial Experience in Spanish America, 1492–1700* (New York: Cambridge University Press, 2012), 26–32.

6. See David C. Lindberg, *The Beginnings of Western Science: The European Scientific Tradition in Philosophical, Religious, and Institutional Context, 600 B.C. to A.D. 1450* (Chicago: University of Chicago Press, 2007), 115–17; Nancy G. Siraisi, *Medieval & Early Renaissance Medicine: An Introduction to Knowledge and Practice* (Chicago: University of Chicago Press, 1990), 97; Mary Lindemann, *Medicine and Society in Early Modern Europe* (New York: Cambridge University Press, 1999), 13.

7. Katherine Park and Lorraine Daston, eds., *The Cambridge History of Science: Early Modern Science* (New York: Cambridge University Press, 2006), 3:407–34; Lindemann, *Medicine and Society*, 19, 29; Christopher J. Lukasik, *Discerning Characters: The Culture of Appearance in Early America* (Philadelphia: University of Pennsylvania Press, 2011), 27–29; Fissell, *Vernacular Bodies*, 4–5; Irene Tucker, *The Moment of Racial Sight: A History* (Chicago: University of Chicago Press, 2013), 28–32; Joyce E. Chaplin, *Subject Matter: Technology, the Body, and Science on the Anglo-American Frontier, 1500–1676* (Cambridge, Mass.: Harvard University Press, 2001), 163–75.

8. Lindemann, *Medicine and Society*, 19–25; Magali Marie Carrera, *Imagining Identity in New Spain: Race, Lineage, and the Colonial Body in Portraiture and Casta Paintings* (Austin: University of Texas Press, 2003), 9.

9. Bernard Lynch, *A Guide to Health Through the Various Stages of Life, Etc.* (London: Printed for the author, 1744), 7. See also 226.

10. Thomas Tryon, *The Way to Health, Long Life and Happiness, or, A Discourse of Temperance, and the Particular Nature of All Things Requisite for the Life of Man* (London, 1697), xv, xvi.

11. Siraisi, *Medieval & Early Renaissance Medicine*, 101–4.

12. William Byrd and William Kenneth Boyd, *William Byrd's Histories of the Dividing Line Betwixt Virginia and North Carolina* (Raleigh: North Carolina Historical Commission, 1929), 54, 55, http://archive.org/details/williambyrdshistoobyrd. On food's relation to appearance under a humoral system, see Park and Daston, *Cambridge History of Science*, 3:407–10.

13. Trudy Eden, *The Early American Table: Food and Society in the New World* (DeKalb: Northern Illinois University Press, 2010), esp. chaps. 1–2.

14. Kathleen M. Brown, *Foul Bodies: Cleanliness in Early America* (New Haven, Conn.: Yale University Press, 2011), 26; Fissell, *Vernacular Bodies*, 25.

15. Samuel Auguste David Tissot, *Advice to the People in General, in Regard to their Health* . . . (London; [Boston: Mein and Fleeming], 1767), 108, 190; see also 175, 248; William Wood, *New-England's Prospect* (London, 1639; repr. Boston: Fleet and Green & Russell, 1764), 10.

16. John Mitchell, "An Essay upon the Causes of the different Colours of People in different Climates," in *Philosophical Transactions, Giving Some Account of the Present Undertakings, Studies, and Labours of the Ingenious in Many Considerable Parts of the World* (London: Royal Society, 1746), 105.

17. William Buchan, *Domestic Medicine, or, The family physician* . . . (Philadelphia: Joseph Crukshank, 1774), 329, 416, 21; George Fisher, *The American Instructor*, 10th ed. (Philadelphia: Benjamin Franklin and David Hall, 1753), 359; John Theobold, *Every Man his Own Physician* . . . ([Boston]: Cox and Berry, 1767), 32.

18. Theobold, *Every Man his own Physician*, 39, 26.

19. John B. Reeves, "Extracts from the Letter-Books of Lieutenant Enos Reeves, of the Pennsylvania Line (continued)," *Pennsylvania Magazine of History and Biography* 21, no. 2 (January 1897): 251.

20. William Douglass, *A summary, historical and political, of the first planting, progressive improvements, and present state of the British settlements in North-America* . . . (Boston: Rogers and Fowle, [1749–52]), 159.

21. Lindemann, *Medicine and Society*, 19, 24; Park and Daston, *Cambridge History of Science*, 3:410.

22. Lynch, *A Guide to Health*, 314, 313. As English poet John Dryden wrote, "Our minds are perpetually wrought on by the temperament of our Bodies." John Dryden, *Aureng-Zebe: A Tragedy. Acted at the Royal Theatre, Etc.* (1676; London: J. Tonsen, 1735), n.p. [p. 13]. On humoral interpretations of melancholy in early modern Spain, see Elena Carrera, "Madness and Melancholy in Sixteenth- and Seventeenth-Century Spain: New Evidence, New Approaches," *Bulletin of Spanish Studies* 87, no. 8 (2010): 1–15.

23. Lindemann, *Medicine and Society*, 19.

24. Griffith Hughes, *The Natural History of Barbados in Ten Books* (London: Printed for the author, 1750), 13.

25. *Pennsylvania Gazette* October 13, 1768.

26. Nathaniel Ames, *An Astronomical Diary, or, Almanack for the Year of Our Lord Christ, 1762* . . . ([New Haven, Conn., 1761]). See also Marilyn Yalom, *History of the Breast* (New York: Ballantine Books, 1998), 43, 84–85, 206–7; Jill Lepore, "Baby Food: If Breast Is Best, Why Are Women Bottling Their Milk?" *New Yorker* January 19, 2009, http://www.newyorker.com/magazine/2009/01/19/baby-food.

27. Jonathan Boucher to George Washington, May 21, 1770, in *The New England Historical and Genealogical Register* (Boston: New England Historical Genealogical Society, 1898), 52:331.

28. On the transfer of "vodun" and other religiously based healing practices from West Africa to the Americas, see James H. Sweet, *Domingos Alvares, African Healing, and the Intellectual History of the Atlantic World* (Chapel Hill: University of North Carolina Press, 2011). On Obeah, see Vincent Brown, *The Reaper's Garden: Death and Power in the World of Atlantic Slavery* (Cambridge, Mass.: Harvard University Press, 2008), 144–52.

29. *The History of the Works of the Learned, or, An Impartial Account of Books Lately Printed in All Parts of Europe* (London: H. Rhodes, 1704), 6:724. On parallels between European and African concepts of health and healing, see Jerome S. Handler, "Slave Medicine and Obeah in Barbados, Circa 1650 to 1834," *NWIG: New West Indian Guide/Nieuwe West-Indische Gids* 74, no. 1–2 (2000): 59–61.

30. James H. Sweet, *Recreating Africa: Culture, Kinship, and Religion in the African-Portuguese World, 1441–1770* (Chapel Hill: University of North Carolina Press, 2003), 104–15. On historiography of African medical and spiritual beliefs, see Lyn Schumaker, Diana Jeater, and Tracy Luedke, "Introduction: Histories of Healing: Past and Present Medical Practices in Africa and the Diaspora," *Journal of Southern African Studies* 33, no. 4 (December 1, 2007): 707–14. On integrated well-being, see Randy M. Browne, "'This Bad Business': Obeah, Violence, and Power in a Nineteenth-Century British Caribbean Slave Community" (Master's thesis, University of North Carolina, 2009), 19; Sharla M. Fett, *Working Cures: Healing, Health, and Power on Southern Slave Plantations* (Chapel Hill: University of North Carolina Press, 2002), 36–59, 75.

31. Anthony F. C. Wallace, *The Death and Rebirth of the Seneca* (New York: Knopf, 1970), 62–63.

32. Colin G. Calloway, *New Worlds for All: Indians, Europeans, and the Remaking of Early America* (Baltimore: Johns Hopkins University Press, 1997), 32. For the endurance of such ideas, see Annemarie Anrod Shimony, *Conservatism at the Six Nations Iroquois Reserve* (New Haven, Conn.: Yale University Press, 1961), 261–62. On visions and the curing of diseases, see Ann Marie Plane, *Dreams and the Invisible World in Colonial New England: Indians, Colonists, and the Seventeenth Century* (Philadelphia: University of Pennsylvania Press, 2014), 66–67. On Native American science generally, see Clara Sue Kidwell, "Native Knowledge in the Americas," *Historical Writing on American Science* (Philadelphia: History of Science Society, 1985), 209–28. On the problem of the archive for indigenous histories, see Ashley Glassburn Falzetti, "Archival Absence: The Burden of History," *Settler Colonial Studies* 5, no. 2 (Winter 2015): 128–44. On permeability, see Martha L. Finch, *Dissenting Bodies: Corporealities in Early New England* (New York: Columbia University Press, 2009), 40–46.

33. Chaplin, *Subject Matter*, 120. On early modern Christian views of the relationship between the human body and soul, and their embodiment in Christian history, see Finch, *Dissenting Bodies*, 5–7, 19–21.

34. Benjamin Grosvenor, *Health: An Essay on Its Nature, Value, Uncertainty, Preservation and Best Improvement* (Boston: D. and J. Kneeland, [1761]), 35, 114.

35. William Bates, *The Harmony of the Divine Attributes* (Wilmington: James Adams, 1771), 69. See also Uzal Ogden, *The Theoretical Preceptor* (New York: John Holt, 1772), 204; Samuel Niles, *The True Scripture-Doctrine of Original Sin* (Boston: S. Kneeland, 1757), 114.

36. Lynch, *A Guide to Health*, 324.

37. Samuel Auguste David Tissot, *The Lady's Physician: A Practical Treatise on the Various Disorders Incident to the Fair Sex, with Proper Directions for the Cure Thereof . . .* (London: J. Pridden, 1766), 19.

38. [James Forrester], *The Polite Philosopher* ([New York]: J. Parker and W. Weyman, 1758), 24.

39. John Knox, *An Historical Journal of the Campaigns in North America for the Years 1757, 1758, 1759, and 1760* (London: Printed for the author, 1769), 232.

40. "temperament, n.," *OED*, December 2015, http://www.oed.com/view/Entry/198881, II, #7. For a modern scientific take on the connection between emotional and intestinal health, see Peter Andrey Smith, "Can the Bacteria in Your Gut Explain Your Mood?" *New York Times* June 23, 2015, http://www.nytimes.com/2015/06/28/magazine/can-the-bacteria-in-your-gut-explain-your-mood.html.

41. To Joseph Galloway, June 13, 1767. See also To Richard Jackson, September 1, 1764; To William Franklin, November 25, 1767, all at http://franklinpapers.org/.

42. [Moses Mather], *America's Appeal to the Impartial World* (Hartford: Ebenezer Watson, 1775), 50.

43. Tissot, *Advice to the People*, 87.

44. *The Burlington Almanack, for the Year of our Lord, 1773* (Burlington, N.J.: Isaac Collins, [1772]), n.p.

45. Smith, *The History of the Colony of Nova-Caesaria*, 2.

46. George Sale et al., *An Universal History, from the Earliest Account of Time* (London: S. Richardson et al., 1759), 260.

47. William Clarke, *Observations On the late and present Conduct of the French, with Regard to their Encroachments upon the British Colonies in North America. . . . To which is added, wrote by another Hand;* [Benjamin Franklin,] *Observations concerning the Increase of Mankind, Peopling of Countries, &etc.* (Boston: S. Kneeland, 1755), 15.

48. Quoted in Ana Echevarría, "Eschatology or Biography? Alfonso X, Muhammad's Ladder and a Jewish Go-Between," in *Under the Influence: Questioning the Comparative in Medieval Castile*, edited by Cynthia Robinson and Leyla Rouhi (Leiden: Brill, 2005), 140.

49. For example, *Twelfth Night*, I, v, line 220; *The Rape of Lucrece*; Sonnet 130.

50. Thomas Jefferson, *Notes on the State of Virginia* (London: John Stockdale, 1787), 230. On red and white in traditional notions of European beauty, see Hall, *Things of Darkness*, 130–31; Jordan, *White over Black*, 8–10, 459. On masks, see Maria Michela Sassi, *The Science of Man in Ancient Greece* (Chicago: University of Chicago Press, 2001), 58. On peaches and cream complexion in the Old Testament, see Athalya Brenner, *The Intercourse of Knowledge: On Gendering Desire and "Sexuality" in the Hebrew Bible* (Leiden: Brill, 1997), 47.

51. For just a few examples of historians' long-lasting attention to color-based terminology for Native American– and European-descended people, see Alden T. Vaughan, "From White Man to Redskin: Changing Anglo-American Perceptions of the American Indian," *American Historical Review* 87, no. 4 (October 1982): 917–53; Nancy Shoemaker, *A Strange Likeness: Becoming Red and White in Eighteenth-Century North America* (New York: Oxford University Press, 2004); Andrew R. Graybill, *The Red and the White: A Family Saga of the American West* (New York: Liveright Publishing, 2014). On the evolution of the term "redskin," see Ives Goddard, "I AM A RED-SKIN: The Adoption of a Native American Expression (1769–1826)," *Native American Studies* 19, no. 2 (2005): 1–20.

52. *Bickerstaff's Boston Almanack, for the year of our redemption, 1774* (Boston: Mills and Hicks, [1773]), 27, italics added.

53. Mary Floyd-Wilson, *English Ethnicity and Race in Early Modern Drama* (Cambridge: Cambridge University Press, 2003), i.

54. Thomas Shadwell, *The Libertine: A Tragedy: Acted by His Royal Highness's Servants* (London: Printed by T.N., 1676), 33. Example originally from *OED*. In the decades before the American Revolution, the use of both "species" and "race" would dramatically increase in British publications, with "species" rising significantly faster than "race"—at least in Google Ngram results. There is less of an uptick in American publications in the period—but the multiple meanings of race (e.g., a track one runs) mean that this, while intriguing, requires further detailed investigation.

55. Nicholas Hudson, "From 'Nation' to 'Race': The Origin of Racial Classification in Eighteenth-Century Thought," *Eighteenth-Century Studies* 29, no. 3 (Spring 1996): 247–64. For an overview of eighteenth- and nineteenth-century intellectual debates on human origins, including the development of race and racism, see Reginald Horsman, *Race and Manifest Destiny: The Origins of American Racial Anglo-Saxonism* (Cambridge, Mass.: Harvard University Press, 2009), esp. 43–53. For a cogent literary analysis that rejects the notion of race as a settled discourse, see George Boulukos, *The Grateful Slave: The Emergence of Race in Eighteenth-Century British and American Culture* (Cambridge: Cambridge University Press, 2008). On early modern Iberian views of race, particularly in reference to genealogy, see María Elena Martínez, *Genealogical Fictions: Limpieza de Sangre, Religion, and Gender in Colonial Mexico* (Stanford, Calif.: Stanford University Press, 2011), 53–54.

56. "species, n.," *OED,* June 2015, http://www.oed.com/view/Entry/185995, #9e. John Locke used "species" as a synonym for a "particular Sort, and distinguished from others," in his discussion of (chemical) substances and argued that "species" should be used to categorize substances "according to their real Essences." John Locke, *An Essay Concerning Human Understanding: In Four Books* (London: Awnsham and John Churchill; and Samuel Manship, 1706), 378–79.

57. Daniel Fenning, *The Royal English Dictionary, or, A Treasury of the English Language . . . To Which Is Prefixed a Comprehensive Grammar of the English Tongue, Etc* (London: Printed for R. Baldwin et al., 1763). On French discussions of race and species, see Andrew S. Curran, *The Anatomy of Blackness: Science & Slavery in an Age of Enlightenment* (Baltimore: Johns Hopkins University Press, 2011), x–xi.

58. For example, Jean-Baptiste-Louis Chomel, *An Historical Dissertation on a Particular Species of Gangrenous Sore Throat . . .* (London: E. Comyns, 1753); *An Essay on the New Species of Writing Founded by Mr. Fielding: With a Word Or Two Upon the Modern State of Criticism* (London: W. Owen, 1751); William Weston, *Specimens of Abbreviated Numbers, or, An Introduction to an Entire New Species of Arithmetic, Etc* (London: Printed for the author, 1765); Philip Miller, *The Gardeners Dictionary . . .* (London: Printed for the author, 1735), [species of plants].

59. John Adams to Abigail Smith, April 26, 1764; John Adams diary 1, November 18, 1755–August 29, 1756; John Adams diary, June 1753–April 1754, September 1758–January 1759; John Adams diary 15, January 30, 1768, August 10, 1769–August 22, 1770, all in *Adams Family Papers: An Electronic Archive*, Massachusetts Historical Society, http://www.masshist.org/digitaladams/.

60. John Adams diary 11, December 18–29, 1765, *Adams Family Papers.*

61. Abigail Adams to John Adams, July 31–August 2, 1775; John Adams to Abigail Adams, April 27, 1777; Abigail Adams to John Adams, September 20, 1776, all in *Adams Family Papers.*

62. John Adams diary 12, December 30, 1765–January 20, 1766; John Adams to Abigail Adams, March 7, 1777, both in *Adams Family Papers.* See "race, n.," *OED*, December 2015, http://www.oed.com/view/Entry/157031, 6, II, 6a.

63. *Pennsylvania Gazette* April 24, 1776; *Boston Evening-Post* August 24, 1752; *Independent Reflector* January 25, 1753. See also *New-York Mercury* February 26, 1753.

64. Hughes, *The Natural History of Barbados*, 14n18; William Robertson, *The History of America* (Dublin: Messrs. Whitestone, 1777), 1:109.

65. Bernard Romans, *A Concise Natural History of East and West-Florida . . .* (New York: R. Aitken, [1776]), 105, 111, 56.

66. *London Magazine, or, Gentleman's Monthly Intelligencer . . .* (London: R. Baldwin, 1750), 19:316–18. On Buffon's impact on theories of monogenesis, see Curran, *The Anatomy of Blackness*, 74–76, 107–16. For "species" and "race" used interchangeably, see, e.g., *London Magazine*, 19:316–18; *A New Collection of Voyages, Discoveries and Travels: Containing Whatever Is Worthy of Notice, in Europe, Asia, Africa and America* (London: J. Knox, 1767), 274; *The History of the Bucaniers of America . . . Translated Into English* (London: J. Clark, 1741), 25.

67. *The New Book of Knowledge* (Boston: Zechariah Fowle, [1767?]), 31.

68. Lindemann, *Medicine and Society*, 18, 17; Siraisi, *Medieval & Early Renaissance Medicine*, 101–3.

69. On the environment's perceived relation to health in colonial settings, see Katherine Johnston, "The Constitution of Empire: Place and Bodily Health in the Eighteenth Century," *Atlantic Studies* 10, no. 4 (December 2013): 443–66; Kathleen Donegan, *Seasons of Misery: Catastrophe and Colonial Settlement in Early America* (Philadelphia: University of Pennsylvania Press, 2014), 6–7.

70. Carl von Linné, *Caroli a Linné . . . Systema naturae: Per regna tria naturae, secundum classes, ordines, genera, species, cum characteribus, differentiis, synonymis, locis* (Vienna: Typis Joannis Thomae nob. de Trattnern, 1767), 29.

71. Parrish, *American Curiosity*, 82–85. According to Katy Chiles, beliefs in "transformable race" underlay such fears. Katy L. Chiles, *Transformable Race: Surprising Metamorphoses in the Literature of Early America* (New York: Oxford University Press, 2014).

72. *The Constitution and Laws of England Consider'd . . .* (London: Tim Goodwin, [1701]), 3; James Lockwood, *Religion the Highest Interest* (New London: Timothy Green, 1754), 25.

73. Benjamin Rush, *An Oration, Delivered February 4, 1774* (Philadelphia: Joseph Crucks-hank, [1774]), 67. On the importance of travel narratives to developing and promoting views on racial divisions, see Curran, *The Anatomy of Blackness*, 18–19.

74. Douglass, *A summary, historical and political*, 157–59.

75. Chaplin, *Subject Matter*, 271–72, 274.

76. Mitchell, "An Essay upon the Causes," 146, 150. On the relation of the Torrid Zone to uncivilized behavior, see Donegan, *Seasons of Misery*, 165.

77. Richard Jobson, *The Golden Trade, or, A Discovery of the River Gambra, and the Golden Trade of the Aethiopians* (London: Nikolas Okes, 1623), 117, 46; Anthony Benezet, *Some Historical Account of Guinea* (Philadelphia: Joseph Cruckshank, 1771), 10. On "tawny" and other descriptions of Africans in chronologically earlier works, see Stephanie M. H. Camp, "Chapter Two: Beauties," in "Black Is Beautiful: An American History," unpublished manuscript in author's possession. See also Jordan, *White over Black*, 254. On British discourses on black skin, see Anu Korhunen, "Washing the Ethiopian White: Conceptualising Black Skin in Renaissance England," in *Black Africans in Renaissance Europe*, edited by Thomas Foster Earle and K. J. P. Lowe (New York: Cambridge University Press, 2005), 94–112.

78. Hughes, *The Natural History of Barbados*, 14; see also Franklin in Clarke, *Observations*, 14.

79. Mitchell, "An Essay upon the Causes," 112.

80. Robert Boyle, "Experiment XI," in *Experiments and Considerations Touching Colours* (1664; Project Gutenberg, 2004), 156; Voltaire, *Works*, edited by T. Smollett et al. (London: J. Newberry, 1763), 22:236; Wood, *New-England's Prospect*, 73–74. For "swarthy" used on its own, see John Maylem, *Gallic Perfidy: A Poem* (1758; repr., New York: Garland, 1978), 7, 9

81. *The History of the Works of the Learned*, 724. On various theories, see Catherine Molineux, *Faces of Perfect Ebony: Encountering Atlantic Slavery in Imperial Britain* (Cambridge, Mass.: Harvard University Press, 2012), 94–108.

82. On debates over monogenesis and polygenesis and "neo-Hippocratic" medicine, see Norris Saakwa-Mante, "Western Medicine and Racial Constitutions: Surgeon John Atkins' Theory of Polygenism and Sleepy Distemper in the 1730s," in *Race, Science and Medicine, 1700–1960*, edited by Waltraud Ernst and Bernard Harris (New York: Routledge, 2002), 29–27; Curran, *The Anatomy of Blackness*, 74–87. For nineteenth-century American debates, see Terence D. Keel, "Religion, Polygenism and the Early Science of Human Origins," *History of the Human Sciences* 26, no. 2 (2013): 3–32. For Native American views on origins, see David J. Silverman, "The Curse of God: An Idea and Its Origins Among the Indians of New York's Revolutionary Frontier," *William and Mary Quarterly*, 66, no. 3 (July 1, 2009): 495–534.

83. "Additions a l'Essay sur L'Histoire Generale, &c," *Monthly Review, or, Literary Journal* (Amsterdam: R. Griffiths, 1763), 493. On Voltaire's promotion of polygenesis, see Curran, *The Anatomy of Blackness*, 138–42.

84. On the increase in European debates on racial divisions post-1730, see Curran, *The Anatomy of Blackness*, 2.

85. Robertson, *The History of America*, 1:299; Romans, *A Concise Natural History of East and West-Florida*, 55. For eighteenth-century scientific discussions on this topic, see Wheeler, *The Complexion of Race*, 25–26.

86. Boyle, *Experiments and Considerations Touching Colours*, 164.

87. Voltaire, *Works*, (London, 1763), 22:227.

88. Hughes, *The Natural History of Barbados*, 14.

89. Mitchell, "An Essay Upon the Causes," 115, 121, 114, 131, 125, 136. On Mitchell and Benjamin Franklin's connections through Franklin's Philosophical Society, see Chiles, *Transformable Race*, 68–69, and on Mitchell more generally, Jordan, *White over Black*, 246–47.

90. Mitchell, "An Essay upon the Causes," 109, 117, 111.

91. Curran, *The Anatomy of Blackness*, 1–4, 120. On eighteenth-century anatomical interest in the causes of dark skin color, see 121–27.

92. Byrd and Boyd, *William Byrd's Histories of the Dividing Line*, 4, see also 57, 113; Douglass, *A summary, historical and political*, 159; Romans, *A Concise Natural History of East and West-Florida*, 42. On complicating the development of racial ideologies with a focus on Native Americans, see Kathleen Brown, "Native Americans and Early Modern Concepts of Race," in *Empire and Others: British Encounters with Indigenous Peoples, 1600–1850*, edited by Martin Daunton and Rick Halpern (Philadelphia: University of Pennsylvania Press, 1999), 79–100.

93. Josselyn, *Account of Two Voyages to New-England*, 124; John Norris, *Profitable Advice for Rich and Poor, in a Dialogue, or, Discourse between James Freeman, a Carolina Planter, and Simon Question, a West-Country Farmer. Containing a Description . . . of South Carolina . . . with Propositions for the Advantageous Settlement of People . . . in That . . . Country* (London: J. Baker, 1712), 18; John Penn, "Proclamation," reprinted in the *Providence Gazette* March 17, 1764.

94. Voltaire, *Works*, 22:236; Robertson, *The History of America*, 1:289, 92; Patrick M'Robert and Carl Bridenbaugh, "Patrick M'Robert's 'Tour Through Part of the North Provinces of America,'" *Pennsylvania Magazine of History and Biography* 59, no. 2 (April 1935): 174; Franklin in Clarke, *Observations*, 14.

95. On description versus categorization of Native American skin color, see Nancy Shoemaker, "How Indians Got to Be Red," *American Historical Review* 102, no. 3 (June 1997): 625–44.

96. James Edward Oglethorpe, *A New and Accurate Account of the Provinces of South-Carolina and Georgia: With Many Curious and Useful Observations . . .* (London: J. Worrall, 1733), 28.

97. Chaplin, *Subject Matter*, 134–35, 138. See also 116–56 on climate theories more generally. On the emphasis on a search for Native American origins, see Brown, "Native Americans and Early Modern Concepts of Race," 89.

98. Wood, *New-England's Prospect*, 10.

99. Douglass, *A summary, historical and political*, 158.

100. Chaplin, *Subject Matter*, 1. See also Dror Wahrman, *The Making of the Modern Self: Identity and Culture in Eighteenth-Century England* (New Haven, Conn.: Yale University Press, 2004), 86.

101. Boyle, *Experiments and Considerations Touching Colours*, 172. On medieval climate theories of racial difference, see Robin Blackburn, *The Making of New World Slavery: From the Baroque to the Modern, 1492–1800* (New York: Verso, 1997), 70; Wheeler, *The Complexion of Race*, 22–28.

102. *Pennsylvania Gazette* June 15, 1749. For an additional discussion of Greenlandic Inuits tending toward the European white complexion, see Robertson, *The History of America*, 1:303. For seventeenth-century discussion of their complexion, see Boyle, *Experiments and Considerations Touching Colours*, 156.

103. Thomas Humphreys, *Marriage an Honourable Estate* (Boston: S.I. London, 1752), 7. See also Parrish, *American Curiosity*, 92–93.

104. Lord Henry Home Kames, *Sketches of the History of Man: In Two Volumes* (Edinburgh: W. Creech, 1774), 14.

105. James Adair, *The History of the American Indians: particularly those nations adjoining to the Missisipi* [sic], *East and West Florida, Georgia, South and North Carolina, and Virginia* (London: Edward Dilly et al., 1775), 5.

106. Granville Sharp, *Extract from a Representation of the Injustice . . . of Tolerating Slavery . . .* (Philadelphia: Joseph Cruckshank, 1771), 19.

107. Mitchell, "An Essay Upon the Causes," 148.

108. Kames, *Sketches of the History of Man*, 21.

109. Jane Sharp, *The Midwives Book, or, The Whole Art of Midwifry Discovered* (1671; New York: Oxford University Press, 1999), 92.

110. Boyle, *Experiments and Considerations Touching Colours*, 162, 164–65.

111. Romans, *A Concise Natural History of East and West-Florida*, 111.

112. Douglass, *A summary, historical and political*, 158.

113. Hughes, *The Natural History of Barbados*, 14n18.

114. Byrd and Boyd, *William Byrd's Histories of the Dividing Line*, 4, 120.

115. Kevin Joel Berland, Jan Kirsten Gilliam, and Kenneth A. Lockridge, eds., *The Commonplace Book of William Byrd II of Westover* (Chapel Hill: OIEAHC at the University of

North Carolina Press, 2012), 139–40. Thanks to Kathy Brown for this citation. For a full discussion of this anecdote, see Brown, *Good Wives, Nasty Wenches, and Anxious Patriarchs: Gender, Race, and Power in Colonial Virginia* (Chapel Hill: OIEAHC at the University of North Carolina Press, 1996), 332–33.

116. Byrd and Boyd, *William Byrd's Histories of the Dividing Line*, 4. On the relationship between reproduction and racial difference in Spanish America, see Martínez, *Genealogical Fictions*, 162–70.

117. Franklin in Clarke, *Observations*, 13–14. See also Philip Gleason, "Trouble in the Colonial Melting Pot," *Journal of American Ethnic History* 20, no. 1 (Fall 2000): 3–17.

118. Franklin in Clarke, *Observations*, 15.

119. John Adams to Abigail Adams, October 29, 1775, "There is, in the human breast . . . ," *Adams Family Papers*.

120. Samuel Stanhope Smith, *An Essay on the Causes of the Variety of Complexion and Figure in the Human Species To Which Are Added, Strictures on Lord Kaims's Discourse, on the Original Diversity of Mankind* ([London]; Philadelphia, London: reprinted for John Stockdale, 1789). Neither "humor" nor "humour" appears in the text.

121. Samuel Putnam, *Sequel to the Analytical Reader* (Boston: Hilliard, Gray, Little & Wilkins, 1828), 191.

Chapter 2

1. On interpreting gendered bodies as in relation, see Judith Butler, *Undoing Gender* (New York: Routledge, 2004), 38–43.

2. Karen E. Fields and Barbara J. Fields, *Racecraft: The Soul of Inequality in American Life*, reprint ed. (London: Verso, 2014), 16–19.

3. David J. Newman and Sharon Block, "Probabilistic Topic Decomposition of an Eighteenth Century American Newspaper," *Journal of the American Society for Information Science and Technology* 57, no. 6 (April 2006): 759.

4. Daniel Meaders, *Dead or Alive: Fugitive Slaves and White Indentured Servants Before 1830* (New York: Garland, 1993), 37.

5. Ibid. Meaders found that 86 percent of *Pennsylvania Gazette* runaways were listed as being between sixteen and thirty years of age. On the listed age of runaways in the early national period, see Newman, *Embodied History*, 85–87. On runaway men's similar ages in Maryland and Virginia newspapers, see Allan Kulikoff, *Tobacco and Slaves: The Development of Southern Cultures in the Chesapeake, 1680–1800* (Chapel Hill: University of North Carolina Press, 1986), 376.

6. On the historical meanings of numeracy, see Rebecca Jean Emigh, "Numeracy or Enumeration? The Uses of Numbers by States and Societies," *Social Science History* 26, no. 4 (Winter 2002): 653–98. For numeracy in early America, see Patricia Cline Cohen, *A Calculating People: The Spread of Numeracy in Early America* (Chicago: University of Chicago Press, 1982), esp. 44–46 on the early modern shift from classical categorization to numerical quantification.

7. Robert J. Myers, "Accuracy of Age Reporting in the 1950 United States Census," *Journal of the American Statistical Association* 49 (1954): 826–31. Some scholars have argued that age heaping can be used to suggest the level of societal numeracy. See Tine de Moor and Jan Luiten van Zanden, " 'Every Woman Counts': A Gender-Analysis of Numeracy in the Low

Countries During the Early Modern Period," *Journal of Interdisciplinary History* 41, no. 2 (2010): 179–208.

8. *Pennsylvania Gazette* June 22, 1758, May 29, 1760.

9. For examples, see *South-Carolina Gazette* May 4, 1752; *Georgia Gazette* November 12, 1766; *Virginia Gazette* August 8, 1751; *South-Carolina Gazette; And Country Journal* December 30, 1766; *Pennsylvania Gazette* June 4, 1772. Approximately 2,500 runaways had their age listed.

10. Brian A'Hearn, Jörg Baten, and Dorothee Crayen, "Quantifying Quantitative Literacy: Age Heaping and the History of Human Capital," *Journal of Economic History* 69, no. 3 (2009): 783–808. For an alternative reading of age-related numeracy, see Emigh, "Numeracy or Enumeration?," 670.

11. On commodification of enslaved people, see the foundational work of Johnson, *Soul by Soul*, 16–18.

12. *South-Carolina Gazette; And Country Journal* December 30, 1766, *South-Carolina Gazette* November 5, 1753. For the one European-descended woman identified as elderly, see *Pennsylvania Gazette* June 4, 1772.

13. *New-York Weekly Journal* July 30, 1750; *South-Carolina Gazette* September 3, 1753; *Virginia Gazette* January 14, 1773; *Georgia Gazette* April 19, 1764; *Virginia Gazette* August 16, 1770, June 12, 1752; *South-Carolina Gazette; And Country Journal* May 29, 1770.

14. Thanks to Jim Downs for this point and citations. Paul Farmer et al., *Reimagining Global Health: An Introduction* (Berkeley: University of California Press, 2013); Paul Farmer, Margaret Connors, and Janie Simmons, eds., *Women, Poverty and AIDS* (Monroe, Me.: Common Courage Press, 2007); Paul Farmer, "An Anthropology of Structural Violence," *Current Anthropology* 45, no. 3 (2004): 305–25. For a modern interpretation of John Henryism, see Sandeep Jauhar, "When Blood Pressure Is Political," *New York Times* August 6, 2016, http://www.nytimes.com/2016/08/07/opinion/sunday/when-blood-pressure-is-political.html.

15. On nineteenth-century ties between age status and laboring ability, see Jim Downs, *Sick from Freedom: African-American Illness and Suffering During the Civil War and Reconstruction* (New York: Oxford University Press, 2015), 125–26.

16. Olaudah Equiano, *The Interesting Narrative of the Life of Olaudah Equiano, or Gustavus Vassa, the African, Written by Himself* (London, 1789), 1:47, 103, http://docsouth.unc.edu/neh/equiano1/equiano1.html.

17. Harriet A. Jacobs, *Incidents in the Life of a Slave Girl, Written by Herself* (Boston: Published for the author, 1861, c. 1860), 84, 111, 123, 252, 256. For a nineteenth-century narrative that emphasized that "Aaron does not know his age correctly, but supposes he was about 29 or 30 years of age when he left Virginia," see *The Light and Truth of Slavery: Aaron's History* (Worcester, Mass.: the author, [1845]), 34, http://docsouth.unc.edu/neh/aaron/aaron.html.

18. William J. Anderson, *Life and Narrative of William J. Anderson, Twenty-four Years a Slave* . . . (Chicago: Daily Tribune Book and Job Printing Office, 1857), 66, http://docsouth.unc.edu/neh/andersonw/andersonw.html. For a Mohegan man's similar notation of specific age at a life transition, see Samson Occum, "A Short Narrative of My Life," in Arnold Krupat, *Native American Autobiography: An Anthology* (Madison: University of Wisconsin Press, 1994), 107.

19. "John Thornton to Samuel and William Vernon, Dec. 20 1773," Charles Yates Letterbook, p. 41, 1773–1783, Harrison Institute and Small Special Collections Library, University of Virginia #3807 (micro M 570-P), http://www2.vcdh.virginia.edu/.

20. "To Gidney Clarke, 20 November 1765," *Papers of Henry Laurens: November 1, 1755–December 31, 1758* (Columbia: University of South Carolina Press, 1970), 357.

21. *South-Carolina Gazette* June 2, 1739, http://www.teachingushistory.org/lessons/Slave Sale.htm.

22. For the long history of the sexualization and adult expectations put onto black children, see Robin Bernstein, "Let Black Kids Just Be Kids," *New York Times* July 26, 2017, https://www.nytimes.com/2017/07/26/opinion/black-kids-discrimination.html; Tressie McMillan Cottom, "How We Make Black Girls Grow Up Too Fast," *New York Times* July 29, 2017, https://www.nytimes.com/2017/07/29/opinion/sunday/how-we-make-black-girls-grow-up-too-fast.html.

23. "Memorandum Division of Slaves, 1762," Founders Online, National Archives, http://founders.archives.gov/documents/Washington/02-07-02-0107 (last update March 20, 2015). Source: *The Papers of George Washington, Colonial Series*, vol. 7, January 1, 1761–June 15, 1767, edited by W. W. Abbot and Dorothy Twohig (Charlottesville: University Press of Virginia, 1990), 172–74.

24. "February 1786," Founders Online, National Archives, http://founders.archives.gov/documents/Washington/01-04-02-0003-0002 (last update March 20, 2015). Source: *The Diaries of George Washington*, vol. 4, September 1, 1784–June 30, 1786, edited by Donald Jackson and Dorothy Twohig (Charlottesville: University Press of Virginia, 1978), 269–87.

25. John Adams diary 27, May–September 10, 1776, *Adams Family Papers*.

26. Some of the more frequent inclusion of men's height was due to the subset of military runaways: about 90 percent of deserters had their numerical height listed, likely because eighteenth-century militaries kept detailed records of their soldiers. For an example, see the notation that "the Commanding Officer of each Company is to keep an exact Size-Roll," in "General Orders, 26 August 1778," Founders Online, National Archives, http://founders.archives.gov/documents/Washington/03-16-02-0413 (last update March 20, 2015). Source: *The Papers of George Washington, Revolutionary War Series*, vol. 16, July 1–September 14, 1778, edited by David R. Hoth (Charlottesville: University of Virginia Press, 2006), 377–78. More generally, see John Komlos and Francesco Cinnirella, "European Heights in the Early 18th Century," Munich Discussion Paper No. 2005–5, p. 2, http://epub.ub.uni-muenchen.de/572/1/european_heights_in_the_early_18th_century.pdf.

27. Carolyn Freeman Travers, "Were They All Shorter Back Then?" Plimoth-on-Web, n.d., http://www.coht.org/resources/persona/Were_They_All_Shorter_Back_Then.doc. Given the context of the article, these measurements appear to be for European-descended colonists. See also Farley Ward Grubb, "Lilliputians and Brobdingnagians, Stature in British Colonial America: Evidence from Servants, Convicts, and Apprentices," *Research in Economic History: An Annual Compilation of Research* 19 (1999): 139–203; Richard H. Steckel, "Health and Nutrition in the Pre_Industrial Era: Insights from a Millennium of Average Heights in Northern Europe," in *Living Standards in the Past: New Perspectives on Well_Being in Asia and Europe*, edited by Robert C. Allen, Tommy Bengtsson, and Martin Dribe (Oxford: Oxford University Press, 2005), 231; Robert A. Margo and Richard H. Steckel, "The Heights of American Slaves: New Evidence on Slave Nutrition and Health," *Social Science History* 6, no. 4 (Fall 1982): 518–19. For a summary of the argument that living conditions led to nineteenth-century slaves' growth being stunted, see Steven Mintz, "Childhood and Transatlantic Slavery," in *Children and Youth in History*, Item #57, https://chnm.gmu.edu/cyh/case-studies/57; Joseph M. Prince

and Richard H. Steckel, "The Tallest in the World: Native Americans of the Great Plains in the Nineteenth Century" (Working paper, National Bureau of Economic Research, December 1998), http://www.nber.org/papers/h0112; John Komlos and Leonard Carlson, "The Anthropometric History of Native Americans, c. 1820–1890" (CESifo Working Paper Series, Munich, 2012), https://ideas.repec.org/p/ces/ceswps/_3740.html.

28. *Virginia Gazette* May 12, 1768; *Pennsylvania Gazette* November 29, 1750, June 30, 1768.

29. "Henry Laurens to Valentine Powell, 20 Nov 1756," *Papers of Henry Laurens: November 1, 1755–December 31, 1758*, 2:358; "To Smith & Clifton, July 17, 1755," *Papers of Henry Laurens: 1746–1755*, edited by David Chesnutt (Columbia: University of South Carolina Press, 1968), 1:295. On the commodification of body parts in the European trade in Africans, see Stephanie E. Smallwood, *Saltwater Slavery: A Middle Passage from Africa to American Diaspora* (Cambridge, Mass.: Harvard University Press, 2008), 82.

30. On European slave traders' calculus of the minimum nutrition needed for their captives, see Smallwood, *Saltwater Slavery*, 43–49; Marcus Rediker, *The Slave Ship: A Human History* (New York: Penguin, 2007), 126, 232.

31. "II., 10 December 1754," Founders Online, National Archives, http://founders.archives.gov/documents/Washington/02-01-02-0115-0003 (last update, March 20, 2015). Source: *The Papers of George Washington, Colonial Series*, vol. 1, *7 July 1748–14 August 1755*, edited by W. W. Abbot (Charlottesville: University Press of Virginia, 1983), 229–30.

32. Byrd and Boyd, *William Byrd's Histories of the Dividing Line*, 3; William Smith, *An Historical Account of the Expedition against the Ohio Indians in the Year MDCCLXIV . . .* (Philadelphia: T. Jefferies, 1766), 38; John Lawson, *A New Voyage to Carolina* (1711; repr. Chapel Hill: University of North Carolina Press, 1984), 54, 174, 185.

33. Romans, *A Concise Natural History of East and West-Florida*, 42; M'Robert and Bridenbaugh, "Patrick M'Robert's 'Tour Through Part of the North Provinces of America,'" 173–74. For an exceptional claim that Native Americans were "not tall," see Robertson, *The History of America*, 1:92.

34. *New-York Gazette* August 10, 1761; *South-Carolina Gazette* August 17, 1765.

35. *Pennsylvania Gazette* April 23, 1772; *Boston Gazette* November 10, 1760; *New-York Journal* September 10, 1767; *Virginia Gazette* March 7, 1766. For just a few additional examples, see *South-Carolina Gazette; And Country Journal* May 30, 1769; *Virginia Gazette* June 23, 1768.

36. *South-Carolina Gazette* March 28, 1761; *Virginia Gazette* November 16, 1769, January 10, 1771, November 12, 1772. For the only two examples of "well made" European-descended women I found, see *New-York Journal* October 17, 1771; *Pennsylvania Gazette* August 18, 1763.

37. *Virginia Gazette* February 5, 1767.

38. *Virginia Gazette* June 17, 1775; *Pennsylvania Gazette* October 30, 1746; *New-York Journal* September 24, 1767; *Boston Post-Boy* May 5, 1760.

39. *A New Gift for Children* (Boston: D. Fowle, [ca. 1756]), 12. For an advertisement emphasizing a man's deformed limbs, see *Pennsylvania Gazette* January 25, 1770.

40. Byrd and Boyd, *William Byrd's Histories of the Dividing Line*, 114; Smith, *An Historical Account of the Expedition*, 38; M'Robert and Bridenbaugh, "Patrick M'Robert's 'Tour Through Part of the North Provinces of America,'" 173–74; Robertson, *The History of America*, 1:92; Oglethorpe, *A New and Accurate Account of the Provinces of South-Carolina and Georgia*, 28; Romans, *A Concise Natural History of East and West-Florida*, 42; Wood, *New-England's Prospect*, 73–74.

41. William Arens, *The Man-Eating Myth: Anthropology and Anthropophagy* (Oxford: Oxford University Press, 1979), 27 (thanks to Alisa Wankier for the citation); Johann Reinhold Forster, *A Voyage Round the World, in the Years MDCCXL, I, II, III, IV*, edited by George Anson and Richard Walter (New York: Cambridge University Press, 2014), 339, 153.

42. For example, *Virginia Gazette* March 7, 1771; *South-Carolina Gazette; And Country Journal* February 6, 1770; *Pennsylvania Gazette* March 25, 1755; *South-Carolina Gazette; And Country Journal* April 17, 1770. South Carolina newspapers seemed to use the phrase "stout limbed" more than other papers. Throughout the book, quotation marks are used around specific words or terms being analyzed for their usage and meaning. On occasion, this may mean that spelling has been modernized and standardized (for example, "limbed" instead of "limb'd").

43. George Cooke, *The Complete English Farmer, or, Husbandry Made Perfectly Easy, in All Its Useful Branches. Containing What Every Farmer Ought to Know and Practice. . . . By George Cooke, Farmer, at West-End, in Hertfordshire* (1771), 30; John Jay and Sarah Livingston Jay, *Selected Letters of John Jay and Sarah Livingston Jay: Correspondence by or to the First Chief Justice of the United States and His Wife* (Jefferson, NC: McFarland, 2005), 83. For mention of "well-limbed" horses in conversation with Thomas Jefferson, see "Thomas Jefferson to Nathanael Greene, 24 March 1781," Founders Online, National Archives, http://founders.ar chives.gov/documents/Jefferson/01-05-02-0302 (last update March 20, 2015), note. Source: *The Papers of Thomas Jefferson*, vol 5, *25 February 1781–20 May 1781*, edited by Julian P. Boyd (Princeton, N.J.: Princeton University Press, 1952), 5:229–31.

44. *Pennsylvania Gazette* November 13, 1766, May 30, 1765, July 19, 1775.

45. *Boston Post-Boy* December 23, 1765; *South-Carolina Gazette* January 23, 1755. For the only African-descended man described as "fat," see *Boston Evening-Post* May 31, 1756.

46. *The Diary of Elizabeth Drinker: The Life Cycle of an Eighteenth-Century Woman Abridged Edition*, edited by Elaine Forman Crane (Boston: Northeastern University Press, 1994; reprint Philadelphia: University of Pennsylvania Press, 2010), 97; Sarah Wister, *Sally Wister's Journal: A True Narrative; Being a Quaker Maiden's Account of Her Experiences with Officers of the Continental Army, 1777–1778* (Philadelphia: Ferris & Leach, 1902, 195; Philip Vickers Fithian, *Journal & Letters of Philip Vickers Fithian, 1773–1774: A Plantation Tutor of the Old Dominion* (Charlottesville: University of Virginia Press, 1978), 192–93.

47. *South-Carolina Gazette* June 10, 1751; *Newport Mercury* February 7, 1774; *Georgia Gazette* January 26, 1764; *Boston Evening-Post* July 31, 1769; *Pennsylvania Gazette* February 8, 1770; *Virginia Gazette* June 23, 1775, February 15, 1770.

48. For examples of "well-set" or "well-made" "stout" men, see *South-Carolina Gazette* July 5, 1760; *Virginia Gazette* August 11, 1774; *Pennsylvania Gazette* May 17, 1770; *New-London Gazette* August 11, 1775.

49. For example, *South-Carolina Gazette* April 12, 1760; *Georgia Gazette* October 25, 1764.

50. "lusty, adj.," *OED*, March 2016, http://www.oed.com/view/Entry/111424, #5a. "Lusty" was also occasionally used in reference to prolific vegetable growth. See also *A New Complete English Dictionary: Containing a Brief and Clear Explication of Most Words in the English Language . . .* (Edinburgh: David Paterson, 1770), 326.

51. *Georgia Gazette* August 6, 1766; *Maryland Gazette* May 3, 1770; *Virginia Gazette* January 24, 1752; *Pennsylvania Gazette* October 20, 1763, October 18, 1775, December 23, 1772, December 26, 1752, August 18, 1763, October 18, 1770; *Virginia Gazette* March 20, 1752, August 27, 1756.

52. Wood, *New-England's Prospect*, 10; William Fleming and Elizabeth Fleming, *A Narrative of Sufferings and Deliverance* (Philadelphia, 1756; New York: Garland, 1978), 6; William Snelgrave, *A New Account of Some Parts of Guinea, and the Slave Trade* (London, 1734), cited in George Francis Dow, *Slave Ships and Slaving* (1927; repr. Mineola, N.Y.: Dover, 2013), 120. For young and "lusty" runaways, see *Virginia Gazette* October 10, 1755.

53. *Virginia Gazette* March 4, 1773; *Maryland Gazette* September 13, 1749; *Pennsylvania Gazette* July 8, 1756.

54. *New-York Gazette* January 17, 1763; *Pennsylvania Gazette* September 22, 1768; *Pennsylvania Gazette* July 4, 1771; *New-York Gazette* February 7, 1763; *Pennsylvania Gazette* December 2, 1762, December 23, 1772, November 10, 1768, November 13, 1766.

55. *South-Carolina Gazette* March 26, 1750; *Virginia Gazette* July 9, 1772; *Pennsylvania Gazette* February 20, 1772.

56. *New-York Gazette; and the Weekly Mercury* August 22, 1768; *New-York Gazette, or Weekly Post-Boy* April 3, 1758.

57. *New-York Gazette* October 4, 1773; *Pennsylvania Gazette* June 5, 1760, April 23, 1752; *Virginia Gazette* September 24, 1772.

58. "likely, adj. and adv.," *OED*, June 2015, http://www.oed.com/oed2/00133238, A, #5.

59. For example, *South-Carolina Gazette* September 2, 1751; *Virginia Gazette* July 19, 1770; *South-Carolina Gazette* July 1, 1751.

60. For "likely Negro wench" examples, see *Pennsylvania Gazette* January 16, 1750, February 8, 1770; *New-York Gazette* February 3, 1752; *Virginia Gazette* April 30, 1772; "To Smith & Clifton, July 17, 1755," 1:295; *Broadside, Georgia, 1774*, Library of Congress, Prints and Photographs Division, LC-USZ62-16876, http://www.loc.gov/exhibits/odyssey/archive/01/0102001r .jpg.

61. Smallwood, *Saltwater Slavery*, 52; see also 63.

62. *Virginia Gazette* January 30, 1752; *Maryland Gazette* May 4, 1769.

63. *Virginia Gazette* August 2, 1775; *Pennsylvania Gazette* March 19, 1751, November 8, 1770; *Virginia Gazette* December 22, 1768. See also *Virginia Gazette* October 25, 1770, August 1, 1771, August 2, 1775.

64. *New-York Gazette, or Weekly Post-Boy* June 1, 1752. Thanks to Terri Snyder for this point.

65. *New-York Gazette, or Weekly Post-Boy* July 3, 1758; *Virginia Gazette* April 11, 1755; *Pennsylvania Gazette* November 8, 1764. Similarly, see the advertisement for "likely young HORSES," *Pennsylvania Gazette* October 21, 1756.

66. *Virginia Gazette* May 23, 1771; *Boston Gazette* April 17, 1769; *Virginia Gazette* December 22, 1768; *South-Carolina Gazette; And Country Journal* August 12, 1766; *Pennsylvania Gazette* February 19, 1751; *Virginia Gazette* April 13, 1769.

67. *Virginia Gazette* September 24, 1772; *Pennsylvania Gazette* April 15, 1762, June 17, 1756; *Virginia Gazette* September 27, 1770 [2 examples]; *New-York Gazette, or Weekly Post-Boy* November 27, 1752; *Pennsylvania Gazette* July 5, 1775, April 16, 1752; *South-Carolina Gazette* August 9, 1773. Given the dearth of women described as "well made," there is a corresponding absence of women described as both "likely" and "well made." Overall, there are too few European-descended women described as "likely" to warrant definitive conclusions.

68. On the centrality of health to colonial Americans' written records, see Rebecca Jo Tannenbaum, *Health and Wellness in Colonial America* (Santa Barbara, Calif.: Greenwood Press, 2012), 218.

69. *Pennsylvania Gazette* May 17, 1750; *Virginia Gazette* October 24, 1751; *Virginia Gazette* August 12, 1775. See also *South-Carolina Gazette* September 24, 1753; *Pennsylvania Gazette* July 19, 1775.

70. *South-Carolina Gazette* January 23, 1755.

71. Alexander Chalmers, *The Guardian* (1713; London, 1802), 143.

72. Thin and long visage examples include *Boston Gazette* January 9, 1758; *Pennsylvania Gazette* September 19, 1771; *Virginia Gazette* May 9, 1751; *South-Carolina Gazette; And Country Journal* April 17, 1770. Round- and full-faced examples include *Pennsylvania Gazette* October 18, 1750; *South-Carolina Gazette; And Country Journal*, June 5, 1770; *Boston Post-Boy* December 24, 1764; *Connecticut Journal*, September 16, 1774. For the use of a thin visage as a sign of ill health or a reflection of exhaustion, see Daniel Turner and Samuel Palmer, *Syphilis: A Practical Dissertation on the Venereal Disease* . . . (London, 1724), 271; Richard Burn, *Sermons on Practical Subjects: Extr. Chiefly from the Works of Divines of the Last Century* (London, 1774), 3:207.

73. *Virginia Gazette* November 8, 1770; *South-Carolina Gazette* December 3, 1750; *New-London Summary* June 13, 1760; *Pennsylvania Gazette* April 22, 1762; *Pennsylvania Gazette* April 4, 1771. See also *South-Carolina Gazette* May 29, 1762; *Pennsylvania Gazette* October 1, 1767.

74. *Boston Gazette* December 17, 1770. See also *Virginia Gazette* October 7, 1773; *Virginia Gazette* January 24, 1752; *Pennsylvania Gazette* January 7, 1755.

75. *Virginia Gazette* June 1, 1769; *Pennsylvania Gazette* February 20, 1772.

76. *Virginia Gazette* September 29, 1775.

77. Wikipedia contributors, "Saethre–Chotzen syndrome," *Wikipedia, The Free Encyclopedia*, https://en.wikipedia.org/wiki/Saethre–Chotzen_syndrome.

78. For example, Richard Saunders, *Saunders Physiognomie, and Chiromancie, Metoposcopie* . . . (London: H. Bragis, 1671), 171; Prosper Alpini, *The Presages of Life and Death in Diseases: In Seven Books. In Which the Whole Hippocratic Method of Predicting the Various Terminations and Events of Diseases* . . . (London: G. Strahan and J. Clarke, 1746), 2:37.

79. *Pennsylvania Gazette* July 11, 1771. Besides sore eyes, he boasted of cures for any complaint, including venereal disease and miscarriages. *Albany Gazette* July 28, 1800; Kenneth F. Kiple, *The Caribbean Slave: A Biological History* (New York: Cambridge University Press, 2002), 90; Thomas Shepard, *The Day Breaking* (1647), cited in Laura M. Stevens, *The Poor Indians: British Missionaries, Native Americans, and Colonial Sensibility* (Philadelphia: University of Pennsylvania Press, 2010), 68.

80. *Virginia Gazette* June 2, 1774; *Pennsylvania Gazette* August 21, 1754, August 21, 1754.

81. *Pennsylvania Gazette* May 15, 1760; *Virginia Gazette* November 4, 1763; *Pennsylvania Gazette* September 7, 1774. See also *Virginia Gazette* November 21, 1755.

82. *Pennsylvania Gazette* February 17, 1773.

83. *Pennsylvania Gazette* April 25, 1754, June 18, 1752, April 12, 1753, September 6, 1764, June 12, 1776, July 19, 1775. See also *Pennsylvania Gazette* September 13, 1753.

84. *New-York Gazette* October 24, 1768; *South-Carolina Gazette; and Country Journal* November 21, 1769, April 17, 1770; *Virginia Gazette* May 2, 1766; *South-Carolina Gazette; And Country Journal* January 9, 1770; *Virginia Gazette* February 17, 1774, December 28, 1769; *South-Carolina Gazette; And Country Journal* June 5, 1770; *Virginia Gazette* November 4, 1773; *Boston Gazette* August 27, 1759.

85. *Virginia Gazette* January 10, 1771.

86. David M. Goldenberg, *The Curse of Ham: Race and Slavery in Early Judaism, Christianity, and Islam* (Princeton, N.J.: Princeton University Press, 2005), 187–91.

87. For example, of four dozen bow-legged runaways, only one-quarter were runaways of European descent, and about one-third of 133 mentions of leg injuries were about runaways of European descent.

88. *Georgia Gazette* August 29, 1765; *Pennsylvania Gazette* October 7, 1772; *New-York Journal* January 1, 1767. See also *Virginia Gazette* June 16, 1774; *New-England Chronicle*, July 13, 1775. Women were virtually absent from commentaries on misshapen leg form, perhaps in part because their legs were generally not publicly visible beneath voluminous skirts. In one of the only known exceptions, a runaway enslaved woman was described as having "remarkable bow Legs," her exceptionality written into the description. *Virginia Gazette* November 21, 1771.

89. *Virginia Gazette* September 21, 1769. See also *Pennsylvania Gazette* May 8, 1766.

90. *Boston Evening-Post* October 19, 1761; *Virginia Gazette* September 15, 1768, January 16, 1761. See also *South-Carolina Gazette* November 28, 1771, November 27, 1755, October 9, 1762.

91. W. Lowther, *A Dissertation on the Dropsy* . . . (London, 1771), 5. For nineteenth-century commentary on slave mortality from "dropsy," see Kiple, *The Caribbean Slave*, 98–99.

92. On swollen feet resulting from leg irons, see Kirsten Fischer, *Suspect Relations: Sex, Race, and Resistance in Colonial North Carolina* (Ithaca, N.Y.: Cornell University Press, 2001), 159.

93. *Pennsylvania Gazette* September 21, 1774; *Virginia Gazette* August 26, 1773; *Pennsylvania Gazette* August 23, 1770. See also *Pennsylvania Gazette* October 30, 1755.

94. *Virginia Gazette* November 14, 1771; *South-Carolina Gazette* July 12, 1770.

95. For example, *Connecticut Courant* October 31, 1774; *New-York Gazette* December 3, 1764; *Providence Gazette* September 21, 1771; *Virginia Gazette* November 10, 1774.

96. *Virginia Gazette* August 12, 1775, July 15, 1773; *Pennsylvania Gazette* March 19, 1761. See also *Pennsylvania Gazette* October 31, 1771, June 11, 1772; *Virginia Gazette* June 17, 1775.

97. *Pennsylvania Gazette* April 11, 1754, January 16, 1766.

98. Searches were performed for the terms "run away," "servant," and "stoop" without "Negro" in the *Pennsylvania Gazette, Virginia Gazette,* and *South-Carolina Gazette.* Similarly, even though *The Geography of Slavery in Virginia* (www2.vcdh.virginia.edu/gos/) contains twice as many slave as servant runaways, it contains more than twice as many colonial advertisements for "round-shouldered" servants as for enslaved runaways.

99. For modern analogues that deny African Americans' subjectivity and self-definition of illness, see Abby Goodnough, "Minorities Suffer from Unequal Pain Treatment," *New York Times* August 9, 2016, http://www.nytimes.com/2016/08/10/us/how-race-plays-a-role-in-patients-pain-treatment.html. At least one advertiser connected two overrepresented descriptors of European-descended runaways as stooping and having signs of smallpox, noting that his servant "stoops and straddles much in his Walk, caused by his having the Pox." *Virginia Gazette* October 6, 1752.

100. *Boston News-Letter* December 4, 1772; *South-Carolina Gazette* May 24, 1770; *Maryland Gazette* February 23, 1758.

101. On the raced discourse of nineteenth-century smallpox, see Downs, *Sick from Freedom*, 95–119. On smallpox frequency in early modern England and colonial America, see Elizabeth A. Fenn, *Pox Americana: The Great Smallpox Epidemic of 1775–82* (New York: Hill and Wang, 2002), 27–29.

102. Kenneth Hughes, "Fatality, Facial Scarring and Blindness from Smallpox in Bangladesh," World Health Organization, May 15, 1978, http://apps.who.int/iris/bitstream/10665/68229/1/WHO_SE_78.101.pdf.

103. "From George Washington to Lund Washington, 10–17 December 1776," *Founders Online*, National Archives, last modified June 29, 2017, http://founders.archives.gov/docu ments/Washington/03-07-02-0228. Source: *The Papers of George Washington, Revolutionary War Series*, vol. 7, *21 October 1776–5 January 1777*, edited by Philander D. Chase (Charlottesville: University Press of Virginia, 1997), 289–92.

Chapter 3

1. *New-London Summary* January 16, 1761, September 2, 1763.

2. *Pennsylvania Gazette* January 17, 1765, April 18, 1765.

3. *Pennsylvania Gazette* October 30, 1755.

4. For examples of the variety of complexions, see *Pennsylvania Gazette* May 29, 1755, June 28, 1764, February 13, 1772, July 16, 1772, June 17, 1756, September 28, 1752, February 12, 1754, August 20, 1761.

5. For example, *South-Carolina Gazette* January 1, 1763; *New-York Mercury* October 14, 1754; *Pennsylvania Gazette* July 8, 1756; *Connecticut Journal*, May 8, 1772; *New-York Mercury* January 7, 1760; *New-London Gazette* August 11, 1775; *Virginia Gazette* April 20, 1769.

6. For example, *Pennsylvania Gazette* October 10, 1754; *Rivington's New-York Gazetteer* July 1, 1773; *Pennsylvania Gazette* July 19, 1750; *Virginia Gazette* August 27, 1756, December 10, 1767; *South-Carolina Gazette* December 31, 1764; *Virginia Gazette* July 22, 1773; *Massachusetts Spy* August 9, 1775.

7. *Pennsylvania Gazette* August 8, 1771, December 5, 1771; *Virginia Gazette* April 16, 1767; *Boston News-Letter* December 6, 1764; *Georgia Gazette* May 24, 1764; *Virginia Gazette* March 22, 1770. See also *Pennsylvania Gazette* February 14, 1765.

8. For a range of black-complexioned nationalities, see *Pennsylvania Gazette* March 18, 1756; *Virginia Gazette* November 11, 1773; *Pennsylvania Gazette* November 3, 1757, December 6, 1770, September 6, 1759; *South-Carolina Gazette* June 6, 1771; *Virginia Gazette* November 21, 1755.

9. *New-York Gazette* October 22, 1764; *Virginia Gazette* December 5, 1755; *New-York Gazette* December 6, 1773; *Pennsylvania Gazette* November 3, 1757; *New-York Gazette, or Weekly Post-Boy* June 8, 1752; *Pennsylvania Gazette* November 3, 1757, December 6, 1770, February 12, 1754.

10. For black Irish, see "black, adj. and n.," *OED*, June 2016, http://www.oed.com/view/ Entry/19670, S, #5a. For fabric, see *Pennsylvania Gazette* March 18, 1755.

11. "Negro, n. and adj.," *OED*, June 2017, http://www.oed.com/view/Entry/125898, B, #5; https://books.google.com/ngrams/graph?content = Negro + complexion&case_insensitive = on&year_start = 1700&year_end = 1900&corpus = 15&smoothing = 10&share = &direct_url = t4%3B%2CNegro%20complexion%3B%2Cc0%3B%2Cs0%3B%3Bnegro%20complexion%3B %2Cc0%3B%3BNegro%20complexion%3B%2Cc0. For a corresponding absence of a fixed notion of whiteness in renaissance Europe, see Valentin Groebner, "Complexio/Complexion: Categorizing Individual Natures, 1250–1600," in *The Moral Authority of Nature*, edited by Lorraine Daston and Fernando Vidal (Chicago: University of Chicago Press, 2004), 373–82.

12. *Boston Post-Boy* June 1, 1761.

13. *A New Complete English Dictionary . . . : Wherein Difficult Words and Technical Terms, in All Faculties and Professions . . . Are Fully Explained . . .* (London: J. Fuller, 1760), n.p.

14. *A New Complete English Dictionary*, n.p. On early modern human-animal taxonomies, see Wheeler, *The Complexion of Race*, 29–31; Winthrop Jordan, *The White Man's Burden:*

Historical Origins of Racism in the United States (New York: Oxford University Press, 1974), 107–8. For ongoing connections between apes and African heritage, see Brent Staples, "The Ape in American Bigotry, from Thomas Jefferson to 2009," *New York Times* February 27, 2009, http://www.nytimes.com/2009/02/28/opinion/28sat4.html.

15. John C. Brigham, "The Role of Race and Racial Prejudice in Recognizing Other People," in *Motivational Aspects of Prejudice and Racism*, edited by Cynthia Willis-Esqueda (New York: Springer, 2008), 68–110; Christian A. Meissner and John C. Brigham, "Thirty Years of Investigating the Own-Race Bias in Memory for Faces: A Meta-Analytic Review," *Psychology, Public Policy, and Law* 7, no. 1 (2001): 3–35.

16. *Virginia Gazette* July 30, 1752; *Pennsylvania Gazette* August 12, 1756, December 2, 1762; *Boston Evening-Post* September 27, 1762; *Pennsylvania Gazette* March 28, 1765.

17. For just some examples, *Pennsylvania Gazette* September 12, 1765, June 2, 1763; *Boston Gazette* May 2, 1763; *South-Carolina Gazette* December 1, 1758; *Boston Evening-Post* December 17, 1759; *South-Carolina Gazette* October 29, 1764.

18. *Boston Post-Boy* February 5, 1759; *Pennsylvania Gazette* June 30, 1763. See also *Boston Weekly News-Letter* February 15, 1759.

19. *South-Carolina Gazette* December 12, 1774, *South-Carolina Gazette; And Country Journal* July 11, 1775.

20. *Pennsylvania Gazette* March 27, 1754 (an advertisement on March 12, 1754, alternatively described him as "white," suggesting that the writer rethought that description when offering "whitish" two weeks later); *Virginia Gazette* April 11, 1771; Supplement to the *Virginia Gazette* May 26, 1775.

21. *Pennsylvania Gazette* February 24, 1773; *South-Carolina Gazette; And Country Journal* November 22, 1774; *Virginia Gazette* February 18, 1773, January 28, 1768. See also *Providence Gazette* August 28, 1773.

22. *Boston Post-Boy* August 26, 1751; *Pennsylvania Gazette* October 5, 1758 (2 examples); *South-Carolina Gazette* September 21, 1767. See also *New-York Weekly Journal* August 20, 1750; *Pennsylvania Gazette* October 31, 1771; *New-York Gazette* October 15, 1759; *Pennsylvania Gazette* October 5, 1758, June 21, 1770, October 18, 1775, and similar commentary in Peter Gordon, *The Journal of Peter Gordon, 1732–1735* (Athens: University of Georgia Press, 1963), 56, 59.

23. *Boston Gazette* May 15, 1753; *Boston Evening-Post* July 11, 1763. See also *Georgia Gazette* August 1, 1765.

24. *Pennsylvania Gazette* October 31, 1765. John claimed that the collar was a punishment for being caught in bed with a married woman—which implicitly connected marks of slavery to sexual immorality. In the early Republic, such collars were used on Philadelphia prisoners. Jen Manion, *Liberty's Prisoners: Carceral Culture in Early America* (Philadelphia: University of Pennsylvania Press, 2015), 18.

25. *Virginia Gazette* October 6, 1752; *South-Carolina Gazette* August 17, 1765, June 25, 1772.

26. Philip Troutman, "'Black' Concubines, 'Yellow' Wives, 'White' Children: Race and Domestic Space in the Slave Trading Households of Robert & Mary Lumpkin and Silas & Corinna Omohundro,'" http://www.academia.edu/2305937/; Edward E. Baptist, "'Cuffy,' 'Fancy Maids,' and 'One-Eyed Men': Rape, Commodification, and the Domestic Slave Trade in the United States," *American Historical Review* 106, no. 5 (December 2001): 1619–50. Joshua Rothman found more than sixty skin color descriptions for African-descended people from 1830 to the 1840s, suggesting that the application of colors other than yellow flourished in that

century. Joshua D. Rothman, *Notorious in the Neighborhood: Sex and Families Across the Color Line in Virginia, 1787–1861* (Chapel Hill: University of North Carolina Press, 2003), 204.

27. Search in *America's Historical Newspapers* on June 30, 2014, for the terms "yellow complexion" and "yellow comple*" in newspaper advertisements from 1750 to 1775, with over 150 results. Approximately fourteen individuals (many with multiple advertisements) were specifically identified as having a European background; another eight had no specific ethnic background mentioned, but circumstances (e.g., being an apprentice, listed surname) suggest an unstated European background.

28. *New-York Mercury* October 1, 1753; *Pennsylvania Chronicle* June 22–June 29, 1767; *Pennsylvania Gazette* November 28, 1751. See also *Pennsylvania Gazette* July 9, 1767.

29. *Pennsylvania Gazette* September 11, 1776; *New-York Mercury* July 1, 1776. See also *South-Carolina Gazette* December 8, 1766.

30. Thomas Stewardson, "Extracts from the Letter-Book of Benjamin Marshall, 1763–1766," *Pennsylvania Magazine of History and Biography* 20, no. 2 (January 1896): 205. For John Adams's commentary on Spanish complexions, see John Adams to Abigail Adams, December 12, 1779, *Adams Family Papers*.

31. *Pennsylvania Gazette* April 28, 1773, November 25, 1772; *Virginia Gazette* July 21, 1775; *Georgia Gazette* March 28, 1770.

32. *Virginia Gazette* March 7, 1766; *New-York Gazette* April 21, 1760; *Maryland Gazette* August 8, 1762. See also *New-England Chronicle* November 9, 1775.

33. *Pennsylvania Gazette* January 20, 1773; *Virginia Gazette* January 3, 1771; *South-Carolina Gazette* November 20, 1762; *New-York Gazette* October 4, 1762; *South-Carolina Gazette* May 15, 1755; *Virginia Gazette* March 27, 1752. See also *New-York Mercury* March 5, 1759, January 11, 1762.

34. *Pennsylvania Gazette* August 19, 1762; *Georgia Gazette* June 12, 1769, August 16, 1769; *South-Carolina Gazette; And Country Journal* October 6, 1767, August 1, 1769.

35. *Virginia Gazette* April 7, 1774; *Georgia Gazette* June 7, 1769; *Pennsylvania Packet* December 7, 1772; *Pennsylvania Gazette* August 12, 1772.

36. Expressed as comparative percentages, 29 percent of 1,792 "Negro" runaways versus 21 percent of 349 "mulatto" or "mustee" runaways had their complexions described.

37. *Virginia Gazette* December 9, 1775, March 11, 1775; *South-Carolina Gazette* February 22, 1768. See also *New-York Journal* November 12, 1767.

38. See Shoemaker, "How Indians Got to Be Red"; Christopher L. Miller and George R. Hamell, "A New Perspective on Indian-White Contact: Cultural Symbols and Colonial Trade," *Journal of American History* 73 no. 10 (September 1986): 311–28, esp. 323–24.

39. Commentary mentioning "red" and "Indian" together might more often mention dye than skin color. For example, George Fisher, *The American instructor, or, Young man's best companion* (Philadelphia: B. Franklin and D. Hall, 1748), 251; John Hawksworth, *A new voyage, round the world, in the years 1768, 1769, 1770, and 1771 . . .* (New York: James Rivington, 1774), 135.

40. Thomas Hutchinson, *The history of the province of Massachusets-Bay, from the charter of King William and Queen Mary, in 1691, until the year 1750* (Boston: Thomas & John Fleet, [1767]), 139.

41. *Virginia Gazette* June 30, 1768; *New-York Gazette* October 22, 1764; *Virginia Gazette* April 19, 1770; *South-Carolina Gazette* February 6, 1762; *Virginia Gazette* April 19, 1770; *New-York Journal* January 1, 1767; *Providence Gazette* May 27, 1775; *Maryland Gazette* May 3, 1770.

See also *Essex Journal*, July 6, 1774; *Boston Gazette* December 3, 1754. For an East Indian man described as tawny, see *New-York Journal* October 8, 1772.

42. *Pennsylvania Gazette* June 27, 1765.

43. On Native American freedom suits from wrongful enslavement that hinged on heritage, see Sachs, " 'Freedom by a Judgment,' " 173–203; Tiya Miles, "The Narrative of Nancy, a Cherokee Woman," *Frontiers: A Journal of Women Studies* 29, no. 2–3 (2008): 59–80. The minimization of Native American heritage is discussed at length in Chapter 4.

44. *Boston Gazette* October 28, 1765; *Boston News-Letter* September 8, 1768; *South-Carolina Gazette* January 23, 1755; *Virginia Gazette* February 8, 1770; *Pennsylvania Gazette* September 6, 1775, August 19, 1772.

45. For example, *Virginia Gazette* July 30, 1772; *Boston Post-Boy* October 8, 1759; *South-Carolina Gazette* November 5, 1753; *Pennsylvania Gazette* September 2, 1772, December 22, 1763; *New-York Journal* May 11, 1769; *South-Carolina Gazette* April 15, 1751.

46. *Pennsylvania Gazette* September 25, 1755, October 20, 1763, February 27, 1766, April 14, 1773, June 20, 1754, October 28, 1762. See also *Connecticut Gazette* August 18, 1775.

47. "Letter from Isabella Marshall Graham, 1773[?]," in Isabella Graham, *The Unpublished Letters and Correspondence from the Year 1767 to 1814: Exhibiting Her Religious Character in the Different Relations of Life* (New York: J. S. Taylor, 1838), 115; U.S. Continental Congress, *Journal of the Proceedings of the U.S. Continental Congress, 1774* [September 5–October 26, 1774 (New York, 1774), backmatter, n.p.; *The American Calendar, or, An Almanack, for the year of our Lord, 1770* (Philadelphia: William Thomas Bradford, [1769]), n.p., December.

48. John Mitchell, "An Essay upon the Causes of the different Colours of People in different Climates . . . ," in *Philosophical Transactions . . . 1744–1745* (London: C. Davis, 1746), 43:108–9.

49. *Pennsylvania Gazette* January 22, 1761, October 10, 1754; *Virginia Gazette* March 24, 1774; *Pennsylvania Gazette* July 5, 1759, May 21, 1761, April 19, 1770.

50. *A New Gift for Children*, 11; Buchan, *Domestic Medicine*, 390; Byrd and Boyd, *William Byrd's Histories of the Dividing Line*, 151.

51. Lady Mary Wortley Montagu, *Letters: Written During her Travels in Europe, Asia and Africa*, 4th ed. (New York, 1766), 86, 110, 197; Rush, *An Oration*, 96; *Hutchin's Improved: Being an Almanack and Ephemeris . . . for the Year of Our Lord, 1765 . . .* (New York: Hugh Gaine, [1764]), n.p. See also *The Universal American almanac . . . For the year of our Lord 1762 . . .* (Philadelphia: Andrew Steuart, [1761]), n.p.; *Boston Chronicle*, March 29, 1768.

52. *South-Carolina Gazette; And Country Journal* May 26, 1767; *Pennsylvania Gazette* June 21, 1770; *New-York Mercury* February 2, 1756; *New-York Journal* March 29, 1770; *Rivington's New-York Gazetteer* June 22, 1774; *New-York Gazette* March 9, 1761.

53. *Pennsylvania Gazette* May 5, 1763; *South-Carolina Gazette; And Country Journal* February 4, 1766; *Pennsylvania Gazette* July 2, 1772.

54. Chalmers, *The Guardian*, 143; *Massachusetts Spy* April 25, 1771. See also *Boston Gazette* September 22, 1747; *New-Hampshire Gazette* June 29, 1759; Wister, *Sally Wister's Journal*, 110.

55. John Adams to Abigail Smith, April 13, 1764, *Adams Family Papers*.

56. *Pennsylvania Chronicle* October 23, 1769.

57. *Pennsylvania Gazette* May 5, 1763, May 3, 1764.

58. *New-York Gazette* July 4, 1763; *Boston Evening-Post* April 14, 1755. For one "Negro" exception, see *Boston Evening-Post* May 31, 1756.

59. *Virginia Gazette* November 23, 1775. See also *South-Carolina Gazette* November 12, 1763; *South-Carolina Gazette; And Country Journal* September 19, 1769; *Boston News-Letter* October 20, 1768.

60. On the fusion of "slave health and property concerns," see Sharla M. Fett, *Working Cures: Healing, Health, and Power on Southern Slave Plantations* (Chapel Hill: University of North Carolina Press, 2002), 25.

61. *South-Carolina Gazette* December 3, 1750, September 24, 1753; *Georgia Gazette* February 4, 1767.

62. *Pennsylvania Gazette* August 12, 1756; *Virginia Gazette* July 2, 1767. For "red faced" or "reddish," see *Virginia Gazette* April 11, 1771; *Connecticut Courant* July 12, 1774; *New-York Gazette, or Weekly Post-Boy* January 9, 1758; *Boston Evening-Post* March 21, 1768; *Story & Humphreys's Pennsylvania Mercury* July 21, 1775.

63. *Pennsylvania Gazette* May 30, 1765; *Virginia Gazette* June 21, 1770; Peter Force, ed., *American Archives*, 9 vols. (Washington, D.C., 1837–53), 4th ser., 6:1162, cited in "To George Washington from Colonel James Clinton, 27 June 1776," *Founders Online*, National Archives, last modified June 29, 2017, http://founders.archives.gov/documents/Washington/03-05-02 -0075. Source: *The Papers of George Washington*, Revolutionary War Series, vol. 5, *16 June 1776?–?12 August 1776*, ed. Philander D. Chase (Charlottesville: University Press of Virginia, 1993), 116–18; *Pennsylvania Gazette* March 13, 1750. See also *Boston Gazette* November 27, 1775; *Pennsylvania Gazette* April 18, 1754.

64. Augustin Calmet, *Dissertations Upon the Apparitions of Angels, Daemons, and Ghosts: And Concerning the Vampires of Hungary, Bohemia, Moravia, and Silesia, Translated from the French* (London: M. Cooper, 1759), 251.

65. *South-Carolina Gazette* September 28, 1767.

66. *The Complete English Dictionary, or, General Repository of the English Language . . . By the Rev. Frederick Barlow . . .* (London: T. Evans et al., 1772).

67. Joseph Randall, *A System of Geography, or, A Dissertation on the Creation and Various Phaenomena of the Terraqueous Globe . . .* (London: Joseph Lord, [1744]), 566.

68. Chelter, a runaway described as mulatto, had "something of a reddish complexion." *Virginia Gazette* November 1, 1770.

69. *Virginia Gazette* March 7, 1771.

70. *Virginia Gazette* February 6, 1772; *New-York Gazette, or Weekly Post-Boy* October 2, 1758; *Virginia Gazette* May 7, 1772; *Boston Post-Boy* December 29, 1766; *Pennsylvania Gazette* July 2, 1767; *Virginia Gazette* January 21, 1773, October 31, 1751; *Pennsylvania Gazette* May 5, 1763. Black hair color accounted for more than one-third of hair color mentions of European-descended servants.

71. For example, *South-Carolina Gazette* December 3, 1753; *New-York Gazette, or Weekly Post-Boy* January 8, 1750; *Boston Evening-Post* September 27, 1762; *Providence Gazette* January 1, 1774; *Pennsylvania Gazette* October 30, 1755.

72. *Virginia Gazette* December 21, 1769; *South-Carolina Gazette* June 1, 1765; *New-York Journal* November 19, 1772; *New-York Mercury* September 3, 1764.

73. Jonathan Dickinson, *God's protecting providence, man's surest help and defence in the times of the greatest difficulty, and most eminent danger . . .* (Philadelphia: William Bradford, 1751), 2.

74. *Pennsylvania Gazette* September 12, 1771, September 19, 1771, November 15, 1764; *New-York Mercury* July 15, 1754.

75. *Virginia Gazette* January 10, 1771; *Pennsylvania Gazette* May 11, 1769.

76. The hair of more than two hundred runaways was described as straight or curly, and more than one thousand had their hair color described. On African American hairstyles, see Shane White and Graham White, "Slave Hair and African American Culture in the Eighteenth and Nineteenth Centuries," *Journal of Southern History* 61, no. 1 (February 1995): 45–76; Jordan, *White over Black*, 7–8.

77. Voltaire, *The works of M. de Voltaire, Translated from the French: With notes, historical and critical* (London: J. Newberry et al., 1763), 22:227. On early commentaries (often admiring) of African (women's) hair, see Camp, "Chapter Two: Beauties." See also Jennifer L. Morgan, *Laboring Women: Reproduction and Gender in New World Slavery* (Philadelphia: University of Pennsylvania Press, 2004), 12–13.

78. *Virginia Gazette* December 21, 1769; *Pennsylvania Gazette* June 5, 1760.

79. Edward Long, *The History of Jamaica, or, A General Survey of the Antient and Modern State of That Island: With Reflexions on Its Situation, Settlements, Inhabitants, Climate, Products, Commerce, Laws, and Government* (London: T. Lowndes, 1774), 374.

80. *New-York Gazette, or Weekly Post-Boy* October 9, 1752; *Boston Gazette* June 25, 1770; *Virginia Gazette* March 7, 1771.

81. *South-Carolina Gazette* March 28, 1761; *Virginia Gazette* March 26, 1767.

82. *Providence Gazette* May 27, 1775; *Virginia Gazette* November 5, 1772.

83. For example, *Virginia Gazette* February 2, 1775; *New-York Journal* November 26, 1772; *New-York Gazette or Weekly Post-Boy* December 18, 1752; *Pennsylvania Gazette* June 17, 1756; *Boston Post-Boy* October 8, 1759; *New-York Gazette* September 26, 1763.

84. *Connecticut Journal* September 16, 1774; *Virginia Gazette* January 14, 1775; *Providence Gazette* January 2, 1768; *South-Carolina Gazette* March 14, 1771.

85. *South-Carolina Gazette; And Country Journal* September 14, 1773; *New-London Gazette* July 1, 1774. See also *South-Carolina Gazette; And Country Journal* July 11, 1775.

86. *New-York Gazette* May 6, 1765; *Boston Gazette* July 10, 1753; *Virginia Gazette* December 2, 1775, December 5, 1755. See also *New-York Gazette* May 27, 1765.

87. *Pennsylvania Gazette* November 10, 1763.

88. Romans, *A Concise Natural History of East and West-Florida*, 42; James Adair, *The History of the American Indians: particularly those nations adjoining to the Missisippi* [sic], *East and West Florida, Georgia, South and North Carolina, and Virginia* (London: E. & C. Dilly, 1775), 6.

89. Wood, *New-England's Prospect*, 75.

90. For example, Peter Williamson, *The life and curious adventures of Peter Williamson, who was carried off from Aberdeen, and sold for a slave* (Aberdeen: Lewis Smith & Son, 1885), 26–27; M'Robert and Bridenbaugh, "Patrick M'Robert's 'Tour Through Part of the North Provinces of America,'" 174.

91. *South-Carolina Gazette* March 28, 1761; *Virginia Gazette* November 26, 1772; *Newport Mercury* March 6, 1775; *Virginia Gazette* November 11, 1773. For emphasis on hair to describe a Native American woman in a turn-of-the-century freedom suit, see the 1802 description of a woman as "'a perfect Indian, with long and straight hair,'" in Sachs, "'Freedom by a Judgment,'" 196.

92. For straight black: *Pennsylvania Gazette* November 15, 1764; *New-York Mercury* November 8, 1756; *Boston Evening-Post* June 8, 1767; *Pennsylvania Gazette* July 16, 1772; *Rivington's New-York Gazetteer* May 5, 1774. For lank black: *Boston Weekly News-Letter* November 2, 1753; *Pennsylvania Gazette* April 14, 1773; *South-Carolina Gazette* November 12, 1763.

93. The most common complexion colors used for European-descended people (brown, dark, fair, fresh, pale, and swarthy) had accompanying hair color and style/texture descriptions relatively similar percentages of the time.

94. Voltaire, *Works*, 22:236.

95. Londa Schiebinger, "The Anatomy of Difference: Race and Sex in Eighteenth-Century Science," *Eighteenth-Century Studies* 23, no. 4 (July 1990): 391. On the historically and culturally contingent meanings of the beard, see Afsaneh Najmabadi, *Women with Mustaches and Men Without Beards: Gender and Sexual Anxieties of Iranian Modernity* (Berkeley: University of California Press, 2005), 15–17.

96. Romans, *A Concise Natural History of East and West-Florida*, 42–43; David Jones, *A Journal of two Visits made to some nations of Indians on the west side of the River Ohio, in the years 1772 and 1773* (Burlington, N.J.: Isaac Collins, [1774]), 63; Adair, *The History of the American Indians*, 6.

97. Kathleen M. Brown, "The Anglo-Algonquian Gender Frontier," in *Negotiators of Change: Historical Perspectives on Native American Women*, edited by Nancy Shoemaker (New York: Routledge, 2012), 37.

98. "A Faithful Narrative of the many *Dangers* and *Sufferings*, as well as wonderful *Deliverances* of ROBERT EASTBURN . . . ," *A Faithful Narrative* (Philadelphia, 1758; repr., New York: Garland, 1978), 17; Wood, *New-England's Prospect*, 75; Erik R. Seeman, *Death in the New World: Cross-Cultural Encounters, 1492–1800* (Philadelphia: University of Pennsylvania Press, 2011), 323n4; H. F. McGee, *Native Peoples of Atlantic Canada: A History of Indian-European Relations* (Toronto: McGill-Queen's University Press, 1974), 28.

99. *New-York Gazette, and Weekly Mercury* October 8, 1770; *Virginia Gazette* March 14, 1751, June 1, 1775; *Pennsylvania Gazette* January 11, 1770; *Virginia Gazette* July 7, 1774; *New-York Gazette, or Weekly Post-Boy* February 26, 1770.

100. *Virginia Gazette* December 12, 1755; *South-Carolina Gazette; And Country Journal* April 17, 1770; *Georgia Gazette* December 20, 1769. See also *South-Carolina Gazette; And Country Journal* June 5, 1770.

101. *Pennsylvania Gazette* June 28, 1770; *New-York Gazette, or Weekly Post-Boy* December 26, 1757; *Virginia Gazette* April 14, 1751. See also *Boston Evening-Post* June 11, 1770.

102. "eye, n.1," *OED*, June 2017, http://www.oed.com/view/Entry/67296. Similarly, Google Books returns almost no results for "eye color" from 1600 to 1780. In contrast, "hair colour," likely referring to a common brown hair color, was used as early as the seventeenth century. "hair, n.," *OED*, June 2017, http://www.oed.com/view/Entry/83299.

103. This is particularly notable given that the term "iris" was named after the Greek goddess who personified a rainbow. For modern research that tries to objectively identify iris coloration, see Luuk Franssen et al., "Grading of Iris Color with an Extended Photographic Reference Set," *Journal of Optometry* 1, no. 1 (July 2008): 36–40. On variation in eye color, see P. Frost, "European Hair and Eye Color: A Case of Frequency-Dependent Sexual Selection?" *Evolution and Human Behavior* 27 (2006): 85–103; R. A. Sturm and T. N. Frudakis, "Eye Colour: Portals into Pigmentation Genes and Ancestry," *Trends in Genetics* 20 (2004): 327–32. On the (modern) rate of "light" eye color in Europe, see http://www.eupedia.com/europe/maps_of_europe.shtml#eye_colour.

104. *Virginia Gazette* April 5, 1770; *Pennsylvania Gazette* December 12, 1771, October 3, 1771, November 7, 1771, June 9, 1773; *Story & Humphreys's Pennsylvania Mercury* July 21, 1775;

New-York Gazette, or Weekly Post-Boy May 28, 1770. For black eye examples, *Newport Mercury* August 2, 1773; *Virginia Gazette* October 31, 1751; *New-York Weekly Journal* March 18, 1750. For brown eye examples: *Pennsylvania Gazette* July 19, 1770; *Connecticut Courant* May 17, 1774. For blue eyes, *South-Carolina Gazette* September 28, 1765; *New-York Gazette, or Weekly Post-Boy* April 6, 1751.

105. *Boston Weekly News-Letter* July 26, 1750; *Pennsylvania Gazette* July 19, 1770; *New-York Gazette* June 25, 1767; *Virginia Gazette* June 11, 1767; *South-Carolina Gazette* April 9, 1763; *Virginia Gazette* July 30, 1752; *New-York Gazette, or Weekly Post-Boy* November 27, 1758; *New-York Gazette* June 25, 1767; *Pennsylvania Gazette* December 6, 1770; *Rivington's New-York Gazetteer* December 2, 1773.

106. *Virginia Gazette* October 27, 1752, March 5, 1772; *South-Carolina Gazette* February 3, 1757.

107. William Shakespeare, *Othello*, edited by Roma Gill (Oxford: Oxford University Press, 2002), Act III, Scene 3, lines 168–69.

108. *Pennsylvania Gazette* October 30, 1755, April 28, 1773; *Norwich Packet* August 21–28, 1775; *New-York Gazette, or Weekly Post-Boy* October 31, 1768; *Boston Evening-Post* May 31, 1756. For examples of adjacent eye and "look" descriptions, see *Virginia Gazette* June 23, 1768, September 24, 1772; *Pennsylvania Gazette* September 8, 1763, November 13, 1766.

109. For instance, *Providence Gazette* July 16, 1774; *South-Carolina Gazette; And Country Journal* January 15, 1771; *Virginia Gazette* January 30, 1752.

110. Voltaire, *Works*, 22:227.

111. Jefferson, *Notes on the State of Virginia*, 228–40 (quotations on 230, 229). In the section in Query XIV on "Laws," that begins with "To emancipate all slaves born after passing the act" and ends with "When freed, he is to be removed beyond the reach of mixture," Jefferson labeled people as black(s) or white(s) more than a dozen times each but Negro only once.

Chapter 4

1. *Essex Gazette* December 24, 1771; *Georgia Gazette* December 27, 1764; *Virginia Gazette* April 9, 1772.

2. *Newport Mercury* December 30, 1765; *South-Carolina Gazette* January 23, 1762; *Georgia Gazette* January 21, 1767; *Virginia Gazette* June 18, 1772; *Essex Gazette* December 6, 1774.

3. On the descriptive category of "negro" being "long a virtual synonym for slave," see Joanne Pope Melish, *Disowning Slavery: Gradual Emancipation and "Race" in New England, 1780–1860* (Ithaca, N.Y.: Cornell University Press, 1998), 119.

4. *New-York Mercury* August 4, 1755; *Pennsylvania Gazette* November 6, 1755; *Georgia Gazette* May 17, 1764.

5. Briton Hammon, *A Narrative of the Sufferings and Deliverance of Briton Hammon, A Negro Man* (Boston, 1760; repr., New York: Garland, 1978), 6.

6. John Knox and Arthur George Doughty, *Appendix* (Toronto: Champlain Society, 1916), 76.

7. For examples of nationality recorded in military rolls, see Lloyd DeWitt Bockstruck, *Virginia's Colonial Soldiers* (Baltimore: Genealogical Publishing Company, 1988), 63–88.

8. *New-York Gazette* February 7, 1763; *Boston Post-Boy* December 24, 1764; *Pennsylvania Gazette* October 10, 1754.

9. *New-York Gazette, and Weekly Mercury* January 8, 1770; *New-York Gazette, or Weekly Post-Boy* November 5, 1767; *Pennsylvania Gazette* November 15, 1764; *Virginia Gazette* December 5, 1755, August 1, 1771.

10. Herbert Moll, "Negroland and Guinea: With the European settlements explaining what belongs to England, Holland, Denmark &c," [1732], Norman B. Leventhal Map Center, Collection, Boston Public Library, http://ark.digitalcommonwealth.org/ark:/50959/kk91fq372.

11. *The History of the Works of the Learned*, 6:720.

12. For just a few examples, *Maryland Gazette* June 30, 1757; *Virginia Gazette* February 4, 1768. On the imposed temporality of slaves' lives even after death, see Daina Ramey Berry, "'Broad Is de Road dat Leads ter Death': Human Capital and Enslaved Morality," in *Slavery's Capitalism: A New History of American Economic Development*, edited by Sven Beckert and Seth Rockman (Philadelphia: University of Pennsylvania Press, 2016), 146–62.

13. *Pennsylvania Gazette* October 21, 1772.

14. *Pennsylvania Gazette* December 18, 1760; *South-Carolina Gazette; And Country Journal* May 26, 1767; *Virginia Gazette* June 1, 1769. "Clownish" was the Anglicized version of the Irish "Cluain Eois," now spelled "Clones."

15. *Virginia Gazette* September 24, 1755; *New-York Gazette* June 18, 1764; *South-Carolina Gazette; And Country Journal* March 12, 1771; *New-York Evening-Post* August 5, 1751; *South-Carolina Gazette; And Country Journal* March 19, 1771.

16. *Pennsylvania Gazette* February 14, 1765. There is considerable ongoing debate on the sex ratio of Africans in the Atlantic slave trade. See, for example, David Eltis, "The Volume and Structure of the Transatlantic Slave Trade: A Reassessment," *William and Mary Quarterly* 58, no. 1 (January 2001): 17–46.

17. *Georgia Gazette* January 27, 1768, May 17, 1769; *Pennsylvania Gazette* September 1, 1763; *Georgia Gazette* July 21, 1763, August 11, 1763.

18. "To Gidney Clarke, 20 November 1756," *Papers of Henry Laurens: November 1, 1755–December 31, 1758* (Columbia: University of South Carolina Press, 1970), 358, 437; "To Smith & Clifton, July 17, 1755," *Papers of Henry Laurens: 1746–1755*, 1:295.

19. John Carter to Richard Gildart, Esq., August 1, 1738, in John, Charles, Landon Carter Letterbook, 1732–1782, Special Collections, Alderman Library, University of Virginia.

20. Griffith, *The Natural History of Barbados*, 14.

21. *Supplement to South-Carolina Gazette; And Country Journal* October 3, 1769; *South-Carolina Gazette; And Country Journal* December 15, 1767, May 22, 1770, December 30, 1766.

22. *Virginia Gazette* March 21, 1766.

23. *Virginia Gazette, or, Norfolk Intelligencer* June 15, 1775; *Virginia Gazette* March 31, 1774; *Pennsylvania Gazette* May 3, 1753.

24. *Virginia Gazette* November 19, 1771, May 24, 1770, March 7, 1766. Presumably "Comana" referred to Cormona, in southwest Spain.

25. *Pennsylvania Gazette* October 19, 1752; *New-York Gazette, or Weekly Post-Boy* November 27, 1752; *Virginia Gazette* July 4, 1751.

26. *South-Carolina Gazette* January 29, 1750; *Boston Gazette* July 22, 1765; *Georgia Gazette* April 4, 1770.

27. *Maryland Gazette* February 23, 1758.

28. *Pennsylvania Gazette* February 24, 1764.

29. *Virginia Gazette* June 30, 1768.

30. *Pennsylvania Gazette* August 28, 1760.

31. "A full and particular ACCOUNT of the late horrid NEGRO *PLOT*," *Pennsylvania Gazette* March 24, 1737.

32. On the history of slave status following the mother, see Jennifer L. Morgan, "Partus Sequitur Ventrem: Calculating Intimacies in Colonial Slavery," *Small Axe*, forthcoming; Jennifer Spear and Kathleen Brown, "Partus Sequitur Ventrem vs. Nullius Filius: Rethinking the Development of Slave Law in the Atlantic World," *WMQ* & *EMSI* Workshop—Early American Legal Histories, May 29, 2015, Huntington Library.

33. *Virginia Gazette* April 18, 1766; *South-Carolina Gazette; And Country Journal* December 2, 1766. See also *South-Carolina Gazette* December 3, 1750; *Virginia Gazette* October 20, 1774; *New-York Gazette, or Weekly Post-Boy* November 27, 1752; *Virginia Gazette* July 4, 1751.

34. See Trevor Burnard, "Slave Naming Patterns: Onomastics and the Taxonomy of Race in Eighteenth-Century Jamaica," *Journal of Interdisciplinary History* 31, no. 3 (January 2001): 325–46; John C. Inscoe, "Carolina Slave Names: An Index to Acculturation," *Journal of Southern History* 49, no. 4 (November 1983): 527–54; Cheryl Ann Cody, "There Was No 'Absalom' on the Ball Plantations: Slave-Naming Practices in the South Carolina Low Country, 1720–1865," *American Historical Review* 92, no. 3 (June 1987): 563–96; Hennig Cohen, "Slave Names in Colonial South Carolina," *American Speech* 28 (1952): 102–7. For a useful overview, see Junius P. Rodriguez, *Slavery in the United States: A Social, Political, and Historical Encyclopedia* (Santa Barbara, Calif.: ABC-CLIO, 2007), 293–94.

35. *Pennsylvania Gazette* October 16, 1772, August 2, 1750; *Georgia Gazette* August 6, 1766; *Pennsylvania Gazette* June 5, 1760, February 14, 1760, May 10, 1770.

36. *Virginia Gazette* January 20, 1774; *Boston Post-Boy* December 24, 1764; *Pennsylvania Gazette* October 18, 1775, October 14, 1762; *Virginia Gazette* August 4, 1774; *Pennsylvania Packet* June 14, 1773. See also *Pennsylvania Gazette* September 29, 1768; *New-York Gazette, or Weekly Post-Boy* August 1, 1768.

37. *Georgia Gazette* April 12, 1764; *South-Carolina Gazette* October 6, 1758; *New-York Gazette, or Weekly Post-Boy* November 6, 1752.

38. Jerome S. Handler and JoAnn Jacoby, "Slave Names and Naming in Barbados, 1650–1830," *William and Mary Quarterly* 53, no. 4 (October 1996): 690. On slave owners' disregard for enslaved people's chosen surnames, see "Naming Patterns in Enslaved Families," *Thomas Jefferson Monticello*, http://www.monticello.org/site/plantation-and-slavery/naming-patterns -enslaved-families.

39. Venture Smith, *A Narrative of the Life and Adventures of Venture a Native of Africa: But Resident Above Sixty Years in the United States of America* (New London: C. Holt, 1798), 13.

40. Equiano, *The Interesting Narrative*, 1:93, 96.

41. *South-Carolina Gazette* March 24, 1757.

42. *Boston Weekly News-Letter* July 19, 1750; *South-Carolina Gazette* December 11, 1775; *Virginia Gazette* November 25, 1775. See also *New-London Gazette* July 9, 1773; *Pennsylvania Packet* December 7, 1772.

43. *South-Carolina Gazette* September 20, 1760. Also quoted in Meaders, *Dead or Alive*, 42; "Tom, n.1.," *OED*, June 2015, http://www.oed.com/view/Entry/203070, #1a. The first *OED* usage is 1734. For a later usage, see *The Critical Review, or, Annals of Literature* (London: A. Hamilton, 1762), 12:476.

44. For example, *Boston Post-Boy* November 22, 1762; *South-Carolina Gazette* January 14, 1764; *New-York Mercury* July 4, 1757; *Virginia Gazette* July 19, 1754, April 25, 1766; *South-Carolina Gazette* March 4, 1756.

45. *Providence Gazette* July 16, 1774.

46. For examples of the women named Doll, see *South-Carolina Gazette* June 12, 1753; *Virginia Gazette* November 12, 1772. For Kitty, *Virginia Gazette* February 14, 1751, December 21, 1769. For a horse called Kitty, see *Virginia Gazette* October 14, 1773. Tiya Miles, *Ties That Bind: The Story of an Afro-Cherokee Family in Slavery and Freedom* (Berkeley: University of California Press, 2006) tells the history of another woman named Doll.

47. For example, *Virginia Gazette* July 9, 1767; *New-York Gazette* May 2, 1774; *New-York Mercury* July 18, 1757; *South-Carolina Gazette* December 30, 1756; *New-London Gazette* November 6, 1772; *Virginia Gazette* August 18, 1768; *Providence Gazette* October 2, 1773.

48. *Georgia Gazette* May 3, 1769; *Pennsylvania Gazette* March 31, 1773.

49. *South-Carolina Gazette; And Country Journal* December 3, 1771. For Jack versus John, see *Virginia Gazette* March 21, 1766; *Providence Gazette* March 13, 1773; *Georgia Gazette* May 3, 1769; *New-York Mercury* April 12, 1756. One man without an ethnic or national identity specified was named John but apparently went by the alias of Jack, *Pennsylvania Gazette* August 18, 1773. Men of African descent were also the only ones named "Johnny," another diminutive. For example, *Virginia Gazette* July 23, 1767; *South-Carolina Gazette; And Country Journal* March 11, 1766. For the one European-descended "Will," see *Boston Post-Boy* October 8, 1759—like Paddy Joe, he was also described as Irish. For an argument that diminutives of English names were used because they sounded more similar to African names, see Marvin L. Michael Kay and Lorin Lee Cary, *Slavery in North Carolina, 1748–1775* (Chapel Hill: University of North Carolina Press, 2000), 142–43.

50. *Virginia Gazette* September 24, 1755; *South-Carolina Gazette* July 5, 1760; *Georgia Gazette* August 10, 1768, May 23, 1770; *South-Carolina Gazette* February 19, 1753.

51. *Connecticut Courant* June 25, 1771.

52. *New-York Gazette, or Weekly Post-Boy* September 10, 1767; *Virginia Gazette* January 24, 1752; *South-Carolina Gazette* December 3, 1753; *Pennsylvania Gazette* March 26, 1772; *New-York Mercury* May 26, 1766; *Pennsylvania Gazette* September 4, 1755, October 3, 1771, September 4, 1755; *South-Carolina Gazette* January 29, 1750; *Rivington's New-York Gazetteer* December 15, 1774; *Boston Gazette* July 22, 1765; *New-York Mercury* September 24, 1753.

53. *Providence Gazette* July 16, 1763; *Virginia Gazette* November 21, 1771, August 4, 1774.

54. *Virginia Gazette* April 16, 1767, March 9, 1769, February 25, 1775; *Rivington's New-York Gazetteer* December 8, 1774; *New-York Gazette* July 23, 1764; *Pennsylvania Gazette* May 10, 1770.

55. *South-Carolina Gazette* November 7, 1761.

56. *South-Carolina Gazette; And Country Journal* May 22, 1770. On enslaved women's naming practices, see Morgan, *Laboring Women*, 107–43; Deborah Gray White, *Ar'n't I a Woman?: Female Slaves in the Plantation South* (New York: W. W. Norton, 1999), 110.

57. *Pennsylvania Gazette* February 19, 1751; *New-York Gazette, or Weekly Post-Boy* March 5, 1750; *New-York Gazette, and Weekly Mercury* May 7, 1770; *South-Carolina Gazette; And Country Journal* January 23, 1770. The *OED* lists a first use of racially specific "wench" in 1765, but this is likely a very late estimate. One of the earliest colonial newspaper uses of "negro wench" was in an ad for sale of a "likely Negro wench" in the *Boston Gazette* May 30, 1715, and became more common from the 1730s on. "Indian wench" was occasionally used in reference to Native American female servants. For example, *New-York Gazette* November 7, 1757. "wench, n.," *OED*, June 2017, http://www.oed.com/view/Entry/227789, #3b. Noah Webster's 1828 dictionary formalized this racialized definition of wench: http://webstersdictionary-1828.com/. See also Brown, *Good Wives, Nasty Wenches, and Anxious Patriarchs*, 370.

58. *New-York Gazette* May 12, 1760.

59. John Adams to Abigail Adams, August 11, 1777, *Adams Family Papers.*

60. *Pennsylvania Gazette* March 18, 1756. See also Thomas Brown, *A Plain Narrative of the Uncommon Sufferings and Remarkable Deliverance of Thomas Brown* . . . (Boston, 1760; repr., New York: Garland, 1978), 19; *South-Carolina Gazette; And Country Journal* February 16, 1773.

61. *Connecticut Journal, and the New-Haven Post-Boy* May 27, 1774; *New-York Gazette* October 5, 1767. See also *Connecticut Courant* September 8, 1766.

62. On "The idea [that] 'Indian' still implicitly identifies a person physically and culturally separate from colonial" authority, see Joyce E. Chaplin, "Enslavement of Indians in Early America: Captivity Without the Narrative," in *The Creation of the British Atlantic World,* edited by Elizabeth Mancke and Carole Shammas (Baltimore: Johns Hopkins University Press, 2005), 46.

63. For uncommon mentions of "Englishwoman" or "Irishwoman," see *Virginia Gazette* September 29, 1752; *Pennsylvania Gazette* September 19, 1754.

64. *Pennsylvania Gazette* October 10, 1754, April 6, 1774. See also *Pennsylvania Gazette* July 21, 1768, September 6, 1753.

65. *Virginia Gazette* February 8, 1770; *South-Carolina Gazette; And Country Journal* May 26, 1767; *Pennsylvania Gazette* October 18, 1775; *New-York Mercury* July 18, 1757; *Virginia Gazette* August 19, 1773; *Pennsylvania Gazette* October 16, 1772.

66. *Newport Mercury,* September 18, 1775; *Virginia Gazette* February 14, 1751; *Boston Gazette* March 25, 1755; *Virginia Gazette* June 12, 1752; *New-London Summary,* June 26, 1761; *Virginia Gazette* February 25, 1775; *Pennsylvania Gazette* December 5, 1771.

67. *South-Carolina Gazette* September 5, 1771; *New-London Gazette* September 7, 1764.

68. For just one modern example of invisibility of whiteness, see Laura Seay, "@AP Describes @BreeNewsome as 'Black Woman' & Her Ally as 'Another Man.' No Mention of His Race, Hers Made Central," Twitter Post, June 27, 2015, 6.30 a.m., pic.twitter.com/6XpCVxSsQg. See also Paula S. Rothenberg, *White Privilege: Essential Readings on the Other Side of Racism,* 5th ed. (New York: Macmillan, 2016).

69. "mulatto, n. and adj.," *OED,* June 2017, http://www.oed.com/view/Entry/123402. On the zoological vocabulary used for people of mixed continental heritages in Spanish America, see Martínez, *Genealogical Fictions,* 164–65.

70. New Jersey, Legislature, *[Journal, 1762 Sept,] Votes and proceedings of the General Assembly of the province of New-Jersey* (Woodbridge: James Parker, [1762]), 16. On the development of the use of "mulatto," see Jack D. Forbes, *Africans and Native Americans: The Language of Race and the Evolution of Red-Black Peoples* (Urbana: University of Illinois Press, 1993), 131–220.

71. *Virginia Gazette* April 10, 1752.

72. *Virginia Gazette* April 11, 1766; William Logan, "William Logan's Journal of a Journey to Georgia, 1745," *Pennsylvania Magazine of History and Biography* 36, no. 1 (1912): 3.

73. *Virginia Gazette* March 27, 1752; *Pennsylvania Gazette* October 31, 1771; *South-Carolina Gazette; And Country Journal* July 17, 1770; *Virginia Gazette* July 25, 1751. On the impact of white people's association to blackness, see Baz Dreisinger, *Near Black: White-to-Black Passing in American Culture* (Amherst: University of Massachusetts Press, 2008).

74. *Maryland Gazette* May 24, 1759.

75. William Waller Hening, ed., *The Statutes at Large; Being a Collection of All the Laws of Virginia from the First Session of the Legislature, in the Year 1619* (New York: R. & W. & G. Bartow, 1823), 3:453. See also Terri L. Snyder, "Marriage on the Margins: Free Wives, Enslaved Husbands, and the Law in Early Virginia," *Law and History Review* 30, no. 1 (February 2012): 141–71.

76. *Virginia Gazette* May 6, 1773.

77. On southern trade in Native American slaves, see Alan Gallay, *The Indian Slave Trade: The Rise of the English Empire in the American South, 1670–1717* (New Haven, Conn.: Yale University Press, 2003), esp. 305–14. In some colonies, more than one-third of Native Americans lived in Euro-American households. See Margaret Ellen Newell, "Indian Slavery in Colonial New England," in *Indian Slavery in Colonial America*, edited by Alan Gallay (Lincoln: University of Nebraska Press, 2009), 60.

78. For example, *Pennsylvania Gazette* February 20, 1750.

79. *Pennsylvania Gazette* December 6, 1764, July 5, 1759; *South-Carolina Gazette; And Country Journal* February 1, 1774.

80. *New-York Gazette, or Weekly Post-Boy* August 29, 1757; *Connecticut Journal* September 16, 1774; *New-London Gazette* May 28, 1773; *New-York Mercury* June 26, 1758.

81. *New-York Mercury* July 11, 1757; *New-York Gazette* May 6, 1765; *South-Carolina Gazette* December 19, 1754; *Virginia Gazette* August 8, 1777, January 6, 1776; *South-Carolina Gazette* May 15, 1755.

82. *Virginia Gazette* January 21, 1775, March 11, 1775.

83. *South-Carolina Gazette* April 30, 1771; January 14, 1772.

84. *Providence Gazette* August 28, 1773; *Virginia Gazette* May 29, 1752, September 24, 1772. See also *Boston Gazette* August 27, 1759; *Pennsylvania Gazette* February 20, 1772.

85. Sachs, " 'Freedom by a Judgment,' " 177. See also Claudio Saunt, *Black, White, and Indian: Race and the Unmaking of an American Family* (New York: Oxford University Press, 2005); Miles, *Ties That Bind*.

86. *Pennsylvania Gazette* August 6, 1767; *New-York Mercury* September 3, 1767.

87. *New-York Gazette* April 26, 1773; *Pennsylvania Gazette* March 14, 1765; *Virginia Gazette* April 29. 1773. See also *South-Carolina Gazette* April 30, 1771.

88. *South-Carolina Gazette* February 21, 1761, September 10, 1750. See also *Georgia Gazette* December 7, 1768, May 20, 1767.

89. Peter H. Wood, *Black Majority: Negroes in Colonial South-Carolina from 1670 Through the Stono Rebellion* (New York: Knopf, 1974), 99. Thanks to Josh Piker for this citation. For other uses of "mustee," see Ruth Wallis Herndon and Ella Wilcox Sekatau, "The Right to a Name: The Narragansett People and Rhode Island Officials in the Revoltuionary era," in *After King Philip's War: Presence and Persistence in Indian New England*, edited by Coling G. Calloway (Hanover, New Hampshire: University Press of New England, 2000), 114–43, 136n10, 140n63; Lathan A. Windley, *A Profile of Runaway Slaves in Virginia and South-Carolina from 1730 Through 1787* (New York: Routledge, 2014), 52. For a Virginia law specifying that African and Native American heritage made someone a mulatto, see "An act declaring who shall not bear office in this country," Laws of Virginia, October 1705, Hening, *Statutes*, p. 252, http://vagenweb.org/hening/vol03-16.htm.

90. Determined by a search for "mustee" in those newspapers. One was found in *America's Historical Newspapers* for New York, two mentions were found in the *Pennsylvania*

Gazette, and one in the *Virginia Gazette.* For exceptional mentions of "mustee," see *Providence Gazette* January 26, 1771; *Virginia Gazette* June 14, 1770; *Pennsylvania Gazette* May 14, 1772; August 4, 1773; *New-York Gazette* July 27, 1761. For a map of Native American borders, see Julianna Barr, "Geographies of Power: Mapping Indian Borders in the 'Borderlands' of the Early Southwest," *WMQ* Interactive Digital Project, January 2011, https://oieahc.wm.edu/wmq/Jan11/Barr/figure2/index.html.

91. Chaplin in *The Creation of the British Atlantic World,* edited by Mancke and Shammas, 63. On the historiographic minimization of the Anglo-American enslavement of Native Americans, see 54–58. For reformulations of North American slavery, see James F. Brooks, *Captives and Cousins: Slavery, Kinship, and Community in the Southwest Borderlands* (Chapel Hill: University of North Carolina Press, 2002); Barbara Krauthamer, *Black Slaves, Indian Masters: Slavery, Emancipation, and Citizenship in the Native American South* (Chapel Hill: University of North Carolina Press, 2013); Margaret Ellen Newell, *Brethren by Nature: New England Indians, Colonists, and the Origins of American Slavery* (Ithaca, N.Y.: Cornell University Press, 2016).

92. *North-Carolina Magazine; or, Universal Intelligencer* June 7, 1764; *South-Carolina Gazette* August 18, 1758; *Georgia Gazette* May 20, 1767; *South-Carolina Gazette* July 28, 1759; *Providence Gazette* January 26, 1771. See also *Boston Evening-Post* April 14, 1755.

93. "mustee, n.," *OED,* June 2017, http://www.oed.com/view/Entry/124249.

94. *Pennsylvania Gazette* October 23, 1760; *Virginia Gazette* July 22, 1773, May 2, 1771. See also *South-Carolina Gazette* April 26, 1773; *Maryland Gazette* May 21, 1752; *South-Carolina Gazette* May 15, 1755, *Virginia Gazette* November 26, 1772.

95. *South-Carolina Gazette; And Country Journal* December 30, 1766.

96. *Virginia Gazette* November 30, 1759, July 19, 1770; *New-England Chronicle* December 21, 1775. Also Henry Stedman Nourse, *The Military Annals of Lancaster, Massachusetts, 1740–1865* . . . (Clinton, Mass.: W. J. Coulter, printer, 1889), 107.

97. Ebeneezer Cooke, *The Maryland Muse* (Annapolis: W. Parks, 1731), 8.

98. Hobbs, *A Chosen Exile,* 36; David Waldstreicher, "Reading the Runaways: Self-Fashioning, Print Culture, and Confidence in Slavery in the Eighteenth-Century Mid-Atlantic," *William and Mary Quarterly* 56, no. 2 (April 1999): 257.

Chapter 5

1. *Virginia Gazette* May 2, 1751.

2. *Virginia Gazette* November 3, 1768.

3. *South-Carolina Gazette* June 22, 1765; *Pennsylvania Gazette* August 23, 1775; *New-York Journal* September 10, 1767; *Pennsylvania Gazette* February 7, 1760; *Pennsylvania Gazette* October 20, 1763; *Maryland Gazette* November 26, 1767; *Pennsylvania Gazette* May 7, 1772; *Boston Gazette* October 1, 1770; *Virginia Gazette* August 26, 1773; *Connecticut Courant* June 15, 1773; *Boston News-Letter* October 20, 1763; *Pennsylvania Gazette* November 8, 1775.

4. *Pennsylvania Gazette* November 16, 1758; *New-York Journal* September 10, 1767; *Virginia Gazette* January 20, 1774. See also *Virginia Gazette* January 16, 1761; *Pennsylvania Gazette* February 16, 1769. For an unusual positive countenance, see *New-York Gazette* September 8, 1760.

5. *Virginia Gazette* April 14, 1768. For a runaway with an "Indian look," see *Pennsylvania Gazette* September 5, 1765.

6. *Pennsylvania Gazette* June 28, 1750; *Virginia Gazette* June 15, 1769; *Norwich Packet* April 21–28, 1774; *New-London Summary* January 16, 1761. See also *New-London Summary* September 7, 1759; *Virginia Gazette* June 15, 1769.

7. *Virginia Gazette* August 3, 1775, September 7, 1769, December 24, 1772; *Pennsylvania Gazette* September 5, 1754; *Virginia Gazette* June 17, 1775; *Pennsylvania Gazette* May 11, 1774.

8. Approximately 7 percent of European-descended people and 2 percent of non-European-descended people had "looks" mentioned. Native American runaways were too small in number to produce separate meaningful statistics.

9. *The Geography of Slavery in Virginia*, http://www2.vcdh.virginia.edu/gos/.

10. Meaders, *Dead or Alive*, 33–34. In my own database of advertisements, women were also described as bold at least twice as often as they appeared in advertisements.

11. *Pennsylvania Gazette* February 16, 1769. See also *Pennsylvania Gazette* February 24, 1773, October 31, 1771; *Virginia Gazette* November 2, 1769. On women's transgressive speech, see Jane Kamensky, *Governing the Tongue: The Politics of Speech in Early New England* (New York: Oxford University Press, 1999); Lynda E. Boose, "Scolding Brides and Bridling Scolds: Taming the Woman's Unruly Member," *Shakespeare Quarterly* 42, no. 2 (1991): 179–213.

12. For examples of down-looking Toms or Thomases, see *Essex Gazette* December 24, 1771; *New-York Journal* March 2, 1775; *Pennsylvania Gazette* November 29, 1753; *Virginia Gazette* June 11, 1767, November 8, 1770, May 16, 1771.

13. Alex Bontemps, *The Punished Self: Surviving Slavery in the Colonial South* (Ithaca, N.Y.: Cornell University Press, 2008), 13; White and White, "Slave Hair," 69–70; Newman, *Embodied History*, 93–94; Peter Charles Hoffer, *Cry Liberty: The Great Stono River Slave Rebellion of 1739* (New York: Oxford University Press, 2010), 47n16.

14. *A New Complete English Dictionary* . . . (London: J. Fuller, 1760).

15. Abel Boyer, *The Royal Dictionary Abridged . . . : French and English. English and French* . . . (London: Messieurs Innys, Brotherton, Meadows, 1755).

16. Francis Bragge, *Of Undissembled and Persevering Religion: In Several Sermons, Etc.* (London: John Wyat, 1713), 356.

17. *New-York Mercury* February 2, 1756; *Virginia Gazette* July 23, 1772; *Pennsylvania Gazette* August 6, 1767, March 29, 1759, October 29, 1761, June 21, 1770, July 8, 1762, September 8, 1768.

18. "ill-looking, adj.," *OED*, March 2016, http://www.oed.com/view/Entry/91488.

19. Daniel Defoe, *The Novels and Miscellaneous Works of Daniel De Foe* (1725; repr. London: Henry G. Bohn, 1856), 268; *Pennsylvania Gazette* July 7, 1763. For other examples of a down and ill look, see *Pennsylvania Gazette* September 6, 1753, July 17, 1755.

20. A search in the *Pennsylvania Gazette* and *Virginia Gazette* resulted in dozens of European-descended but no African-descended runaways described with the terms "ill look" or "ill looking." For an exception, see *South-Carolina Gazette* December 3, 1750.

21. *Pennsylvania Gazette* June 30, 1773; February 13, 1772; July 4, 1771.

22. *Pennsylvania Gazette* March 18, 1756, May 29, 1755; *South-Carolina Gazette* April 6, 1752; *Virginia Gazette* April 11, 1766.

23. *Pennsylvania Gazette* June 21, 1770, October 30, 1766, November 2, 1767. For the only African-descended runaway identified with an accent, see *Virginia Gazette* June 22, 1775, where Road was described as speaking in the New England dialect.

24. *South-Carolina Gazette* June 4, 1750; *New-York Journal* February 15, 1770; *Virginia Gazette* November 3, 1775; *Pennsylvania Gazette* May 28, 1760; *Georgia Gazette* July 2, 1766; *New-York Gazette* October 15, 1759; *Virginia Gazette* June 27, 1771.

25. *New-York Gazette, or Weekly Post-Boy* May 28, 1750. See also *Pennsylvania Gazette* May 30, 1754; *New-York Gazette* January 2, 1758; *Virginia Gazette* January 7, 1768.

26. *Georgia Gazette* January 21, 1767; *Pennsylvania Gazette* June 28, 1770; *Virginia Gazette* November 12, 1772. See also *Pennsylvania Gazette* April 22, 1762.

27. *New-York Gazette* October 17, 1763; *Virginia Gazette* July 4, 1771; *Georgia Gazette* July 13, 1768, February 7, 1765; *New-York Gazette* June 4, 1767; *Pennsylvania Gazette* September 2, 1762. For other examples of African-descended people lacking English skills, see *Pennsylvania Gazette* November 4, 1762; *Virginia Gazette* September 10, 1772; *South-Carolina Gazette* August 4, 1757; *Georgia Gazette* July 13, 1768; *New-York Journal* November 26, 1772; *Boston Gazette* September 7, 1761.

28. For specific African origins, see *South-Carolina Gazette; And Country Journal* August 12, 1766; *New-York Journal* October 15, 1767; *Georgia Gazette* April 12, 1764; *Virginia Gazette* January 30, 1752. For recent arrivals, see *New-York Gazette, or Weekly Post-Boy* November 6, 1752; *Virginia Gazette* November 25, 1775, December 13, 1770; Jacobs, *Incidents in the Life of a Slave Girl*, 49.

29. *Virginia Gazette* September 24, 1755, April 25, 1766; *Boston Evening-Post* October 19, 1761; *Virginia Gazette* October 3, 1771. See also *New-York Weekly Journal* March 18, 1750; *Boston Gazette* October 19, 1772; *Georgia Gazette* September 21, 1768; *New-York Gazette* April 21, 1760; *Georgia Gazette* December 20, 1764.

30. Christof Migone, "Sonic Somatic: Performances of the Unsound Body" (PhD diss., New York University, 2007), 167–69. Studies of antebellum slavery have identified speech impediments in anywhere from 8 percent to nearly one-third of runaways. Franklin and Schweninger, *Runaway Slaves*, 225; Wilma A. Dunaway, *The African-American Family in Slavery and Emancipation* (New York: Cambridge University Press, 2003), 84.

31. *New-York Gazette, or Weekly Post-Boy* September 4, 1758; *Story & Humphreys's Pennsylvania Mercury* July 21, 1775; *Virginia Gazette* March 18, 1773. See also *Boston Gazette* May 27, 1771; *Virginia Gazette* September 15, 1768.

32. For example, *Norwich Packet*, August 4, 1774; *New-York Mercury* July 2, 1753; *Boston Evening-Post* October 14, 1754; for "had on and took with him," *Pennsylvania Gazette* September 20, 1764; *Virginia Gazette* January 30, 1752, August 14, 1752. On enslaved people's clothing specifically, see Shane White and Graham White, "Slave Clothing and African-American Culture in the Eighteenth and Nineteenth Centuries," *Past & Present*, no. 148 (August 1, 1995): 149–86; Katherine Egner Gruber, "Slave Clothing and Adornment in Virginia," *Encyclopedia of Virginia*, http://www.encyclopediavirginia.org/Slave_Clothing_and_Adornment_in_Virginia.

33. For textile scholars, see Patricia K. Hunt, "Osnaburg Overalls, Calico Frocks and Homespun Suits: The Use of 19th Century Georgia Newspaper Notices to Research Slave Clothing and Textiles," *Clothing and Textiles Research Journal* 14 (1996): 200–203; Linda Baumgarten, *What Clothes Reveal: The Language of Clothing in Colonial and Federal America: The Colonial Williamsburg Collection* (Williamsburg, Va.: Colonial Williamsburg Foundation in association with Yale University Press, 2002), 133; Barbara Martin Starke, Lillian O. Holloman, and Barbara K. Nordquist, *African American Dress and Adornment: A Cultural Perspective* (Dubuque, Iowa: Kendall/Hunt Publishing, 1990), 87–88. On the importance of runaways' clothing to their identification, see Waldstreicher, "Reading the Runaways," 252.

34. *Virginia Gazette* February 24, 1766; *Pennsylvania Gazette* January 30, 1766; *Virginia Gazette* July 18, 1771. For additional examples, see *Pennsylvania Gazette* June 30, 1768; *New-York Journal* March 14, 1771; *Connecticut Gazette* October 27, 1759; *Virginia Gazette* July 25, 1771; *Boston Gazette* April 8, 1771.

35. *Pennsylvania Gazette* April 9, 1772. See also *Virginia Gazette* November 8, 1770, June 9, 1774.

36. *New-York Gazette* June 25, 1750; *Boston Gazette* June 25, 1770; *Pennsylvania Gazette* November 25, 1762.

37. These data include approximately 120 individuals from 100 advertisements in 1760. If advertisements that do not describe clothing are included, the average number of words describing clothing drops to 35 and other aspects of appearance to 31.

38. For European-descended men: 33 bodily versus 39 clothing words; for African-descended men: 31 bodily versus 36 clothing words. For European-descended women: 28 bodily versus 34 clothing words. African-descended women were too small in number for a meaningful average.

39. Based on 180 advertisements in the *Virginia Gazette* in 1766 that focused on at least 65 individuals. European-descended servants' non-clothing-related appearance was described with approximately 36 words, African-descended slaves' with 33, affirming that there was a much larger difference in clothing descriptions.

40. This is based on *South-Carolina Gazette* advertisements for 81 people in 1763. Only a few of these ads involved runaway servants.

41. South Carolina, *The Statutes at Large of South Carolina: Containing the Acts Relating to Charleston, Courts, Slaves, and Rivers, Volume Seventh* (Columbia, S.C.: A. S. Johnston, 1840), 396.

42. *Pennsylvania Gazette* January 22, 1756, May 13, 1756, March 5, 1751; *Connecticut Courant* November 6, 1775. For examples of worn or old clothing, see *Virginia Gazette* September 21, 1775, June 27, 1771; *Pennsylvania Gazette* April 8, 1762. See also Baumgarten, *What Clothes Reveal*, 122.

43. *Virginia Gazette* July 25, 1751, January 31, 1771, November 8, 1776. See also *Maryland Gazette* March 7, 1771.

44. For instance, see *Virginia Gazette* January 14, 1773, November 5, 1767 (regarding a slave in a North Carolina jail). The *Pennsylvania Gazette* had three advertisements mentioning "Negroe Cloth," and two of them referred to events in South Carolina. See *Pennsylvania Gazette* August 17, 1769, December 20, 1770. See also *New-York Gazette, and Weekly Mercury* November 20, 1769. In addition to the thousands of advertisements I read, I searched for ["negro cloth"] and ["negroe cloth"] in *America's Historical Newspapers* and *Accessible Archives* from 1750 to 1775.

45. For example, *South-Carolina Gazette* January 1, 1756, May 31, 1760, December 8, 1766; *Georgia Gazette* October 10, 1765, September 30, 1767, March 28, 1770.

46. *South-Carolina Gazette* November 7, 1754, February 26, 1756, May 31, 1760.

47. For example, *South-Carolina Gazette* October 16, 1762, September 6, 1760, May 23, 1761. A few mentions of "negro cloth" appeared in the *Virginia Gazette*, usually in the context of Revolutionary-era efforts at promoting homespun over import. For example, *Virginia Gazette* September 28, 1769, October 4, 1770. On the rise of homespun clothing for slaves, see

White and White, "Slave Clothing," 166–73. On clothing and the construction of race, see Fischer, *Suspect Relations,* 162–164.

48. White and White, "Slave Clothing," 152–53. Even African traditions of adopting some European garb were not a wholesale importation of European standards. See Pernille Ipsen, " 'The Christened Mulatresses': Euro-African Families in a Slave-Trading Town," *William and Mary Quarterly* 70, no. 2 (April 2013): 371, 377, 395. On the transformation of Native American clothing styles, including resistance to European clothing, see Linda Welters, "From Moccasins to Frock Coats and Back Again: Ethnic Identity and Native American Dress in Southern New England," in *Dress in American Culture,* edited by Patricia A. Cunningham and Susan Voso Lab (Bowling Green, Ohio: Popular Press, 1993), 10–25.

49. Baumgarten, *What Clothes Reveal,* 106. On runaways' attempts to self-fashion through clothing manipulation, see Waldstreicher, "Reading the Runaways," 252–54. For an example of sumptuary law directed specifically at slaves, see I. Bennett Capers, "Cross Dressing and the Criminal," *Yale Journal of Law & the Humanities* 20, no. 1 (2008): 8; Eulanda Sanders, "The Politics of Textiles Used in African American Slave Clothing," *Textile Society of America Symposium Proceedings,* September 1, 2012, http://digitalcommons.unl.edu/tsaconf/740.

50. *New-York Gazette* March 18, 1751; *Virginia Gazette* October 26, 1769; *Pennsylvania Gazette* May 19, 1773.

51. "genteel," *OED,* June 2017, http://www.oed.com/view/Entry/77636.

52. *Pennsylvania Gazette* April 29, 1762, December 1, 1763, September 1, 1763; *Virginia Gazette* August 29, 1766; *Pennsylvania Gazette* May 31, 1775. See also *Pennsylvania Gazette* August 9, 1775; *Virginia Gazette* June 30, 1768; *South-Carolina Gazette* January 1, 1763; *Pennsylvania Gazette* February 19, 1761, April 16, 1761.

53. On the cultural significance of Native American clothing, see Carole Cory Silverstein, "Clothed Encounters: The Power of Dress in Relations Between Anishnaabe and British Peoples in the Great Lakes Region, 1760–2000" (PhD thesis, McMaster University, 2000); Timothy J. Shannon, "Dressing for Success on the Mohawk Frontier: Hendrick, William Johnson, and the Indian Fashion," *William and Mary Quarterly,* 53, no. 1 (January 1996): 13–42.

54. *Pennsylvania Gazette* May 9, 1751, July 2, 1752, November 10, 1763.

55. *Virginia Gazette* March 17, 1774, September 5, 1755.

56. *Virginia Gazette* April 5, 1770, August 28, 1752; *Pennsylvania Gazette* February 20, 1753. On cross-dressing in Western culture, see Marjorie Garber, *Vested Interests: Cross-Dressing and Cultural Anxiety* (New York: Routledge, 1997). On colonial America, see Elizabeth Reis, *Bodies in Doubt: An American History of Intersex* (Baltimore: Johns Hopkins University Press, 2009), 14–16; Jen Manion, "The Queer History of Passing as a Man in Early Pennsylvania," *Historical Society of Pennsylvania Legacies,* special issue, "Pennsylvania Pride: LGBT Histories of the Commonwealth," 16, no. 1 (Spring 2016): 6–11.

57. Kate Haulman, *Politics of Fashion in Eighteenth-Century America* (Chapel Hill: University of North Carolina Press, 2011), 19–33.

58. "Extracts from the Journal of Sarah Eve . . . 1772–1773," *Pennsylvania Magazine of History and Biography* 5, no. 1 (1881): 24n2; Wister, *Sally Wister's Journal,* 182.

59. Byrd and Boyd, *William Byrd's Histories of the Dividing Line,* 46, 47.

60. *South-Carolina Gazette* January 29, 1756, January 6, 1757. For wig examples, see *South-Carolina Gazette* March 5, 1750; *Pennsylvania Gazette* April 29, 1762; *Virginia Gazette* April 11,

1751; *New-York Gazette, or Weekly Post-Boy* August 29, 1757; *Pennsylvania Gazette* November 22, 1770. For other examples, see *Pennsylvania Gazette* February 13, 1772; *Virginia Gazette* July 15, 1773; *Boston Gazette* July 22, 1765; *New-York Gazette* September 17, 1764; *Georgia Gazette* April 4, 1770. For an exceptional female runaway wearing "a black hair hat," see *Pennsylvania Gazette* October 5, 1758. On wigs, see Haulman, *Politics of Fashion*, 62–64.

61. *Pennsylvania Gazette* September 12, 1771, September 26, 1751; *Boston News-Letter* January 11, 1770; *Pennsylvania Gazette* October 8, 1767, July 2, 1772. For examples of short haircuts, see *Pennsylvania Gazette* November 8, 1775; *Virginia Gazette* June 6, 1766, May 23, 1771. For a diarist's extended description of a man's hairstyle, see "Extracts from the Journal of Sarah Eve," 26–27.

62. For example, *Pennsylvania Gazette* June 11, 1767; *New-York Mercury* June 26, 1758; *Virginia Gazette* October 6, 1752.

63. *Pennsylvania Gazette* September 6, 1759, February 17, 1773.

64. This lack of attention to women's hairstyles parallels Laurel Thatcher Ulrich's comparisons of how differently Ephraim Ballard and Martha Ballard noted women's economic labor in their respective written records. Laurel Thatcher Ulrich, "Martha Ballard and Her Girls: Women's Work in Eighteenth-Century Maine," in *Work and Labor in Early America*, edited by Stephen Innes (Chapel Hill: University of North Carolina Press, 1988), 70–105. For men cutting their hair, see *Virginia Gazette* May 9, 1751, July 2, 1767, December 10, 1772. See also Kate Haulman, "A Short History of the High Roll," *Common-Place* 2, no. 1 (October 2001), http://www.common-place.org/vol-02/no-01/lessons/.

65. My analysis contradicts the finding that eighteenth-century advertisements "very frequently" described runaway slaves' hair. It may be that longer post-Revolutionary and nineteenth-century advertisements were more likely to focus on details like hair. It may also be that the often-cited compelling descriptions of African American hairstyles were exceptions rather than the rule. White and White, "Slave Hair," 50; Waldstreicher, "Reading the Runaways," 254.

66. *Pennsylvania Gazette* September 1, 1773; *Virginia Gazette* June 22, 1775, July 21, 1774. See also *Boston Evening-Post* February 20, 1764; *Virginia Gazette* November 5, 1772.

67. *Providence Gazette* December 14, 1771; *Virginia Gazette* January 21, 1775; *New-York Gazette* February 23, 1761. See also *New-York Gazette* July 4, 1763, May 11, 1772.

68. For examples of "mulatto" runaways' hairstyles, see *South-Carolina Gazette; And Country Journal* April 3, 1770; *South-Carolina Gazette* March 14, 1771; *Providence Gazette* August 28, 1773; *Virginia Gazette* February 25, 1775, December 13, 1770, March 11, 1775. For Frank, see *South-Carolina Gazette; And Country Journal* August 30, 1774. On enslaved women's hair fashions in the nineteenth century, see Stephanie M. H. Camp, *Closer to Freedom: Enslaved Women and Everyday Resistance in the Plantation South* (Chapel Hill: University of North Carolina Press, 2004), 84.

69. George Washington, *Rules of Civility & Decent Behaviour in Company and Conversation: A Book of Etiquette* (Williamsburg, Va.: Beaver Press, 1971), http://www.history.org/almanack/life/manners/rules2.cfm.

70. Carol E. Henderson, *Scarring the Black Body: Race and Representation in African American Literature* (Columbia: University of Missouri Press, 2002), 3–7, 23–36, quotations on 3, 23; Putzi, *Identifying Marks*, 1; Toni Morrison, *Beloved*, repr. ed. (New York: Vintage, 2004), 79; "Gordon (slave)," *Wikipedia*, May 26, 2015, https://en.wikipedia.org/wiki/Gordon_(slave).

71. *New-York Journal* May 11, 1769; *Pennsylvania Gazette* February 4, 1752, April 5, 1750; *Boston Gazette* July 17, 1769; *Pennsylvania Gazette* October 30, 1755, January 22, 1767; *South-Carolina Gazette* May 4, 1752; *Pennsylvania Gazette* July 2, 1772; *Virginia Gazette* June 7, 1770. See also *Pennsylvania Gazette* November 3, 1757.

72. *Boston Gazette* January 9, 1758; *Virginia Gazette* October 15, 1772; *Pennsylvania Gazette* June 2, 1763; *Boston Gazette* March 13, 1753.

73. *Virginia Gazette* December 3, 1772; *Pennsylvania Gazette* February 14, 1765; *Virginia Gazette* April 14, 1774; *New-York Journal* September 10, 1767. See also *South Carolina Gazette; And Country Journal* January 9, 1770; *Virginia Gazette* June 24, 1773, July 9, 1767; *Boston Weekly News-Letter* September 16, 1762. Although Native American–identified runaways are too few to analyze systematically, for one "half Indian" whose teeth were rotted and nose was broken by a blow, see *Virginia Gazette* March 17, 1774.

74. *South-Carolina Gazette* February 26, 1750; *Pennsylvania Gazette* January 22, 1761. See also *Virginia Gazette* October 29, 1772.

75. *Virginia Gazette* September 29, 1775; *South-Carolina Gazette; And Country Journal* January 16, 1770; *Virginia Gazette* March 7, 1766, April 10, 1752, July 9, 1767, April 16, 1767; *Pennsylvania Gazette* June 29, 1774.

76. *Pennsylvania Gazette* July 11, 1771; *New-York Journal* October 15, 1767; *South-Carolina Gazette; And Country Journal* January 5, 1768; *Georgia Gazette* August 4, 1763; *Pennsylvania Gazette* October 20, 1763; *New-York Gazette* June 18, 1764. For a more modern study of West African ritual scarification, see Ekhaguosa Aisien, *Iwu, the Body Markings of the Edo People* (Benin City, Nigeria: Aisien Publishers, 1986). On African ritual scars as marking temporality and kinship before enslavement, see Fuentes, *Dispossessed Lives*, 14.

77. *Pennsylvania Gazette* September 19, 1754, June 30, 1763.

78. *Virginia Gazette* March 26, 1767; *Pennsylvania Gazette* October 20, 1773; *Georgia Gazette* August 24, 1768; *Virginia Gazette* May 29, 1752.

79. *Virginia Gazette* June 16, 1774, October 8, 1767, August 8, 1771. See also *Virginia Gazette* February 7, 1771.

80. *Pennsylvania Gazette* November 13, 1766. See also *Pennsylvania Gazette* July 17, 1755; *Virginia Gazette* August 1, 1771.

81. *Virginia Gazette* August 26, 1773.

82. Terri L. Snyder, "Suicide, Slavery, and Memory in North America," *Journal of American History* 97, no. 1 (June 2010): 50.

83. South Carolina Ar Council Journal #23, April 16, 1754, pp. 192–93, South Carolina Department of Archives and History, Columbia, S.C; Trial of Tom, Lancaster County Order Book, Sept. 14, 1775, XVI, 1778–1783 (despite the mismatched dates), 8 (upper left), 14 (lower right), Virginia State Library, Richmond; *Virginia Gazette* May 2, 1751; Sharon Block, *Rape and Sexual Power in Early America* (Chapel Hill: OIEAHC at University of North Carolina Press, 2006), 194; Fischer, *Suspect Relations*, 185–86.

84. *South-Carolina Gazette* April 30, 1753; *Virginia Gazette* August 1, 1766.

85. *Virginia Gazette* December 9, 1775, January 28, 1768, January 10, 1771. See also *Virginia Gazette* August 18, 1738; *Pennsylvania Gazette* June 23, 1763.

86. *South-Carolina Gazette* September 5, 1771; *South-Carolina Gazette; And Country Journal* December 15, 1767.

87. Johnson, *Soul by Soul*, 142.

88. *Pennsylvania Gazette* October 28, 1772, August 26, 1772, August 28, 1760, March 17, 1768; *New-York Gazette, and Weekly Mercury* May 1, 1769; *Virginia Gazette* November 10, 1774. See also *Pennsylvania Gazette* April 12, 1770.

89. For instance, *South-Carolina Gazette; And Country Journal* December 30, 1766, October 19, 1773; *Georgia Gazette* July 25, 1765.

90. *Georgia Gazette* September 3, 1766; *Pennsylvania Gazette* May 12, 1773; *Virginia Gazette* May 7, 1772; *Boston Evening-Post* October 19, 1761; *Pennsylvania Gazette* May 10, 1770; *Virginia Gazette* October 27, 1752; *Pennsylvania Gazette* June 29, 1774; *Georgia Gazette* August 10, 1768; *Virginia Gazette* June 1, 1775.

91. *Virginia Gazette* October 7, 1773, December 2, 1773; *Pennsylvania Gazette* February 14, 1765.

Epilogue

1. Joanne Barker, Jodi A. Byrd, Jill Doerfler, Lisa Kahaleole Hall, LeAnne Howe, J. Kēhaulani Kauanui, Jean O'Brien, Kathryn W. Shanley, Noenoe K. Silva, Shannon Speed, Kim TallBear, and Jacki Thompson Rand, "Open Letter from Indigenous Women Scholars Regarding Discussions of Andrea Smith," *Indian Country Today* July 7, 2015, https://indiancountry medianetwork.com/news/opinions/open-letter-from-indigenous-women-scholars-regarding -discussions-of-andrea-smith/.

2. Thelma Wills Foote, *Black and White Manhattan: The History of Racial Formation in Colonial New York City* (New York: Oxford University Press, 2004), 190.

3. George Yancy, "Walking While Black in the 'White Gaze,'" *New York Times* September 1, 2013, expanded in George Yancy, *Black Bodies, White Gazes: The Continuing Significance of Race* (Lanham, Md.: Rowman and Littlefield, 2008).

4. Jason Felch and Maura Dolan, "How Reliable Is DNA in Identifying Suspects?" *Los Angeles Times* July 19, 2008, http://articles.latimes.com/2008/jul/20/local/me-dna20.

5. CNN Newsroom Transcripts, Aired February 6, 2011, 22:00 ET, http://www.cnn.com/ TRANSCRIPTS/1102/06/cnr.03.html; "Surprise! You're African-America," http://www.cnn .com/video/us/2011/02/05/nr.african.american.cnn.640x360.jpg; "A Genetic Puzzle: 'Black' and 'White' Twins Are Born to Mixed Couple in London," *Ebony* (December 1980): 80–84; Joanna Moorhead, "Different But the Same: A Story of Black and White Twins," *Guardian* September 23, 2011, https://www.theguardian.com/lifeandstyle/2011/sep/24/twins-black-white; "These 4 Girls Are the Rarest Siblings in the World, a One-in-a-Million Family," http://goingviralposts .biz/these-4-girls-are-the-rarest-siblings-in-the-world-a-one-in-a-million-family-2/; John Shammas, "Black and White Twins: Meet the Sisters Who 'Couldn't Look More Different if They Tried," *Mirror* March 2, 2015, http://www.mirror.co.uk/news/real-life-stories/black -white-twins-meet-sisters-5256945.

6. For example, *New-York Journal, or, the General Advertiser* January 23, 1768; *Pennsylvania Gazette* January 28, 1768; *Boston Post-Boy & Advertiser* February 15, 1768; *Virginia Gazette* February 4, 1768; "From the Gentleman's Magazine, for June 1752," *New-York Gazette, or Weekly Post-Boy* October 9, 1752, original in *Gentleman's Magazine and Historical Chronicle* 22 (June 1752): 271; *Georgia Gazette* September 27, 1769. On theorizing ghosts and hauntings in archives, see Avery F. Gordon, *Ghostly Matters: Haunting and the Sociological Imagination*, 2nd ed. (Minneapolis: University of Minnesota Press, 2011).

7. "Those Perceived as Black Arrested Three Times More Often: UC Irvine-Stanford Study," *OC Weekly* June 19, 2015, http://www.ocweekly.com/news/those-perceived-as-black

-arrested-three-times-more-often-uc-irvine-stanford-study-6448833; Andrew M. Penner and Aliya Saperstein, "Disentangling the Effects of Racial Self-Identification and Classification by Others: The Case of Arrest," *Demography* 52, no. 3 (May 27, 2015): 1017–24. See also Jonathan B. Freeman et al., "Looking the Part: Social Status Cues Shape Race Perception," *PLoS ONE* 6, no. 9 (September 26, 2011), https://doi.org/10.1371/journal.pone.0025107.

8. Andrew Noymer et al., "Cause of Death Affects Racial Classification on Death Certificates," *PLoS ONE* 6, no. 1 (January 2011), https://doi.org/10.1371/journal.pone.0015812.

9. For sample aggregation of this coverage, see Carimah Townes and Dylan Petroholos, "Who Police Killed in 2014," *ThinkProgress* December 12, 2014, https://thinkprogress.org/who -police-killed-in-2014-44e56b4037a1; "Black Lives Matter | Not a Moment, a Movement," http://blacklivesmatter.com/; Roxane Gay, "On the Death of Sandra Bland and Our Vulnerable Bodies," *New York Times* July 24, 2015, https://www.nytimes.com/2015/07/25/opinion/on -the-death-of-sandra-bland-and-our-vulnerable-bodies.html; https://twitter.com/#Black LivesMatter; #SayHerName. On Native Americans' prominence, see Zak Cheney-Rice, "The Police Are Killing One Group at a Staggering Rate, and Nobody Is Talking About It," *Mic* February 5, 2015, https://mic.com/articles/109894/the-police-are-killing-one-group-at-a-stag gering-rate-and-nobody-is-talking-about-it.

10. Jelani Cobb, "Murders in Charleston," *New Yorker* June 18, 2015, http://www.new yorker.com/news/news-desk/church-shooting-charleston-south-carolina.

11. N. G. Osborne and M. D. Feit, "The Use of Race in Medical Research," *JAMA* 267, no. 2 (January 8, 1992): 275–79; Michael J. Fine, Said A. Ibrahim, and Stephen B. Thomas, "The Role of Race and Genetics in Health Disparities Research," *American Journal of Public Health* 95, no. 12 (December 2005): 2125–28; Catherine Elton, "Why Racial Profiling Persists in Medical Research," *Time* August 22, 2009, http://content.time.com/time/health/article/ 0,8599,1916755,00.html. For an important critiques of sex studies, see Rebecca M. Jordan-Young, *Brain Storm: The Flaws in the Science of Sex Differences*, repr. ed. (Cambridge, Mass.: Harvard University Press, 2011).

12. On the "beautification engine," see Sarah Kershaw, "The Sum of Your Facial Parts," *New York Times* October 8, 2008, http://www.nytimes.com/2008/10/09/fashion/09skin.html. The computer scientists used only images of "white" faces to create a basis for their mathematical assessment of attractiveness.

13. Michael Paulson, " 'Hamilton' Heads to Broadway in a Hip-Hop Retelling," *New York Times* July 12, 2015, https://www.nytimes.com/2015/07/13/theater/hamilton-heads-to-broad way-in-a-hip-hop-retelling.html. It is unclear how "out of favor" these biographies have fallen, given the extensive list of prizes on Brand's Wikipedia page. Wikipedia contributors, "H. W. Brands," *Wikipedia, The Free Encyclopedia*, https://en.wikipedia.org/wiki/H._W._ Brands. For a critique of early American biographies, see Ann M. Little, *The Many Captivities of Esther Wheelwright* (New Haven, Conn.: Yale University Press, 2016), 9–11. Similarly, the *New York Times* regularly runs pieces on the terrifying decline of traditional white men's history. See Fredrik Logevall and Kenneth Osgood, "Why Did We Stop Teaching Political History?" *New York Times* August 29, 2016, https://www.nytimes.com/2016/08/29/opinion/ why-did-we-stop-teaching-political-history.html; Patricia Cohen, "Traditional History Courses: Disappearing or Just Evolving?" *New York Times* June 10, 2009, http://www.nytimes .com/2009/06/11/books/11hist.html. For my own response to the latter, see "Taking Over or Just Undertaking?: A Quantitative Overview of American Women's History," in *Major Problems in American Women's History* (Stamford, Conn: Cengage, 2013), 18–23.

14. Tiya Miles, *The Cherokee Rose* (Winston-Salem, N.C.: John F. Blair, 2015), prologue.

15. Douglas Martin, "Mildred Loving, Who Battled Ban on Mixed-Race Marriage, Dies at 68," *New York Times* May 6, 2008, http://www.nytimes.com/2008/05/06/us/06loving.html.

Appendix 1

1. On advertisements for the return of servants and slaves in England, see Susan Dwyer Amussen, *Caribbean Exchanges: Slavery and the Transformation of English Society, 1640–1700* (Chapel Hill: University of North Carolina Press, 2009), 221–25. See also "Runaway Slaves in Britain," http://www.runaways.gla.ac.uk/ (accessed September 3, 2016).

2. Sharon Block, "Doing More with Digitization," *Common-Place* 6, no. 2 (January 2006), http://www.common-place.org/vol-06/no-02/tales/.

3. *Pennsylvania Gazette* January 16, 1750; Waldstreicher, "Reading the Runaways," 259n62; *Virginia Gazette* October 8, 1736. See also *Pennsylvania Gazette* August 22, 1751; Charles E. Clark and Charles Wetherell, "The Measure of Maturity: *The Pennsylvania Gazette*, 1728–1765," *William and Mary Quarterly* 46, no. 2 (April 1, 1989): 284–86; J. L. Bell, "Colonial Newspaper Advertising Rates," June 6, 2017, http://boston1775.blogspot.com/2017/06/colonial-newspaper -advertising-rates.html.

4. *Virginia Gazette* October 8, 1736.

5. *Boston Evening-Post* October 19, 1761.

6. For example, *The Diary of Elizabeth Drinker*, edited by Elaine Forman Crane (Boston: Northeastern University Press, 1991), 1:97, 160, 161. On the racial terminology used in Drinker's diary, see Alison Duncan Hirsch, "Uncovering 'the Hidden History of Mestizo America' in Elizabeth Drinker's Diary: Interracial Relationships in Late-Eighteenth Century Philadelphia," *Pennsylvania History* 68, no. 4 (2001): 483–506.

7. Of the nearly one thousand incidents of sexual coercion I traced in *Rape and Sexual Power in Early America*, references to an individual's appearance generally only appeared in newspaper reports of a defendant's escape from jail. For example, Charles Calahan in the *Pennsylvania Gazette* November 27–December 2, 1731; James Burnside in the *American Weekly Mercury* December 16–23, 1729.

8. For example, see Entries of Convicts in the State Prison, Charlestown, Mass., 1805–1818; Graham Russell Hodges, ed., *The Black Loyalist Directory: African Americans in Exile After the American Revolution* (New York: Garland in association with the New England Historic Genealogical Society, 1996). See also http://www.blackloyalist.info/runaways/. For an article on early republic bodily descriptions in citizenship applications, see Simon P. Newman, "Reading the Bodies of Early American Seafarers," *William and Mary Quarterly* 55, no. 1 (January 1998): 59–82.

9. On the importance of using popular sources for analysis of bodily descriptions, see Rebecca Herzig, *Plucked: A History of Hair Removal* (New York: New York University Press, 2015), 9.

10. For sample collections, see Lathan A. Windley, *Runaway Slave Advertisements: A Documentary History from the 1730s to 1790* (Westport, Conn.: Greenwood Press, 1983); Graham Russell Hodges and Alan Edward Brown, *"Pretends to Be Free": Runaway Slave Advertisements from Colonial and Revolutionary New York and New Jersey* (New York: Taylor & Francis, 1994); Billy G. Smith and Richard Wojtowicz, *Blacks Who Stole Themselves: Advertisements for Runaways in the Pennsylvania Gazette, 1728–1790* (Philadelphia: University of Pennsylvania Press, 1989). In addition to behind-paywall digitized newspaper collections such as *Accessible*

Archives and Readex's *Early American Newspapers*, online runaway advertisement corpuses include *North Carolina Runaway Slave Advertisements*, http://libcdm1.uncg.edu/cdm/landing page/collection/RAS; *Geography of Slavery in Virginia*, http://www2.vcdh.virginia.edu/gos/; and *Runaway Connecticut*, https://wesomeka.wesleyan.edu/runawayct/ (an excellent student project). The newer *Freedom on the Move* (http://freedomonthemove.org/) project, although still in development, has received extensive press. For an example of mainstream interest, see Eve M. Kahn, "New Databases Offer Insights into the Lives of Escaped Slaves," *New York Times* February 18, 2016, http://www.nytimes.com/2016/02/19/arts/design/new-databases -offer-insights-into-the-lives-of-escaped-slaves.html. For scholarship, see Gerald W. Mullin, *Flight and Rebellion: Slave Resistance in Eighteenth-Century Virginia* (New York: Oxford University Press, 1972); Wood, *Black Majority*, 239–68; White and White, "Slave Hair"; Michael Gomez, *Exchanging Our Country Marks: The Transformation of African Identities in the Colonial and Antebellum South* (Chapel Hill: University of North Carolina Press, 1998), 38–40, 68–70; Waldstreicher, "Reading the Runaways."

11. For work incorporating runaway servant advertisements, see Sharon Salinger, *"To Serve Well and Faithfully": Labor and Indentured Servants in Pennsylvania, 1682–1800* (Cambridge: Cambridge University Press, 1987); Robert J. Steinfeld, *The Invention of Free Labor: The Employment Relation in English and American Law and Culture, 1350–1870* (Chapel Hill: University of North Carolina Press, 2014); Manion, *Liberty's Prisoners*; Newman, *Embodied History*. For work comparing servants and slaves, see Jonathan Prude, "To Look upon the 'Lower Sort': Runaway Ads and the Appearance of Unfree Laborers in America, 1750–1800," *Journal of American History* 78, no. 1 (June 1991): 124–59; Foote, *Black and White Manhattan*, 190–209.

12. Smith, "Resisting Inequality," 136. See also his contrast between owners' "subjective beliefs" and "material characteristics" of runaways on p. 137.

13. Newman, *Embodied History*, 95.

14. Sánchez-Eppler, *Touching Liberty*, 23.

15. Newspapers were published in Massachusetts, Rhode Island, Connecticut, New York, Maryland, Pennsylvania, Virginia, North Carolina, South Carolina, and Georgia. For basic information on colonial advertising, see Steven J. Shaw, "Colonial Newspaper Advertising: A Step Toward Freedom of the Press," *Business History Review* 33, no. 3 (October 1, 1959): 409–20, esp. 417–19 (Franklin and *Pennsylvania Gazette*). For the best overview of the place of advertisements in a colonial newspaper, see Clark and Wetherell, "The Measure of Maturity," 279–303, esp. 286.

16. On the sex of runaways, see Smith, "Resisting Inequality," 138. Daniel Meaders found that from 1729 to 1780, 12 percent of *Pennsylvania Gazette* fugitive servants were women and points out that women were a smaller overall proportion of indentured servants than slaves (*Dead or Alive*, 33–34). Scholars working on enslaved runaways in the early republic have found higher numbers of female runaways. See Barbara Krauthamer, "The Possibility of Pleasure: Runaway Slave Women and Sex in the Antebellum South," unpublished manuscript in author's possession. On women's reasons for running away, see Camp, " 'I Could Not Stay There' "; Krauthamer, "The Possibility of Pleasure."

17. *New-York Gazette* January 17, 1763; *New-York Mercury* June 27, 1763.

18. Filemaker database was used for creating individual runaways' records, and JMP Software from SAS was used for statistical analysis.

19. For examples of advertisements that described the missing man in far more detail than the woman, see *Virginia Gazette* March 26, 1767, March 18, 1773. On the importance of intersectional analyses, see Anna Carastathis, "The Concept of Intersectionality in Feminist Theory," *Philosophy Compass* 9, no. 5 (2014): 304–14.

20. *Virginia Gazette* August 26, 1768.

21. Women identified as "Negro" averaged 4.4 items per runaway, and women identified as "Mulatto" had slightly more information provided, with an average of 4.9 pieces of information per runaway. Although the numbers of Native Americans are too small for statistically useful conclusions, they averaged 5.4 pieces for women and 6.0 pieces for men, putting them between European- and African-descended people in the amount of detail provided about them.

22. *Virginia Gazette* January 12, 1775. See also *Virginia Gazette* May 24 1751; *Pennsylvania Gazette* October 14, 1762. For a modern analogue on the invisibility of black women, see Jonathan Capehart, "Michelle Obama Goes Unrecognized on Walks Outside the White House: Black Women Know Why," *Washington Post* January 10, 2017, https://www.washingtonpost.com/blogs/post-partisan/wp/2017/01/10/michelle-obama-goes-unrecognized-on-walks-outside-the-white-house-black-women-know-why/.

23. While it may be tempting to label this "data mining," all advertisements were human-read and hand-entered into a database. Data mining is generally associated with much larger corpuses of documents and involves machine-reading of content.

24. For recent work, see Cameron Blevins, "Topic Modeling Historical Sources: Analyzing the Diary of Martha Ballard," *Stanford Digital Humanities* (2011), http://dh2011abstracts.stanford.edu/; Newman and Block, "Probabilistic Topic Decomposition of an Eighteenth-Century American Newspaper," 753–67; Carol Percy, "Early Advertising and Newspapers as Sources of Sociolinguistic Investigation," in *The Handbook of Historical Sociolinguistics*, edited by Juannuel Hernández-Campoy and Juan Camilo Conde-Silvestre (Chichester, England: John Wiley and Sons, 2012), 191–210; Tze-I Yang, Andrew J. Torget, and Rada Mihalcea, "Topic Modeling on Historical Newspapers," *Proceedings of the Association for Computational Linguistics Workshop on Language Technology for Cultural Heritage, Social Sciences, and Humanities (ACL LATECH)*, June 2011, 96–104, http://mappingtexts.org/whitepaper/Topic_Modeling_History.pdf.

25. In addition to University of California subscriptions to historical newspaper databases, frequently used collections included Readex's *Early American Imprints*, Google Books, and early twentieth-century JSTOR antiquarian publications in state and regional historical journals.

INDEX

Aaron, 133
Aaron (slave narrative), 168n17
Aberdeen, 117
Abram, 42
Adair, James, 28
Adams, Abigail, 20
Adams, James, 102
Adams, John, 20, 32, 41, 74, 100–101
advertisements for runaways: compared to
    modern newspaper, 141; costs of, 143–44;
    genre of, 2–3; quantified overview of, 150f–
    53f; reach of, 143–45; regional variations in,
    37, 39, 91, 121, 122; scholarship on, 5, 146; as
    source, 145–46
Aesop (Greek author), 31
African ethnicities and named groups: Ana-
    mabw, 90; Angola, 39, 40, 68, 89, 90, 91,
    96, 98; Ashanti, 98; Bamba, 62; Calabar, 91;
    Coramantee, 89, 90; Fula/Fulbe, 23, 91, 117;
    Gambian, 82, 90; Gold Coast, 90; Guiney,
    68; Igbo, 50, 68, 89, 90, 91, 93, 96, 98, 117;
    Kinshey, 68; Malimbo, 68; Whiddaw, 90;
    Wolof, 117; Yalunka, 91
Africans, as a group: 2, 15, 21–24, 54, 77, 82;
    called Ethiopians, 31, 63. *See also* West
    Africa
age, 37–41; estimated, 148; as health, 37; heap-
    ing, 37–38; of individuals, 3–4, 5, 10, 37, 38,
    39–40, 41, 47, 50, 52, 60, 75, 84, 95, 112, 118,
    124, 133, 147; older, 37, 39, 40–41, 56; quali-
    tative versus quantitative, 38–40; related to
    value of slaves, 40–44, 58; subjectivity of,
    5, 38, 147; young, 4, 37, 39–41, 48, 49, 50,
    52, 58, 73, 74, 105, 131, 133; youthful, 71–73

Agnew, Thomas, 55
alcohol, effects of, 53, 54, 112, 118, 132, 147
Alexander, James, 84
Algrey, Adam, 125
Alice, 95
Al[i]ce, 41
Aminta, 106
Amy, 98, 123
anatomy, 11, 22, 25–26, 28, 72
animals, non-Europeans compared to, 46–
    47, 50, 64, 77, 97, 103, 105, 133
Annas, 65, 133
Anteno, 42
archives: construction of, 140, 161n32, 195n6;
    digital, 56, 69
arms, 129, 130, 131
Ashton, William, 76
Ashworth, James, 102
Aston, Charlotte Anne, 87, 130

B (woman), 79
Bacchus, 117
back, 129, 132–33
Ball, William, 50
Bamba Born, 62
Barbara, 42
Barnaby, 3–7, 38
Barnes, James, 110, 136
Barsterie, John, 93, 99
beard. *See* hair, facial
Beaver, Elizabeth, 72, 124
Bedlo, Harry, 68
behavior of runaways, 4, 5, 95, 111–16, 118, 127,
    135. *See also* character
Belinda (VA), 4

ACKNOWLEDGMENTS

I would like to express my gratitude to the programmers and archivists who developed the digital sources on which this book relies. Thanks to several archivists for providing images in record time: Cliff Parker at Chester County Archives; Marianne Martin at Colonial Williamsburg; and Nicole Joniec at the Library Company of Philadelphia.

I consider myself lucky to participate in social media communities where I regularly learn from those generous enough to share their intellect and their politics. I am grateful to the virtual universe of the National Center for Faculty Development and Diversity, which gave me new productivity strategies that helped this book get written, even with overwhelming professional and family demands on my time. Those thirty minutes a day really do add up!

The content of *Colonial Complexions* benefited greatly from audience feedback on papers I gave at the Australian and New Zealand American Studies Association conference, the EMSI American Origins Seminar, the Organization of American Historians conference, the Western Association of Women Historians annual conference, and the *William and Mary Quarterly*–Early Modern Studies Institute Women's History Workshop; as well as presentations at New York University and the University of Oregon. It also benefited from the work of outstanding student researchers, including Andrea Milne, Jeffrey Muir, Jason Sellers, Melissa Sigona, Danielle Vigneaux, and Alisa Wankier. Max Speare improved the final version with on-point and on-call proofreading. Colleagues were generous with their time. Allison Perlman pointed me toward a new argument at a crucial moment, and Renee Raphael generously shared her knowledge of early modern European medicine. Longtime friends and colleagues, including Matt Dennis, Josh Piker, and Jacki Rand, were happy to respond to random online questions in their area of expertise. Randy Sparks saved me hours of last-minute citation checking with his access to an online database. Gary

Hewitt not only offered Dutch translations from Amsterdam but he even asked his neighborhood shopkeeper about the connotations of "neérgeslaagen." Once a historian, always a historian.

Stephanie Camp was one of the first people to be excited about this project. She did not get to see the final product, but her scholarship, friendship, and early suggestions permeate this book. Several readers, some anonymous, offered sage advice that greatly improved the final manuscript and gave me the courage to jettison a chapter at a rather late date (aka: Chapter Everything But the Kitchen Sink) and write something entirely new. I was lucky to have many people willing to read draft chapters, often on a ridiculously short turnaround: Steven Amsterdam, Beth Anderson, Jim Downs, Jennifer Morgan, Patricia Sloane-White, Emily Thuma, and Vicki Ruiz all gave cogent comments on not-quite-coherent chapters. Special thanks to Lizzie Reis, who repeatedly reminded me to not bury the lede.

Terri Snyder has been an amazing friend and brilliant colleague. She has offered incisive advice on every chapter in this book, sometimes more than once. Terri has that remarkable skill of framing critiques as an opportunity, which I appreciated more than I can say. Her support and wise counsel have been a gift. Ann Little and I have traveled a long way together since the days when we were the two outspoken feminists in a graduate colonial history class. I cherish Ann's friendship, honesty, and fearlessness; the feminist community she has created among early Americanists; and her detailed and thoughtful feedback on the entire manuscript.

Working with the editors and staff at the University of Pennsylvania Press has been a delight. Kathy Brown's comments on and conversations about the project were incredibly helpful in reconceptualizing and honing the argument. Bob Lockhart has been a longtime (and patient!) supporter. His editing has added clarity and helped me better define the book's narrative arc. He has made the entire process predictable, clear, and even enjoyable. As an added benefit, publishing with Penn has been a lovely homecoming to the institution where I first discovered colonial history with Rick Beeman and Richard Dunn. Thanks to the people at Penn Press who helped turn the manuscript into a book, including Will Boehm, Gavi Fried, Elizabeth Glover, John Hubbard, Amanda Ruffner, and Susan Staggs. Extra thanks to Jennifer Backer and Erica Ginsburg, whose copyediting improved the text tremendously.

Dear friends who provided much-needed succor throughout the years I worked on *Colonial Complexions* include Steven Amsterdam, Rosemarie

Paduano, Daniel Pietenpol, and Melissa Pietenpol. Ashley Glassburn Falzetti and Patricia Sloane-White have been wonderful long-distance supporters and compatriots. Thanks to all the World Elite trampoline moms
who, despite my never-ending scribbling on typed pages at practices and
meets, still cajoled me out to dinners and drinks. Thanks also to the So Cal
friends and colleagues who have made my days brighter: Bobbie Allen,
Anita Casavantes Bradford, Sarah Farmer, Doug Haynes, Adria Imada, Allison Perlman, Ann Plane, Sharon Salinger, James Steintrager, Emily Thuma,
and Linda Vo.

I consider myself exceptionally lucky to have had Vicki Ruiz as a friend
and mentor. Vicki has offered me advice and opportunities, critique and
support, and has modeled what true success looks like. If that weren't
enough, she also came up with the title of *Colonial Complexions*. As anyone
who is lucky enough to be her friend knows, Vicki is truly in a class by
herself.

A shout-out to Taz, who did not really help with the book but has
served as my online avatar (you look great in reading glasses, pup!) and
dozes patiently by my desk. Heidi Block Barishman gamely took a first
crack at cleaning up my footnotes. I owe an ongoing debt to my mother,
Anne Block, whose generous assistance with family responsibilities allowed
me to eke out writing time. Thanks for the many ways you understand the
daughter who took a different path. Two-plus decades on, David Newman
still makes me laugh. Leaving homemade lattes in front of my computer at
7:00 a.m. every morning was a brilliant work-starting strategy. And I can't
count the cups of lovely tea that appeared at my elbow throughout work
days and nights. Thanks, too, for all the non-ingestible ways you sustain my
soul, including the welcome reminders of life beyond a computer screen.

I dedicate this book to my children, Casey Newman Block and Ripley
Block Newman. In my last monograph, I thanked the childcare providers
who looked after you. Now you are nearly adults. Casey, I admire both the
fantastical feats of aerial majesty you have accomplished with your body
and the thoughtful, original person you have become. Rip, you have taught
me new ways to see a body's relationship to the world, and I'm in awe of
your talents and fearlessness. I have loved watching you each come into
your own identities. Thanks for the immeasurable joy you bring to our
family.

CPSIA information can be obtained
at www.ICGtesting.com
Printed in the USA
BVHW051720310822
646002BV00005B/251

9 780812 224924